SLIP-UP

Also by Anthony Delano

BREATHLESS DIVERSIONS

SLIP-UP

*Fleet Street, Scotland Yard,
and The Great Train Robbery*

ANTHONY DELANO

Quadrangle/The New York Times Book Co.

Designed by Tere LoPrete

Library of Congress Cataloging in Publication Data

Delano, Anthony.
    Slip up: Fleet Street, Scotland Yard, and the Great
Train Robbery.

    1. Train robberies—Great Britain. 2. Great
Britain. Metropolitan Police Office. Criminal Investi-
gation Dept. I. Title.
HV6665.G72D44 1963   364.1'55   75-8289
ISBN 0-8129-0576-8

For all of my friends and colleagues who were lucky enough to play a part in this dazzling and unforgettable romp. I know they'll get me for this.

Illustrations follow page 124.

SLIP-UP

1

"I think I have had a very, very, very successful assignment to Brazil. My instructions were to trace and detain Ronald Biggs. That is what the assignment was all about and I did it. "I'm very disappointed not to have brought Biggs back with me, but I'm confident that he will be back in Britain within a few weeks."

Detective Chief Superintendent Slipper,
London, February 5, 1974

•

The thousands of miles of doubt, suspense, discomfort and humiliation had come down to a few feet of elevator shaft. But even in that distance plenty could go wrong. For one thing, the elevator was not working properly.

They wanted the ninth. But the elevator had a mind of its own. It stopped at every floor whether the button had been pressed or not. Sometimes the doors flew open unbidden. Sometimes they just shuddered and groaned pneumatically before the car lofted up again. And sometimes they even had to be wrenched apart or forced together before the elevator would move.

The hotel air conditioning had dried off the sweat wrung from the men in an hour of sitting in a car parked in the midsummer lunchtime sun of Copacabana Beach. Their throats were dry and metallic with anxiety. They were hoarse. They were beginning to breathe faster. The ascending hotel guests with whom they unconvincingly mingled got on or off with nervous and sometimes knowing side-glances at them.

They were a purposeful and powerful-looking lot. Although their precise purpose could only be guessed at, their general one was perfectly clear. Most Brazilians could see a Brazilian policeman straight through his Italian suit. And here they saw two. They were the only men of the six in the party who looked as though they could possibly belong in Rio and who were not plainly suffering from strain.

The *agentes* were poised, patient and, behind their dark glasses, aloof. They were still puzzled by the incomprehensible theatrics in which they had suddenly become involved. But they could afford to wait until they saw what came of it all. Foreigners were puzzling enough at any time. But especially at this time of year with Rio's fabled *carnaval* in the offing. It was half an hour past noon on January 31, 1974. In Rio the police could afford to wait. In Rio the police were always right.

The least comfortable of the four was Mr. Henry Neill, the British Consul. He had already withdrawn into the glum and disapproving torpor which so often envelops Her Majesty's plenipotentiaries on the rare occasions that the performance of a professional duty is actually required of them. Besides, there was no air conditioning in the elevator, and it was almost as hot as outside—101 degrees. And he wanted desperately to go to the bathroom.

In classic detective fiction the younger of the remaining men would have been the unassertive but faithful sergeant, ever alert to transmute into action the wishes—however inscrutable—of his ponderous superior. The part was being played with eager fidelity by one Peter Jones—even though he had recently been promoted to Inspector in the rolls of London's Metropolitan Police Force and was quite entitled to be ordering around a Detective Sergeant of his very own.

Despite the sweat pouring from beneath his carefully tended dark hair and down his flushed face, Jones felt cheerfully privileged to be awaiting the professional pleasure of the man who clearly dominated the elevator—the hook-nosed, thick-chested, six-foot-four-inch tall, richly moustached and resonantly titled Detective Chief

Superintendent John Slipper, aged forty-nine and at the pinnacle of a proud career of enforcement, persuasion and relentless thief-taking as the active head of Scotland Yard's finest, the legendary Flying Squad. The Heavy Mob. The Sweeney Todd.

The old firm of Slipper and Jones felt far from at ease. And not merely because they were 10,000 miles from their familiar manor. As the elevator lurched uncertainly upward once again, the strain they had endured over the past few weeks burst from Slipper in spouts of fruity and portentous supra-Cockney tones, a style of speech that Rio, for all its cosmopolitan ways, rarely hears.

"Peter," he said, policemanlike, his lips barely parted, his eyes to the front. "There's still time for that cunning blighter to give us a miss."

"Which cunning blighter?" asked Jones. It was a timely and apposite question. There were more than one about.

Only a few minutes earlier, from their bakeoven of a car on the promenade of Copacabana Beach, this curiously assorted clutch of hunters—the sixth man was the British Vice-Consul—had sighted their quarry for the first time. To the *agentes* the moment meant nothing. As far as they had been able to gather from the hasty and piecemeal explanations offered by the others, there was a fleeing English thief to be picked up—a routine matter and hardly one that seemed to justify the personal attention of a delegation as distinguished as this seemed to be.

There were many fleeing thieves in Rio lured, as the tourists were to *carnaval*, by the welcome negligence of Brazil in never bothering to sign extradition treaties with the countries of which they were citizens. If their papers were in order, if they had money and if they behaved themselves they were allowed to stay. When one of these conditions ceased to apply they were expelled. Everyone knew that. It was not an international mystery.

There must be more to this high-powered intervention, the *agentes* suspected. The man they were seeking was not even a murderer, of whom at least 120 were still going about their work in Rio each month, alarming orderly citizens and giving the police a great deal of unwelcome overtime. In recent years the Brazilian police had been compelled to develop somewhat direct methods of dealing with the rising crime statistics. They had found it most effective to go out themselves and murder the criminals. Spectacular results had been achieved by these *Esquadroes da Morte.* Their colleague, the *Senhor* from Scotland Yard, would no doubt be interested to hear of them when he had completed his true mission. Whatever that was.

Consul Neill knew that it all meant trouble. The serene routines of a British Consulate are rarely disturbed by anything more demanding than seeing a merchant seaman into or out of hospital, refusing entry permits to colored citizens of the Commonwealth or burying a superannuated Scots nanny. Men and women might serve out long, comfortable and worthy careers in the game without suffering anything as burdensome as a call to action at lunchtime. Without, in fact, ever leaving their office. Neill's instincts for detecting a damn nuisance in the making were as acute as any in the Diplomatic Service. He could foresee with mournful certainty the stream of explanation, translation, certification, authentification, and ratification that was about to be set flowing between the Consulate and the Foreign and Colonial office in distant Whitehall, disturbing the clerks and attracting far more attention than was welcome on this remote and peaceful outpost. Bad show. Especially not being able to get to a bathroom.

But Slipper and Jones had squinted up from the promenade at a ninth-floor balcony of the Hotel Trocadero as greedily as a pair of big game hunters on their first day in the bush, their deprived and hungry eyes measuring up a trophy for which any copper in Britain worth his funny hat would instantly have renounced a lifetime's hope of gain or preferment.

For an honest rozzer—even a dishonest one—of whom there is no shortage despite the public relations job done by blinkered generations of mystery writers and tourists in making British policemen wonderful—the past nine years had held out no greater chance of fame and fulfillment than to be the one who would feel the collar of the man that the intrepid pair of stalkers had seen step out on the balcony and, with gratitude and relief beyond assessment, had instantly recognized. It was Ronald Arthur Biggs, aged forty-four, carpenter, painter and decorator, latter-day highwayman, professional fugitive, indefatigable seducer, would-be *bon vivant*, sentimental father. And the most wanted man in Britain since Jack the Ripper.

If Slipper and Jones stuck with the erratic elevator, how could they be certain, so near their mark now, that they would not be trapped in it? That Biggs, instead of unsuspectingly awaiting their arrival at his door, might not simply decide to walk down the stairs and lose himself for another nine years? And if they abandoned the elevator? Took to the stairs? Biggs might even summon it up for himself and ride down past them. At the end of the long and humbling ordeal that had brought the Yard men to within collar-feeling reach those thoughts were the keenest torture.

At the seventh floor it looked as though the elevator was taking no more orders from anyone. The berserk doors rattled apart and stayed there twitching for a while. The lesser members of the group stabbed nervously at the buttons. Then Slipper, energizing his enormous frustration into the kind of decisive action that had in his time subdued many a bold and obstreperous villain, stepped forward and smote the dilapidated control panel again and again with his meaty right fist. The elevator groaned and went quietly, heading with no more hesitation for the ninth.

The Brazilian detectives appraised their companions with more interest than they had previously been willing to show. The hotel guests shrank back against the shabby walls of the car. Slipper drew from his pocket a tiny comb and bestowed a couple of complacent strokes upon his well-modeled moustache.

At the threshold of Room 909 Slipper's right to the initiative went unquestioned. He knocked mightily and when the door opened, walked squarely through the turmoil the intrusion caused inside the room, to tower over Biggs, who was sitting on the edge of the bed wearing only a pair of natty scarlet trunks and an expression like a stunned mullet.

From his intimidating height Slipper looked down at him with a slave-trader's leer. The remark he was preparing to deliver had been carefully rehearsed that morning before the mirror of his hotel room in a judicious search for just the right balance of confidence and informality in which to epitomize the moment. After all, he would be addressing an old acquaintance; a professional equal in a way. And he wanted to wear his triumph lightly rather than to gloat. The line he had savored longest and finally settled for seemed to have just the kind of offhand, stylish ring that would appeal to the boys back at the Yard. It would make a good headline.

"Hello, Ronnie," said Slipper, ponderously separating the words like someone trying to pronounce an eye chart. "Long time, no see."

Biggs too had had plenty of time to polish up a gem of dialogue to exchange when his borrowed time finally ran out, and some sort of Slipper-shaped nemesis got him up against a wall. All through Biggs's studious efforts to shape a rewarding criminal career, people had argued whether he was really genius or oaf and he had provided both sides with evidence in support of their case. Much of his thinking was naive in the extreme, although adventurous, and his language, especially when dealing with his many womenfolk, was smart-ass adolescent. Mawkish. But he had a low-pitched, sardonic delivery, a style widely cultivated in the outskirts of the London underworld to which he once so touchingly aspired and, sometimes, an appealing, self-mocking wit. He might have managed a crisper riposte to Slipper's roundarm slash had his thoughts not been so occupied recently by certain unusually agreeable prospects for the future. But he did his best.

"Fuck me!" he said ruefully. "How did *you* get here?"

It may not have been a memorable comeback. But it was another very good question.

The crime that made an international celebrity of Biggs—and that Slipper could reasonably assume would do the same for him—was the greatest robbery of all time. Ever. Anywhere. By anyone. Six million dollars in satisfyingly grubby and anonymous banknotes—seven million at today's rate of exchange—had been snatched and dispatched with a dash and daring never equaled. That was then topped by a spectacular prison breakout and getaway that should have won an Oscar for its script and—(more!) —Biggs, the last of the villains at large, pulled off another melodramatic bound to freedom when five years of a neatly fabricated new identity fell apart on him in far-off Melbourne, Australia. The whole thing plunged Scotland Yard into the sulks for nigh on a decade. But to connoisseurs it was unchallengeably the Crime of the Century.

Slipper and Jones knew for certain that when they got their man back to Britain, they would be welcomed like returning moonwalkers. Who, at that moment, could begrudge them their alluring visions of what must surely happen next? The interviews, the television appearances, the heartwarming editorials acclaiming their initiative and resourcefulness. The grateful glow of reflected glory on the brows of their superiors. The grudging compliments of their colleagues. The ingratiating and calculated adulation of their narks. Their stoolies.

Up and down the bars of the low-life pubs that they frequented in the course of their duties, tankards of mahogany-colored bitter beer would be pressed upon them. Epic lunches would be arranged for their boasts to be recycled over carafes of the rough red house wine in trattorias of the second rank. And through those happy hours who could be surprised if Slipper, at least, allowed himself a peek of the daydream that is every faithful civil servant's final consolation and reward. . . .

"Sit down, old chap. You know they start collecting names for the List about this time each year. The New Year's Honors List, you know."

And a few months later there would be the deferential crush in the huge anteroom listening to the easy-mannered briefing of the Gentlemen Ushers.

"And when Her Majesty is sure that the decoration is firmly attached, she may decide to make a remark to you. Do not be afraid to respond." A Commander of the Order of the British Empire, at least. C.B.E. after your name and a gold medallion on a pink and grey ribbon to hang around your neck on ceremonial occasions. A richly deserved award. A thoroughly believable prospect. Detective Chief Superintendent Tommy Butler had been made a Member of the Order for tracking down far less sought after members of the gang.

Ronnie Biggs, home at last, would be unceremoniously banged up in a cell and the clock that was stopped when he went so boldly over the wall of Wandsworth Prison in 1959 would be restarted. There were 28 years left on the dial. Slipper and Jones would become the most celebrated pair of heavies to pound the streets of London since the days of the Bow Street Runners. The crime that won Biggs his credentials as a crook to be taken seriously undoubtedly deserved its subtitle. So his arrest had to be the Collar of the Century.

Nowhere in the world do people read more newspapers than in Britain. The nation of 55 million people buys 30 million papers—national, local, morning, evening—every working day of the week. And even more on Sundays. By comparison, the United States, with a population approaching 215 million, reads only 60 million papers a day. In Britain on an average day nearly 90 percent of the adult population read at least one newspaper.

Only in Japan is there a similarly devoted readership and for very similar reasons. Both Japan and Britain are densely populated island nations with communications sufficiently well developed to allow newspapers produced in central points during the night to be distributed everywhere in the country before morning. Both have had more than a century of compulsory literacy.

Mass newspaper reading—and therefore selling—owes its present-day development in Britain to the Elementary Education Act of 1870, a worthy piece of legislation that required every child in the United Kingdom to go to school between the ages of five and thirteen. This had, generally speaking, the effect of teaching them how to read. It did not, of course, teach them *what* they should read, an observation first made very thoughtfully by Alfred Harmsworth, the first of a hustling bunch of press magnates to perceive the enormous possibilities of profit offered by these millions of aroused but unsatisfied consumers of the printed word.

The first newspaper on earth to sell two million copies a day was the *Daily Herald*, a crusading union-backed broadsheet, in 1939. By 1956 ten London-based national dailies were selling a total of 16 million papers and a similar number of Sundays selling 30 million. There were also three London evening papers adding up to well over two million copies and a double handful of provincial giants in places like Liverpool, Leeds, Manchester, Newcastle, Bristol, Glasgow, Belfast and Cardiff.

Television and modern industrial economics have had their effect over the years. But even now, despite the corresponding statistics that Britons are among the most dedicated television-viewers on earth (sets in 95 percent of households), the provincial ranks have not noticeably thinned, and there are still nine national dailies and seven Sunday papers operating in a spirit of diminished but far from deadened competitiveness.

The country first heard of the sensational bagging of Ronnie Biggs from only one of them—the *Daily Express*. And even though only the *Express* (read—although not necessarily bought—by 34 percent of British adults, according to the Institute of Practitioners in Advertising) could tell the story at first, word swept the nation with the speed of a new flu virus. While the forlorn remainder of the news industry—television and radio as well as other papers—scrambled breathlessly, desperately to catch up. There was no hope. The *Express* and only the *Express* had the whole thing signed and sewn up, as well as delivered.

There were pictures of Biggs in custody. A statement from Slipper. A detailed account of the arrest. There were Biggs's own words, the story of his roamings since the last time he briefly surfaced, a scoundrellish odyssey so unlikely that it could only be the gospel truth. There was an interview with his extraordinary wife in Australia. And more pictures. Pictures of Biggs with—a final twist of the scissors in an editor's heart—beautiful girls who were, it seemed, also devoted to him. Two of them. The other papers had known it was coming—there had been hazy, late warning signals—but it was far worse than anyone had feared. After their own hurried checks, the rest could do no more than peck morosely through the stubble of the *Express*'s rich harvest and come up with tight-lipped rewrites for their own early editions. Television newsreaders hitting the screen with extra bulletins simply gave up and read out the first edition of the *Express* to viewers, holding the clamorous headlines up to the cameras, so they could see for themselves.

Train Robber Biggs Captured in Rio, said the devastating front page, underscoring the triumph with a gloating kicker, *Our Men Are There*.

The competition stood no chance of dismissing it as an insignificant tactical defeat. Public fascination was almost tangible enough to photograph. Britons have always had a healthy appetite for crime stories, and the Train Robbery had fascinated them like nothing else in living memory, even the morbidly enthralling adventures of horror-show celebrities like John Haig, the acid bath king or

Christie, the ghoulish mummy-maker of Notting Hill. Every word served up about Ronnie Biggs would be devoured. And they would be asking for more.

In the megatonnage of exclusivity the *Express* had done something akin to pulling off a whole-day beat on the beginning of the Third World War or the Second Coming of Christ. It was the Scoop of the Century as well.

The chagrin, the outrage, the righteous indignation that swept the ranks of the defeated competitors attained truly awesome force. Dog does not merely bite dog on Fleet Street. Given half a chance any one of the dogs would tear the throat out of another and refuse to leave the carcass until it had been gnawed to inky shreds. Only a certain reciprocal vulnerability prevents such a thing from happening too often. The first exultant copies of the *Express* had hardly reached the open air before the rest of the pack aligned itself in rare unity, the gruff and aging bark of *The Times* and the spiteful snapping of *The Sun*, marking opposite extremes of language, taste and mores. But both of them and all the others in between were demanding to be told the same things. The questions were getting better all the time.

Could the country—let alone the media—really be expected to believe the only explanation the *Express* seemed willing to offer of how they had done it? That its men just *happened* to reach Biggs at the same time that Slipper and Jones also caught up with him? A charitable disposition to believe what they read in the papers comes naturally to newspapermen. But that was asking too much.

Therefore, could the *Express* have managed to persuade senior Metropolitan Police officers to so far depart from the traditions of reticence that had for so long guided the Force in its relations with the press to enter into collusion with reporters?

Or could the *Express* have been tempted to breach the most adamant provision of the code of ethics to which all the papers—however reluctantly—publicly acknowledged and paid a convicted criminal to cooperate with them?

Rival editors found the silence on the first of these possibilities and the loud and hasty denial with which the second was met equally suspicious. Tame Members of Parliament, of which every paper has a few, were briefed to repeat them in the House of Commons at the first opportunity, although when they did the

Home Secretary, the Cabinet Minister ultimately in charge of the Metropolitan and all other police forces was not much more forthcoming than the *Express* itself.

Nor could the outpaced editors obtain anything but a vicarious sense of revenge when, in the execution chamber gloom of their own offices, they put these and other questions a good deal less politely to the men on whom they could most easily pin the blame—their own crime reporters. For the only question that really mattered, of course, was—why didn't WE get Biggs?

Something else occurred to most editors, though, sooner or later in the long night, while each successive edition of the *Express* widened a gap that simply could not be bridged by the frantic efforts being made on the wavering telephone link with Rio and the grilling of sullen and embarrassed contacts at Scotland Yard.

To journalists the by-line on a story, the signature of the man who wrote it has almost as much significance as the headline that proclaims its essence or the dateline that tells where it came from and when. The name is usually familiar even if the person of the reporter is not.

But as they browsed moodily through the packed and boastful pages of the *Express* and tried to weigh up the likely damage done to their own circulation in the morning, several editors (or deputy editors, since it was a Friday night, traditionally a night off for department chiefs) finally had to ask someone.

"Who in bloody hell is Colin MacKenzie, anyway?"

2

"Clearly our security arrangements have been unsatisfac-
tory."

Reginald Bevins, Postmaster General,
after the Great Train Robbery

•

To this day the Up Special still leaves Glasgow's Central Station at
6:50 every evening. It is now drawn by a diesel locomotive more
modern than the one in service on the night of Wednesday, August
8, 1963. But it is still a Traveling Post Office, one of forty or more
that trundle up and down Britain through the night with mail
sorters working aboard as they go.

The Up—as opposed to Down, naturally—Special on that
particular night was made up of 12 coaches including the guard's
van, or caboose, at the rear. Things are rather different these days,
but at that time "guard" meant simply the lone brakeman who,
together with the two men in the locomotive, comprised the entire
British Rail crew of the train. The sorters, 72 of them, were
employees of the Post Office. Not one among them was armed with
as much as a billy club. This was, after all, Britain, where the police
had always gone unarmed (although that has also changed since)
and the underworld, except for the occasional desperate renegade,
was happy to follow their example.

In keeping with immemorial practice, the coach immediately behind the locomotive was unmanned and carried parcels and packages of an ordinary nature. And the one following that, described with uncomplicated logic as the High Value Coach, also always occupied the same place. When the cargo of mailbags was opened in the rest of the train, any packets among the letters and other contents that were registered or designated in some way valuable had to be passed forward until they reached it. Then they would be recorded, transferred to white rather than ordinary green mailbags and stowed away in wooden lockers strong enough to resist a juvenile delinquent with a penknife for at least five minutes.

Normally the High Value Coach was a special vehicle with reinforced side panels and doors worked by a complicated self-locking mechanism. But there was not one available for that night's Up Special. There were only three to serve the entire Traveling Post Office system and by an extraordinary coincidence all were out of service: two with "hot" axles and one with a "flat"—a wheel out of shape. Nevertheless, the sorters conscientiously observed the regulations and bolted themselves in. There had never been a robbery in the 125 years of Traveling Post Offices. But you never knew, even in Britain.

They worked steadily at their boring duties as the train thundered south at 70 to 80 miles an hour. More mail was collected or dropped as they flashed through stations by a pick-up device rigged from the side of one van like a miniature old-fashioned lifeboat suspended in davits, and another substantial load of bags was taken on when they stopped at Carstairs and Carlisle. But by the time they reached the rough half-way mark in the great rail-junction town of Crewe, the greater part of the night's work had been done. There had been far more stuff than usual for the High Value Coach and the wooden lockers were packed with 68 white bags. Sixty more jammed the narrow space between the lockers and sorting racks, making it hard for the Chief Sorter, Frank Dewhurst, and his four helpers to move around. Most of the packages contained money.

The previous Monday had been August Bank Holiday, the climactic *fiesta* of the British summer, and tourists had poured across the border into Scotland to celebrate it there. The Scots are perfectly happy to accept English currency. But they are more accustomed to dealing in bills that, as a vestigial symbol of their separate nationhood, are issued by their own banks, each to its own design. When the Scottish banks reopened on Tuesday, the principal duty awaiting the staff was to count and package all the alien paper money brought in by merchants and pub owners and send it back to where it had come from.

The packages that would go first to the East Central Post Office near London's Euston Station and from there to the English branches or trading partners of the 58 Scottish banks involved, contained either 10-shilling, 1-pound or 5-pound notes—the denominations circulated in Britain at that time.

The 10-shilling note was small and rust-colored, a little larger than a dollar bill. The 1-pound note was that universal money-green in hue and looked, at best, serviceable. But the fiver of the period was a memorable and moving sight—perhaps the most impressive piece of paper currency ever produced. It measured $8\frac{3}{4}$ x $5\frac{1}{4}$ inches and with inspired understatement was printed on one side only in authoritative glossy black upon vellumlike paper of purest white. Usually it would be carried folded evenly in four. The sight of one diffidently withdrawn from the fortunate owner's inside pocket or purse could have a dramatic effect on people and situations. Possession of an intact vintage fiver made it possible for the skilled practitioner to live quite free without embarrassment for days at a time. His companions would often insist that they should pay rather than witness the disintegration of such highly compacted purchasing power. To some extent, minor transactions like buying cigarettes or taking a taxi were completely out of the question.

Barmen and shopkeepers would likely shake their heads respectfully as though they had been offered settlement in industrial diamonds or gold dust. They would much rather take a check than change a fiver, and when they did agree, it was not uncommon for the cashee to be required to write his name and address on the blank reverse side, just as though it had been a check. The notes went from hand to hand accumulating a chain mail tally of those who had previously enjoyed the privilege, however briefly. In 1963 the average national wage was only about 14 pounds a week and, since most Britons had never been able to rub two fivers together in their lifetime, one alone remained a reassuring token of status. They were already being phased out in favor of a puerile blue note scaled down to fit the wallet. But the potent and unforgettable crackle of the old white ones was still the sound track of many a dream of ease and riches.

At Crewe a new driver, fireman and guard took over the Up Special. On to the footplate of the square-nosed 2,000 horsepower Model IB diesel locomotive climbed Jack Mills, age fifty-eight, long-jawed and large-featured, and his assistant, David Whitby, age twenty-six. Crewe was their home, but they would sleep that night in the snug British Rail hostel at Camden Town in London. Mills settled into the high leather-padded seat on the "near" right side of the cab, tested all the brake systems, read the gauges and, pushing down the spring-loaded, the "Dead Man's Handle," eased open the throttle of the great husky idling at his back.

It was the morning of August 8 now, 30 minutes after midnight, with stops scheduled at Tamworth and Rugby and—nothing for Mills to worry about—more flying drops at the apparatus points of Leighton Buzzard and Berkhamstead. The big green power unit, the golden insignia of the Royal Mail monogrammed on her side, worked smoothly up to over 70 m.p.h., the Up Special's reputation for punctuality in good standing. Fireman Whitby made the tea.

That classless English anodyne was being drunk peacefully in the swaying coaches as well by the time that Driver Mills cocked his educated ear to the thrumming of the rails and realized that he was entering a dead straight, and therefore fast, section of track approaching Sears Crossing in Buckinghamshire. Without looking at the speedometer he knew they were about to touch 80. The sorters, weary now, had finished their work save for the last leather pouches slung out to be netted at Berkhamstead. In less than an hour they would be in Euston where with unfussy efficiency the trainload of mail would be unloaded into red Post Office vans for the last stage of its journey. The High Value packages would get no more special protection there than they had had at any other time.

So inured were the sorters to their monotonous life of shuttling through the night from one end of the country to the other that it rarely crossed their mind to look out of a window. In the waning moon that still lit up the sky, there would have been even less to see as they hurtled along that straight stretch than there was on most of the Up Special's route. There were pleasures to be found there by daylight, though. The track ran across a triangle formed by the borders of the counties of Berkshire, Hertfordshire and Bedfordshire—picturesque countryside of farms, barns, canals, haystacks, the occasional Jacobean manor house and some surviving fragments of 14th-century architecture. They were not tourist pastures, however, and a few days earlier a visitor busy with a movie camera was a rare enough sight to be remembered.

At that moment, the same stranger was there again, watching the glaring yellow eye of the Up Special grow larger as it approached. With him were the tightest knit, best rehearsed, most adventurous and carefully chosen band of thieves that could be got together in Britain. There were, as far as anyone has been able to establish, between 12 and 15 of them. And as the Up Special had been clocking up its punctual progress southward toward destiny's points switch, they had been confidently threading their way through dark, leafy lanes and back roads to Bridego Bridge, a point where a well-surfaced secondary road tunneled through the embankment that supported the fast section of the permanent way.

They had not bothered to travel inconspicuously. They rode in a convoy made up of a three-ton truck and two Land Rovers. But their self-assurance was justified. They had cased the territory soundly. And they wore, with beguiling cheek, British Army battledress. Soldiers on a night exercise if anyone asked. Only the Widow Nappin, peering sleepless after midnight from the window of her cottage on Brill Road, just before the lanes gave into the hardtop, saw them go and wondered if she had dreamed it.

At the bridge there was plenty to do, and each man knew his part. They were already dressed in blue railway overalls beneath the uniforms which they quickly stripped off. Covering their heads and faces, but for the eyes, they wore Balaclava helmets, a kind of cold-weather mask named for the Crimean battle, which was the setting of the charge of the Light Brigade. The Great Train Robbers were far better led than the British cavalry of that melancholy day and every bit as disciplined.

They had walkie-talkie radios with strap-on throat mikes for the sentries, who were posted in either direction along the road. They even had a folding bicycle on which one of them mounted a mobile patrol. Most important of all, there were men among them who had mastered some of British Rail's more elementary secrets and they went to work with gloved and skillful hands. Others cut the public telephone lines strung on posts that marched along the top of the embankment. They had served their vital purpose. Regularly through the early evening the progress of the Up Special had been reported by them to pay phones in nearby villages, and they had brought word from someone shrewdly assessing the pile of bags building up on Glasgow Central's Platform 11 that tonight's train would be the one worth hitting. The robbers had been ready to go the night before but decided against it because the bag count in Glasgow had been too low.

While a couple of "heavies" broke into a small railway store by the bridge to collect the crowbars they knew to be there—and a few railwaymen's caps as well to top off their outfits—others including the "technicians" drove a mile north to attend to the signals on which the entire plot now depended. Roger Cordrey, a forty-one-year-old florist with an unhappy home life, a weakness for gambling and a fascination with trains since boyhood, was the expert here. And what he did was simple, effective and fool-proof.

The first marker that delineated the sector of track controlled by the next station along the line, Cheddington, was called the Distant Signal. Housed low by the side of the roadbed it could show only an amber or a green light. If it was amber the driver of an oncoming train would expect to find that the Home Signal at Sear Crossing, 1,300 yards on, would be red. He was required to reduce speed in the first instance, but in the second, to stop until the light changed to green.

In the cab of the Up Special, Mills was in no way surprised to see the first light at amber, although he was slightly irritated. It was a few seconds before three, and he was still on time. There had been endless maintenance going on along the track even at night and the Cheddington signal box might merely be slowing him down. But when he could see that the Home Signal did stand at red, making him brake in earnest, he wondered, because he could see that far beyond Sear Crossing the further light showed green. Odd.

"Probably something wrong with the lights," he said to Fireman Whitby. "Jump down and see."

Indeed there was. Cordrey had cut the power line to the Distant Signal and illuminated its amber glass with a bulb powered by four six-volt flashlight batteries wired together. He did the same with the red disc of the Home Signal suspended from its gantry over the track. But here he did not snip the power line. He had discovered that this key warning was wired to a malfunction alarm in the Cheddington signal box. The green light was masked by a piece of cardboard and, for good measure, a glove. Beside each lamp was left a spare lamp and batteries. Jimmy White, who had been responsible for much of the details of the operation, was an ex-paratrooper. He knew the value of having two of everything in case something happened to the first. The rails were already vibrating with the oncoming train before the lines of the railway phone that linked points all along the line—and whose breakdown, therefore, might be accidentally discovered—was snipped.

As well as the pair of signal lights the overhead gantry which Mills had brought the front buffers of the locomotive close to also carried a squared-off diamond-shaped white plaque inscribed with a black "T." Mills who knew most British tracks like other men know the way to their office was well aware even without the sign that there was a telephone there. He wanted Whitby to call the Cheddington signal box and ask if this was a genuine delay or if, as frequently happened, the circuit controlling the signals was faulty.

In the weak moonlight it took Whitby a few minutes to locate the box containing the telephone but only seconds to realize that the instrument was silent and dead. He shone his flashlight on it. And for the first time in the Up Special's long haul through that night someone realized that all was perhaps not as it ought to be.

"Jack," he yelled back to the locomotive 20 yards behind him. "The wires are out!"

Whitby was walking back, puzzled rather than alarmed, to the familiar footplate, when he glimpsed a possible explanation or, at least, a source of one. From between the High Value Coach and the one astern of it, stepped a figure whose face could not be seen but whose silhouette showed the unmistakable graceless lines of British Rail cap and dungarees, and who carried a pair of the signal flags used in shunting. We never sleep, thought Whitby commiseratively, before he moved further on past the loco toward the man and asked, "What's up, mate?"

Whitby was never certain whether the man replied by actually saying "Come here," or whether he merely gave a casual gesture that meant the same thing. But still unsuspecting, he went toward the embankment where the other led. By the time he had realized that all he could see of his supposed colleague's face were his eyes, the man lunged forward and projected by a powerful push in his chest, Whitby sailed over the edge, rolled down the thinly grassed slope and came to rest at the feet of two more dark figures. Where their faces should have been there was just "a black mass." Winded and terrified though he was, he did not forget the words that one of them spoke to him.

"If you shout," said the closer of the black masses amiably, "I'll kill you."

Whitby knew when to quit.

"All right, mate," he said. "I'm on your side."

"Thanks," said the black mass.

Back aboard the locomotive the footsteps that the driver Mills heard on the metal steps below the narrow doorway did not, as he assumed, belong to Whitby. The first man of the assault force came aboard armed with the primary weapon on which the gang had agreed—a pick handle padded with cloth as a thoughtful precaution against doing too much harm to anybody who might have to be hit with one.

Mills did not get the implied message.

"I'm not giving in without a fight," he articulated later, re-membering his first chilling glimpse before he leaped to repel the boarder. He had the advantage at first. The robber was still on the steps and Mills towered above him. Though only five years short of retirement age, Mills was still well served by the muscles he had developed during a long apprenticeship of heaving coal in the days of steam. But other robbers came up the steps on the other side of the cab and one of them, lacking a padded club, reluctantly gave him a tap on the head with a small crowbar. He fell, hitting his head again as he did, and suddenly the cab was jammed with impatient men in overalls and Balaclavas.

There were more of them busy at the rear of the High Value Coach as Whitby was brought back up the embankment, pushed aboard again and handcuffed to the bleeding Mills. He was forced to lie down with him, heads to the rear, in the narrow iron passageway that runs from the cab between the engine room of the locomotive and the fan room that provides its cooling.

The robbers down on the track knew their uncoupling drill well. They had learned it from disaffected railwaymen and practiced it clandestinely in darkened marshaling yards. A few nights earlier they had gone through it again in pantomime on that exact spot. They only forgot one thing. So did the man on whom the next part of the operation depended, a rogue railwayman, whose nerves were not under the same impressive standard of control achieved by the full members of the gang. Mills and Whitby could hear him cursing over the controls. And being cursed.

When the hooded shunters had lifted the giant coupling links and unhooked the first two coaches from the ones behind them, the driver, who had backed up a few feet to give them slack, let the locomotive and its lightened load run forward again. The vacuum hose which actuates the braking system along the whole length of the train had been left connected. It snapped away with a report that shattered the tense silence of the night. But while it scared the robbers badly, the sleepy sorters, wise in the waywardness of such things, diagnosed it as a minor technical mishap. Nonetheless, they thought the driver might like to know. And Chief Sorter Dewhurst made use of the only means they had of getting in touch with him, the communication cord or the emergency signal. Not only did this elementary alarm system work an indicator in the cab, but it applied the vacuum brakes, freezing the heavy locomotive to the tracks.

The gang's driver, unnerved and baffled by unfamiliar controls, could not get it to move again. The frustrated robbers unshackled Mills and manhandled him back into the driver's seat, shouldering their own man aside, whimpering and disgraced.

"Start her up," one of them ordered. "And keep going. But slowly."

This was Gordon Goody, the narrow-lipped hairdresser with a record of violence, one of the prime movers. A real *duro*.

Mills rectified the vacuum brake valve and pumped air out of the system to lift the brakes. At first they could only creak away from its standstill. But as the vacuum built up, the brake shoes lightened on the wheels and the truncated Up Special continued to roll toward the next part of its adventure, bandits hanging from its sides as though they had been working on the railroad all their lives.

"When I say stop," Goody told Mills, "you stop—or you'll get some more."

And another Balaclava-encased head bent down and whispered, "For God's sake don't speak. There are some right bastards here."

As the High Value Coach drew away from the rest of the train the oblivious sorters in it, reassured by renewed movement, turned back to their tea. However, left at a standstill an ever increasing distance behind them, Guard Thomas Miller, 20 years on the job at sixty-one, was at last beginning to get worried. He had seen from his tail-end van window the amber and red lights that had brought them to a halt. He had noticed his vacuum gauge drop to zero, informing him he would not be able to apply the brakes in any emergency. He had no way of communicating with the locomotive either. But he decided that even at the risk of being left behind on the track if Mills suddenly got a green light and pulled away, it was time he found out what was going on.

When he discovered that his train now ended abruptly at Coach Number Three and that the telephone was dead, his first thought was not for the locomotive, which could clearly look after itself, but for an eventuality the gang had not even considered. Swinging his lantern, Miller plodded dutifully for a mile back along the permanent way, planting detonators on the line and red flares beside it to warn the next train that might come along.

Just before Bridego Bridge a grubby white towel had been tied to an upright. A bandit, clinging to a ladder, pointed it out to Mills.

"Stop at the marker," he ordered. Mills braked. Once more the handcuffs were clapped on him and Whitby. Again they were bundled out of the cab and down the embankment. At the bottom their noses were pressed into the grass, but they could hear behind them the splintering of wood and the cries of the sorters bestirred at last and under attack. While still keeping their heads down they caught occasional glimpses—their first—of the Up Special's precious burden being passed across them by a human chain of bogus railwaymen.

The robber who had told Mills where to stop stood guard over them. He chatted, asking their names.

To Mills he murmured, "I'll get your address when this is all over and send you a few quid."

To Whitby, he said, "You can smoke if you want to."

And when the fireman lit up awkwardly with his one free hand, the friendly robber said, "I'll have one if you've got one to spare."

He even borrowed Whitby's lighter.

Then, as the engines of the loaded truck and the Land Rovers were started, four robbers lifted the crew back aboard the locomotive yet again.

"Now, Dave," one of them warned Whitby, "don't say anything to any of them. There are some bastards in this lot who will kill you."

The man who had bummed the cigarette waved a cocky good-bye and went off to collect his reward.

Ronald Biggs.

3

"I run the paper purely for the purpose of making propaganda and with no other motive."

Lord Beaverbrook, testifying
before the Royal Commission
on the Press, 1948

•

Fleet Street begins where the Strand ends outside the Royal Courts of Justice. It runs a mere half mile or so to Ludgate Circus at the foot of the hill on which stands Wren's foundering masterpiece, St. Paul's Cathedral. It was named—as was a notorious 18th-century prison nearby—for the Fleet River that still gurgles down to the Thames somewhere beneath its pavements, and it has passed the name on as an allusive label for the whole school and outlook of British national journalism as Wall Street, the Quai d'Orsay and Carnaby Street were called upon in the cause of verbal shorthand.

It is a well-worn part of London, singed around the edge by the Great Fire, battered squarely by the Blitz and marked for its remaining life now by gimcrack 1950s office architecture. It is bounded by seats of learning and influence like the London School of Economics, an obligatory stopover for any revolutionary going places, and two inns of court—The Temple and Lincoln's Inn, which provide a counterbalance by breeding the commissars of the status quo. It has its own adjacent waterfront, the Victoria Embankment, where the ship that took Scott (and a correspondent from *The Times*) to the Antarctic lies preserved and, since it is part of the City of London, a separate administrative territory from the adjacent borough of Westminster, it appears to have its own policemen; they wear a more theatrical helmet than their cousins patrolling in the Strand.

From its upper stories the view takes in both the blindfolded figure of Justice with her scales atop the gilded dome of the Old Bailey (the Central Criminal Court; it is divorce and civil cases in the Royal Courts) and the stark cross surmounting St. Paul's. Editors and newspaper proprietors have been known to take this sight as an oppressive reminder of the forces, spiritual and temporal, that direct their daily judgments. For the press is not "free" in Britain in the sense that it is thought to be in the United States or Italy or Sweden or Israel. Wild, maybe. Libertine, certainly. Free, no. Perils abound.

Despite the indelible synonym, very few of the national newspapers' offices are actually in Fleet Street itself. Most are lodged in the capillaries feeding off the vein—Fetter Lane, Bouverie Street and Shoe Lane. *The Times* recently forewent the gratification of having Printing House Square as its address and moved to Grays Inn Road, territory first deflowered by *The Guardian* when it made its half-hearted move to the Big Smoke from Manchester. But the toilers of such enclaves are not denied citizenship; they are looked on as the *pieds noir* of their time and place; or perhaps the Puerto Ricans.

The offices are spaced out by other landmarks. The mock Gothic Public Record Office in Chancery Lane has the grist of great news events since the quintessential political year of 1066 filed away. Carey Street for long supplied another handy synonym, one uncomfortably haunting to a surrounding community so chronically insecure and improvident, until the Bankruptcy Court was moved to somewhere else, and St. Bride's, which rather pompously bills itself as the mother church of the media, provides yet one more.

A memorial service at Bride's, a Wren *hors d'oeuvre* raised on Roman ruins, is the customary acknowledgment that the Great Circulation Manager got there a step ahead of the first retirement check. Several times a year a full house of grateful survivors gathers there to mark a sudden departure, exchange reminiscences and note each other's symptoms. The rest of the time it is even less frequented than most British churches. Bride's parishioners may not be a long-lived lot but their impiety is unassailable.

There are many buildings other than offices that are indispensable to the recycling of information. And they are lavishly studded through the web of alleys and passageways that laces this village together, for ink is not its only vital fluid. National taste and custom dictates a respectful amount of beer drinking in the public houses, particularly in the ones favored by printing workers, the strongly unionized artisan aristocrats, who often earn more than most of the journalists. Whisky flows and gin. But mostly, Fleet Street drinks wine. Champagne in El Vino, a self-consciously venerable den where women may still not use the bar, or Spanish plonk in the Printer's Pie—a strategic window-front from which to keep lunch-hour movement under observation—it is consumed in industrial quantities every hour of the long, long newspaper day.

If it is too long a wait for the statutory opening hour of 11:30 A.M. the pubs in Smithfield nearby open at five to serve the wholesale meat market. Anyone with blood on their clothes can buy a drink. The evening newspaper offices, remember, have been manned since 6 A.M., and the wire services—Reuters, United Press International, Associated Press, Agence France Presse, Tass, Japan News Agency —work through the night. Soon after noon pubs like Poppins, Barney's, Mother Bunche's, The Red Lion, The Harrow, The Cartoonist, The Bell, The Printer's Devil become swamped by an inexorable prelunch wave. Some of them are virtually annexes of the newspapers they adjoin and some are practically on the premises like the *Daily Mirror*'s local. When the *Mirror* staff discovered that, technically speaking, the place belonged to their firm, they claimed the right to choose its name, and in keeping with the spirit of friendly rivalry so familiar to all in the calling, decided on the Stab in the Back. The brewers who hold the pub's lease, however, preferred something a little less vivid, and from their threadbare approved list came up with the White Hart. It may be the White Hart to John Courage & Sons but to the *Mirror* and to anyone else who has ever breathed its blighted air it will be The Stab forevermore.

Guidebook joints like the Cheshire Cheese and The Cock are frequented only with greatest caution because of the peril of being badgered by Japanese tourists or ladies from Arkansas and Sydney about where Dr. Johnson's pipestand may be seen and whether they are in the right place for a rancid old English delicacy like steak kidney and oyster pudding. But the existence of the Wig and Pen Club and the City Golf Club insures that members and their friends need not be inconvenienced by the strange civic precautionary measure of shutting down pubs for most of the afternoon. In them, just as in all the other places of refreshment during more orthodox hours, members of the only two major industries of the quarter may be found side by side facing the bar but in every other way opposed. Lawyers and journalists are natural enemies, and however much their professional and recreational interests overlap, they are uneasy in each other's company.

Reporters have a weakness, actually, for Managing Clerks, the knowledgeable and wily noncommissioned officers of the calling who are the lynch pins in every legal practice. They are often appealingly Dickensian types, given to watch chains and a lot of dandruff who, thanks to the stealthy dividends yielded by the artfulness with which they go about their masters' business, have no difficulty in matching the openhandedness of a companion with an expense account. Clerks and reporters are likely to have in common, what is more, a considerably superior experience of the eye-level workings of the law.

It is never hard to distinguish between the two communities. Professional vanity drives the barristers to lunch still wearing the peculiar waistcoats that go under their ostentatiously tattered gowns in court and their white neck "tabs," much as an actor will casually leave on some makeup to show that he is employed. They are less worried about being taken for journalists than for solicitors. Solicitors, the other half of the legal world (or rather its submerged nine-tenths), dress with caution but without distinction. The precise opposite is true of most newspapermen. But when the eye cannot perceive the contrast there is a simple test. If a solicitor is asked for a pen or pencil he always has one.

Subdivisions within the dominant tribe are also frequently marked by distinctions of appearance—some the product of emulation and some stimulated by tradition. Visitors to the territory are intrigued to discover that literary editors and critics often do wear bow ties in real life, that motoring experts and sports reporters may be found in check suits verging upon the chromatic, that the man in the dirty trenchcoat actually is a crime reporter, that women writers are usually good-looking and assertive, that velvet suits are a mark of the rising executive or expanding by-line, that foreign correspondents flaunt genuine tans and that gossip columnists often seem to have on the shirt they wore the night before.

El Vino is practically the last place in London to refuse to serve a drink to a man without a jacket or tie, and that simple fact alone forbade Fleet Street the wilder sartorial excesses to which the communications industries abandon themselves. That and the rigid view clung to in some offices that even the most gifted of interviewers might find himself at a disadvantage, if he had suddenly to be sent to see the Archbishop of Canterbury or the Chancellor of the Exchequer when he had arrived at work dressed as a Katmandu yak-master or with the price of a hutful of Bantu brides swathed in beads across his pale bare chest.

Not that everyone wants to go to El Vino every day. There are plenty so disenchanted with its quaint and peremptory ways that they would rather drink milk. (There is, too, the constant danger of capture by bores, although in common with every other desirable rendezvous of its kind it has a well-used back exit.) It is just that Fleet Street natures react to the possibility of exclusion from anywhere like a vampire to a silversmith's sign.

The demography changes at the end of the afternoon. The lawyers and the rest of the noncombatant population do not linger past conventional work hours. Nor does the clerical and managerial staff of the newspapers. Inside the offices the initiative passes from those who have planned and written the paper and provided its contacts with reality to the latecomers whose task it is to give tangible form to the result.

Fleet Street itself is deserted then, although handover ceremonies eddy fitfully through the pubs, but the courtyards and byways are jammed with gaudy delivery vans and expensive cars owned by the printers. Birth takes place at the same time every night, simultaneously duplicated in the case of most papers by a similar event in

Manchester where northern readers are presented with a not-quite-identical twin, but it is never without complications. The pains are at their strongest between a first burst of frenzied straining to wrest stories being written for the first edition out of typewriters, and a second one a couple of hours later to get them off the subeditors' tables where they have been prepared for the printers, allocated a place on a page and adorned with a headline.

Different editions—different versions, in effect—of the papers are prepared for different parts of the country (television programs in East Anglia being different from those in Kent as is the sport, weather and local news). But the printing of the main edition, the definitive version, is the major objective of the night. That is the one the majority of readers will see, and it keeps many tons of heavy machinery busy until dawn. By 11 P.M. the underground rumble of high-speed rotary presses will raise a ripple on the surface of a glass of stout on any bar between Holborn Circus and Tudor Street. The pubs close then. But there is still the Press Club, the final haven for nocturnal theoreticians, allied or opposed, to rerun the night.

A tireless obsession with what they do for a living is not youthful enthusiasm in journalists. Fleet Street's average age is close to forty. Careers are not begun there. Eligibility is purchased with credentials already earned somewhere else. Typically, a man will arrive at age twenty-five and not long married to the prettiest girl from the town where he was the best reporter on the local paper. Women are often a little older than that by the time they get there, going back to work perhaps after a child and a divorce—usually from another journalist.

Many come from the less economically blessed parts of Britain—Scotland, Wales and the North—just as many of their American counterparts are likely to be Jews or small-town Southerners. They saw that more than any other occupation readily available to them journalism promised classless acceptance, swift upward financial and geographical mobility—and glamor.

It can hardly be called a profession, for it lacks the essential elements of controlled entry and exclusive right of practice, let alone a demanding standard of preliminary education (probably no more than 15 percent of Fleet Street people are university graduates). For those who practice it routinely, it remains a trade; for the best of them it becomes a complicated and embracing craft.

But more than anything, for the ones who make it, Fleet Street is a way of life quite unlike any other. Bank managers do not write their names into half the households in the land overnight; advertising copywriters do not get telephoned at home in the morning and told to go to Beirut instead of coming to the office.

The degrees of talent ("*flair*"), experience and determination that gets them there through the formidable competition varies wildly as does the level of dedication, guile and effrontery that must constantly be exerted to stave off the onset of *downward* mobility. But to a man and a woman they are sufferers in common from two distinctive and disabling aberrations. The first one they share in a sense with the stereotype backyard gossip—as well as a large number of the suspects detained by the Flying Squad—an irresistible compulsion to impart to others everything they know. The second is not so widely encountered. Much as they appreciate the money that they earn they could probably—like ace hit men, Evel Knievel and the better type of hooker—be persuaded to do it for nothing.

The *Daily Express* is planted firmly in Fleet Street itself, an ink-black, *art-moderne* glass monument to its only significant proprietor—the first and last Baron Beaverbrook. In Evelyn Waugh's benchmark novel of popular journalism, *Scoop*, the Beaver became Lord Copper and the *Express* the immortal *Daily Beast*.

But the antics of the self-made press lords of the day—self-made not only because they generated their own fortunes but because they blandly used the money one way or another to buy their peerages—practically defied satirization. When Beaverbrook got his title, King George V, in whose name it was granted, was not even consulted. The King's private secretary wrote to Prime Minister Lloyd George with whom the Beaver had negotiated that His Majesty "was surprised and hurt that this honor should have been offered without first obtaining his consent."

The shaky triple alliance of Viscount Northcliffe, who by the First World War owned the *Daily Mail*, the *Evening News* and *The Times*, his brother Baron Harmsworth, to whom he had sold the *Daily Mirror*, and Beaverbrook could not quite manage any king-making. But they gleefully combined to make and unmake political leaders and governments with far more effective help from their reckless and acquiescent editors than they could get from their seats in the House of Lords.

William Maxwell Aitken, as he had been before his ennoblement, was already a millionaire when he arrived in Britain from Canada, convinced that he had a divinely endorsed mission to preserve the British Empire in its far-flung majesty. He never had much luck with that, since it was already well advanced in its decay. But the *Express*, which he bought for a measly 17,000 pounds in 1915, gave up the good fight only when Britain entered the Common Market a few years after his death in 1965.

That was a fairly routine example of the true influence of the *Express* on the great issues of its time. Indeed, it became an unchallengeable axiom years back that no cause was truly lost until it had been taken up by the Beaverbrook Press. Nor, despite indefatigable efforts, was the Beaver ever able to penetrate to the central core of the British Establishment, despite the support he gave to most conservative causes.

But he remained an incurable intriguer and mischief-maker, serenely convinced of his mission and his immense fortune, made from cement, bond-pushing, insurance, and audacity, had left him unbeholden to anyone. He could never be kept away from the action. In his time he became the country's first Minister of Information (and made Northcliffe Director of Propaganda in Enemy Countries), launched the United Empire Party in an effort to head a government (but by splitting the Tory vote insured a Labour victory in 1929), failed to talk King Edward VIII out of abdicating (after masterminding the British newspaper conspiracy of silence over the Wallis Simpson romance) and as Minister of Aircraft Production in the Second World War did as much as any single man to insure Britain's survival.

Once he got a good enough whiff of the heady vapors of Fleet Street, the Beaver developed an addict's taste for popular journalism quite apart from the political uses to which it could be put. He hired generously and cannily, supported his editors and writers with shrewd counsel, provided them with endless targets for campaigns and vendettas and for years built up the *Express* as a lavishly stocked showcase of wonders into which people loved to peer every morning even though common sense told them that most of the glittering baubles there had to be fake. Crisp, witty, chrome-plated human drama and irresistible picture layouts were the specialities of the house. They could be enjoyed even if staccato right-wing editorials and slick, bitchy gossip items were too large a part of the package to be ignored. The most brilliant if not quite the very best of British journalism was on display in the *Express* six days a week, many of the practitioners personally signed up by the restless old Beaver himself.

One of the distinguished specialists the Beaver introduced to *Express* readers in this way was A. J. P. Taylor the Oxford historian. He later became a dutiful biographer of his patron recording Max's precocious fascination with newspapers as a 13-year-old in Maple, Ontario where he founded something called, perhaps in his own honor, "The Leader."

"A restless little boy, always up to mischief," noted Taylor foreshadowing the man—of whom he also wrote, "Max's devices for making money were inexhaustible and ingenious."

Admiringly Taylor recorded the details of the celebrated cement transaction that earned the Beaver the crowning fortune he brought to Britain like a dowry the year after raking it in, emphasizing firmly that there had been "nothing underhanded" about the way it had been acquired; the *chef d'oeuvre*, rather, of a master craftsman of capitalism outsmarting an array of his peers.

In 1934 the paper the grown-up Beaver had bought himself for such a pittance sold 1,708,000 copies a day. By 1947, after wartime restrictions on newsprint had been lifted, it sold 3,706,000, easily the world's highest figure and a tribute to the Beaver's astuteness in keeping one Arthur Christiansen as editor for 25 years and thereby making a Fleet Street legend of him as well.

But Fleet Street was a new world by 1949. The left-wing *Daily Mirror*, driving ahead with the momentum of its wartime popularity with servicemen and managing to cling to the rails, was selling 4,187,000 to the *Express*'s 3,985,000. Behind the black glass, clerks took thousands of letterheads to a guillotine and trimmed off the slogan: "The Largest Sale On Earth."

The Beaver rarely went near the place—he did not even keep an office there. Whoever he wanted to see came to see him wherever he was—in his London apartment off Piccadilly, his estate at Leatherhead on the Surrey Downs, or his villa in Cap d'Antibes. He might equally well have been in Fredericton, New Brunswick, where he had founded a university or aboard the *Queen Elizabeth* at sea. Whoever he wanted to speak to he simply telephoned. Many a far-flung *Express* correspondent carries the cardiac scar to this day from the first time he picked up his telephone and heard an accented voice say, "This is Lord Beaverbrook," and in curious, radio announcer's rhythm and rounded evangelistic periods go on, with something like, "It has been suggested to me that the story on which your name appears in this day's paper is not in accordance with the facts as they have been understood by some respected friends of mine. Could I ask you to provide me with the means of reassuring them?"

Satisfied with the reply he would ring off saying, "It is a gratifying thing to know such men work for the *Daily Express*. You have put my mind at rest."

*Express*men never strayed far from a telephone. They still don't.

By 1974 Fleet Street was an even less recognizable world from those halcyon postwar days. And the *Express* was struggling to stay alive in it; the Beaver's heirs left to tot up the price of half a century of totally self-indulgent proprietorship. Because he had never needed any money from the paper—indeed had always been embarrassed by its considerable profits—he had been delighted to see everything it made soaked up by theatrical editorial expenditure and complacent management.

Unlike its competitors, who had shareholders to satisfy or were run by men wedded to expansion, the commercial evolution of the *Express* and its stablemates, the *Sunday Express* and the *Evening Standard*, had been thwarted by the Beaver's capriciously limited objectives. No kind of serious future planning or diversification into real estate, provincial newspapers, commercial television, magazines and other industries, which had been essential to papers that functioned as the mainspring of public fortunes, was ever begun. The *Express* had never been anything but a useful set of gears in the Beaver's global gadgetry, and when he had gone it stayed that way, its ownership frozen in a trust and control passed to the aging dauphin of the Aitken, who circumspectly declined to become the second Lord Beaverbrook, preferring to be known by the style of the baronetcy that was the family's first honor, as Sir Max.

Five ambitious men succeeded one another in the search for a

worthy replacement of the immortal Christiansen. All that happened was that the draft from the revolving door of the Editor's
office chilled the ardor of the ranks, blasted an irreplaceable
accumulation of infertilizing esprit de corps out into The Street and
crisped the snow under the front skids of the circulation toboggan.

In eight years more than a million copies a day was wiped off the
figures. And even though it still sold nearly three million and was
still manifestly a prime advertising vehicle for the temptation of the
acquisitive, rising middle class, by the beginning of 1974 the *Express*
had hardly enough overdraft left each day to meet the next day's
running costs.

Sixty-four-year-old Sir Max fought as gallantly on the savage
battleground of The Street as he had in the skies over it as an
illustrious wartime R.A.F. fighter pilot. But he had long since sent
for help. It came in the graceful form of Jocelyn Stevens, who in
background and appearance was just the kind of young Englishman
readers of the *Express* would most like to be.

"The newspaper industry is not characterized by people who
could honestly be described as glamorous in the true meaning of the
word," it was observed in an admiring *Sunday Times* profile that
provided a rare instance of one of the dogs taking a friendly sniff at
another in front of the readers. "But Jocelyn is the exception. He is
the archetypal dream hero of True Romance fiction: a fun-loving,
good-looking, high-living, brilliant millionaire with everything
money can buy and much it can't."

Stevens was forty-two. He could hardly be said to have learned
the hard way since he was left a fortune by his uncle, a minor press
nobleman from the sizable group of them that proliferated in the
wake of the Northcliffe–Harmsworth–Beaverbrook pioneers. When
he grew up he used a quarter of a million pounds of it to buy himself
a Vogue-ish magazine called *Queen*. With it he practiced a system
of forthright up-market diagnosis and cure that won some admira-
tion from the Beaverbrooks, and when he was consulted by Sir Max
on the condition of the ailing *Evening Standard*, he went to its
bedside so confidently that no one dared question his qualifications.

The *Standard* soon discovered that beneath the decadent pink
shirts Stevens favored beat a heart of true native stone but that most
of his remedies made good economic sense, despite the languid
Etonian vowels in which they were prescribed. He brought the

patient around, at least for the moment, and was then expected to do the same with the far, far sicker *Express*.

He had radical surgery in the back of his mind; the liquidation of the largely autonomous Scottish *Daily Express* for instance and 1,750 jobs with it. Meanwhile, he warmed up with some therapeutic hiring and firing, chopping off superannuated departmental heads as fast as he could find men to replace them. One of the key changes he approved was the appointment of Brian Vine as Assistant Editor in charge of news—assistant that is to the Editor himself Ian McColl, the supreme and nominally independent overall head of editorial operations in London, Manchester, and Glasgow.

Because home-bound Londoners often got their first sniff of a big story from the evening papers, one of the things Stevens had seen amply demonstrated during his apprenticeship at the *Standard* was the basic adage that nothing sells newspapers like news; at any rate, the kind of news the customers really want to read. The Fleet Street life cycle begins with getting the paper bought. Circulation increases earn higher advertising charges; the income pays for more expensive news gathering and promotion campaigns to urge people to buy the paper because they will like what's in it. The fuel that packs the highest lift-off punch, of course, comes from the exclusive possession of a story any of the other papers would be glad to have so that their regular readers may be lured at least for a moment to pick up an unfamiliar rival that they may even come to prefer.

It was to be up to Vine to insure a steady supply of these elusive treasures, a daunting task in the early days of that dreary January of coal shortages, oil crisis and endless squabbling between Egyptians and Israelis at Kilometre 101. But as it was he hardly had to try. A short conversation one day with one of the few reporters on the general staff that he knew really well, and he realized he had stumbled across the daddy of them all.

4

The Well Situate Compact Small Holding of about 5 acres
Known as Leatherslade Farm, Brill, Bucks.
Real Estate Agents' description

●

When a pack of hooded men fell upon the High Value Coach with
businesslike threats and nifty crowbar work, the sorters inside at last
realized that something was seriously amiss. They reacted with the
instincts of good citizens and began to fight back. One jammed a
precious bagful of notes into the first shattered window. Another
tried to bolt the door that had connected with the abandoned rest
of the train. A robber halfway into the coach spotted him and
yelled, "Some bastard's putting the bolts on! Get the guns!"

There were no guns. But if there had been, they would not have
been needed. Faced with the dozen sinister mobsters who had
levered their way through the flimsy coachwork in seconds, the Post
Office men behaved sensibly. They saw the crowbars, the axes and
the padded pickhandles and meekly lay down on the floor in a
corner as they were told and hid their faces. They heard the locks
being smashed off the wooden doors and the soft, familiar slither of
the canvas bags being dragged away.

Faultlessly the well-drilled robbers fanned out between the coach
and the vehicles parked out of sight beneath the bridge, swinging

the bags from man to man, stowing them away under a false bottom in the Austin truck. Someone was keeping them to a timetable and when the appointed time came—they went, even though it meant abandoning eight full mailbags.

A classic admonition was given to Dewhurst, who had been in some way recognized as the sorters' leader.

"You stay here on the floor for half an hour after we've gone," said one of the Balaclavas. "We're leaving someone behind to make sure you don't move. And God help you if you do."

Sorters and locomotive crew alike heard the engines of the little convoy start, run steadily through their gear changes and fade into the distance. Less than half an hour, all told, since Mills had put the brakes on at his first sight of the red light, the gang was back in the leafy lanes again, sitting on top of the money. Two and a half tons of it. Only the Widow Nappin, watching behind her curtains, saw them coming back and realized that earlier she had not been dreaming.

Dewhurst waited about ten minutes before he climbed down, walked around the train, saw that no one had been left on guard and sent a couple of the sorters for help. One borrowed a bicycle from the nearest farm and pedaled off to find a telephone. But the Cheddington signal box had already realized it had lost a train. The Up Special had been traced through Leighton Buzzard, so the next Down train was asked to cover the section in between slowly and see what had gone wrong. The driver stopped for a sorter waving a flashlight and took the victims aboard—together with poor old Miller, the guard, who by then had caught up with the lost locomotive—aboard. Mills and Whitby were still handcuffed together. They stayed that way until they finally got to the Royal Buckinghamshire Hospital at Aylesbury. At 4:24 A.M., on August 8, Miller telephoned Euston from Cheddington and, in the most routine and orderly manner he could contrive, broke the staggering news.

Right from the beginning, the Great Train Robbery was a smash hit. Although on the first day no one appreciated the true extent of the achievement, it was clearly the kind of crime any country could be proud of. And Britain was almost wantonly ready to be amused.

General de Gaulle had just barred her way into the Common Market, there was considerable embarrassment that Kim Philby, the Middle East correspondent of *The Observer*, had turned up in Moscow as a Communist spy, the winter had been the coldest recorded since 1740 and the summer that followed not much better. The only happenings at which the nation had been able to warm itself at all were the exotic carryings on of Miss Christine Keeler and the Secretary of State for War (among others) but that dazzling spectacle was nearing the end of its run. In terms of popular entertainment the timing of the robbery was perfect. Britons were in the mood to soak up every word about it.

On that first day the timing was a salutary gift for the evening papers since the nationals had finished printing their final editions by the time word reached them from Scotland Yard. The evenings with the story all to themselves—there were no daytime television news programs in Britain then—soon discovered that the robbers had got away with at least a million pounds which was enough to ensure them of both immortality and the largest headlines in which the figure could be expressed. But the story kept getting better by the minute and an entranced and admiring public cleaned out edition after edition, chuckling smugly at the contrast between the primitive dispositions of the bureaucracy and the criminals' brisk and workmanlike demonstration of private enterprise. It seemed like crime in the best of British traditions, with no one really getting hurt—except the driver who, it was widely considered, should have showed the same good sense his mate had; after all, it wasn't *his* money.

Relish deepened even more the next day when the eight banks to which the consignment was going finally tallied up their combined loss at 2,631,000 pounds, with one of them, the Midland Bank shamefacedly having to admit that they never bothered to insure banknote shipments and would therefore have to suffer their share of the loss themselves. Half a million pounds.

What could be done with such an enormous sum? Well, for one thing, the *Daily Mirror* calculated irreverently, it would buy all the beer drunk in Britain every 24 hours. Many a boisterous toast was drunk in pubs to that thought.

A heist of such grandeur compelled international recognition. *The New York Times* obliged.

How pallid our own crime syndicates are made to look, how wanting in imagination. . . . After all we hold the copyright on train robbery. We even put them on film half a century ago in the first movie with a fully developed plot, "The Great Train Robbery," yet now the best we can say about this updating of Jesse James is that we supplied the cultural inspiration. The know-how is distinctly British.

The New York *Herald Tribune* put the story on the front page beneath a six-column headline, *History's Greatest Robbery—There'll Always Be An England.* And its editorial read: "Perhaps because of a long tradition of highly literate writers on sophisticated crime, British criminals tend to avoid the blood-and-thunder style of the James boys and do their work with exceptional finesse."

Many a clerkly British heart fluttered with quiet pride. After all, the best the James boys ever did the Rock Island Line for was $3,000.

British newspapers could hardly praise the robbers. But there was a distinctly respectful tone about the earliest comments. Except in one quarter from which terse and admonitory sentences were snapped out under the heading: *Brutal Plot.*

"There should be no disposition to look on the train robbers as masterminds, or to admire their 'genius' for large-scale crime," it said. "For what happened at Sear Crossing? A gang of armed bandits held up unarmed railmen and postal workers.

"They made a gigantic haul through simple criminal brutality. Their plot depended on terrorizing train drivers into silence. What is daring or brilliant about that?

"The real organizing ability comes from those whose job it is to track down criminals—the police."

The *Daily Express.*

But the police did not have a clue. Literally. Dozens of detectives arrived at the scene with admirable dispatch, but the sorters and railwaymen could not tell them much. The items collected and held by the man appointed Exhibits Officer, Detective Constable Keith Milner, told them even less. A broken coupling from a vacuum hose, a few crowbars and axe handles, a railwayman's cap, a bloodstained bandage and a piece of string. No robber had shown his face nor taken off a glove. Nobody was certain how many of them there had been nor which direction they might have gone in. They had not even left a tiremark, let alone a fingerprint.

For the first 24 hours the police could not be quite sure about fingerprints, for the locomotive promptly disappeared again. British Rail having lost it once were not going to leave it lying around, and although the Buckinghamshire Constabulary particularly asked them to keep it at Cheddington, it was driven all the way back to Crewe where the police did not find it again until the following day.

The Buckinghamshire force was technically in charge of the investigation but Detective Superintendent Malcolm Fewtrell realized that the resources of the Metropolitan Police would have to be mobilized and the ritual call for assistance went off to New Scotland Yard. Yard men were already turning out in impressive numbers in London to share the floodlights with Post Office officials and the Postmaster General, who had been hastily recalled from a Spanish beach. But to the bewilderment of all, Commander George Hatherill, deputy head of the Criminal Investigation Division, decided to send only two men down to take over the search. There was, of course, a strong probability that the gang had already divided the loot and split up. How long did it take to count two-and-a-half million pounds?

The Great Train Robbery was a transcendent masterpiece of criminal planning by men with a gift not only for leadership and organization but for thrift. What they were forced to buy they did, apparently out of the proceeds of an equally inspired but far less ambitious raid at London Airport nearly a year before. But they preferred, naturally, to steal whatever they could, including one of the Land Rovers, a couple of Jaguars for stand-by getaway cars and even their base of operations, Leatherslade Farm. When they realized how perfectly the isolated two-storey house and outbuildings suited their purpose, they offered the owner Bernard Rixon 100 pounds more than the 5,500 for which he had already agreed to sell to a neighbor. They gave him only the usual 10 percent deposit knowing that by the completion date of the contract they would be far away.

It took three months to refine the details of the plot: to decide on the right train; to find the right spot to stop it and work out the means; and to gather the right men together. The idea that the robbers were working to a script prepared for them by some epicurean master theoretician is still cherished by many people with an interest in the matter. And it may be true. But four capable and experienced operators got the practical aspects of it together with flawless efficiency, and there is no reason why they could not have worked the entire thing out from the beginning.

They were Goody, the visionary hairdresser with a record of violence; Charles Wilson, a successful greengrocer (and less successful bookmaker); and the *capos* of two well-established regional mobs in London, Ronald "Buster" Edwards of the South East Gang and Bruce Reynolds of the South West Gang. These two mobs had carved up the territory that lay south of the Thames, the recognized frontier that divided them from the patchwork dominion of the East End gangs (who also laid claim to the rich and productive pastures of the respectable West End). The East Enders specialized in racetrack revels, shady catering and protection rackets with no compunction about violence. The Southerners took pride in their reputation as peaceful and accomplished thieves.

Each of the Big Four recruited followers whose qualifications they could speak for. On his list Reynolds put a six-foot, strongly built, eager and promising Royal Air Force deserter with a reform school past and nine trivial convictions, who had been pestering him for a shot at the big time. Ronald Biggs.

Most of the gang saw Leatherslade for the first time only three days before the raid when they arrived in the guise of the painters and decorators that the purchaser had particularly asked should be allowed to get an early start. They did not stay then, although they brought with them supplies, equipment and amenities in addition to some already delivered. But for weeks, those who had been chosen to do the driving had been discreetly touring the district, accompanied by Reynolds with his movie camera, Goody with his notebook, Cordrey with his railway manuals, and even on occasion, a suborned twenty-nine-year-old solicitor's clerk, Brian Field, who persuaded a namesake, Leonard Field, who had impressive criminal connections, to sign himself up as the prospective buyer of the farm.

The second Field was not the only scoundrel of the first Field's acquaintance. There was, for example, his boss, senior partner of the law firm of Wheater and Lomer and a decorated officer of the Queen's Own Royal West Kent Regiment, who allowed himself to be sucked into the conspiracy by arranging the farm purchase.

When the time came for everyone to move into Leatherslade, the chauffeurs—two men for each vehicle, a prudent precaution in case of accident—under the tutorship of Roy James, an amateur racing driver, had learned every road in the area high and low, lit or not that led to the railroad and could make a perfectly timed journey from any one point to another.

They settled in comfortably, even though there were no beds or other furniture and they had to sleep in sleeping bags on the floors of the six bedrooms. James became attached to a couple of cats who appeared to expect to eat at the kitchen door and fed them regularly.

Still thinking they were going to attack the train of the night of Tuesday the sixth, the main force of robbers assembled at Leatherslade early that evening, and under the command of Goody ran through their plans one last time behind farmhouse windows masked by nailed up army blankets. They practiced with the walkie-talkies—awkwardly because of the gloves they were not allowed to remove.

Shortly after midnight they made their way to Bridego Bridge. But the messages from Glasgow and Carlisle that reached Reynolds at a pay phone brought word that it was not to be the night. They went back to Leatherslade tense and frustrated but even better rehearsed than ever and more confident. They could afford to wait. They had food and comforts that would last them for weeks, vast amounts not chosen with the fastidiousness they had shown in other arrangements but collected by the hijacked piecemeal truckload from Wilson's obliging business contacts in the wholesale food market at Covent Garden . . . 18 dozen eggs, 34 rolls of toilet paper, cases of apples, pears and oranges, sacks of potatoes and onions, cans of soup and beans, packets of tea and sugar. Someone had remembered the can opener—in fact several—and there were, among other camping hardware, a portable gas stove, 15 enamel drinking mugs and 16 eating tools, combined knife-spoon-fork. When the gang realized there was going to be time to kill, Robert Alfred Welch, the owner of a modest London club and therefore an experienced caterer was sent to Bicester to buy ten one-gallon cans of Friary Meux ale known as pipkins—a popular party item.

Someone had supplied paperbacks, a dartboard and a Monopoly set which those with the grandest plans for the future found particularly intriguing. For those at the other end of the intellectual scale, there was a Snakes-and-Ladders board. They played with their gloves on.

Leatherslade had been incomparably well chosen. A sentry with a walkie-talkie posted out in the courtyard could look right down the half-mile of track that joined it to the nearest road. The farmhouse stood on a rise and from its top windows there was a clear view for miles around. Lookouts took turns there with binoculars. Wilson produced a VHF set that could be tuned to the wavelengths used by the Buckinghamshire Constabulary. When a farmer came by to inquire if the new owners would let him lease one of the paddocks a few of them slouched confidently about behaving like painters and the gang just stayed out of sight while Reynolds posed as a foreman and got rid of him.

Afterwards it occurred to them that the visitor might remember the number of the Austin truck which had been parked outside. But they were not worried. After all they had not done anything yet.

Not until 19 hours after the robbers had pulled off their dashing deed did the Scotland Yard team arrive in Buckinghamshire with Detective Superintendent Gerald McArthur and Detective Sergeant Jack Pritchard. The assignment of such a small Yard presence reflected a belief in London that raiders so audacious and accomplished were bound to have made efficient arrangements for getting as far away as fast as possible. But the usual formalities were gone through like alerting ports and airports, although such skilled tacticians as these were hardly likely to attract attention as "suspicious characters." British Rail Police and the Post Office Investigation Branch, in demand as never before, swarmed jealously over the route of the Up Special and the scattered, alienated cross-bred throng of underworld dropouts who earn a dangerous living or a tenuous freedom as police informers began, as they knew they must, to receive visits from The Sweeney.

The Sweeney is as close as Britain comes to having any kind of a national police force or is ever likely to have, even though the number of borough, county and city forces have shrunk since the time of The Great Train Robbery from 158 to 76 in England and Wales and from 33 to 23 in Scotland. It was formed in the 1920s from the plain-clothes Criminal Investigation Branch of Metropolitan Police headquarters at Scotland Yard to overcome demarcation disputes that developed when criminal activities overlapped the Metropolitan boundaries—which extend only in a 15-mile radius from Charing Cross—into neighboring counties and beyond. Tearing about in fast, unmarked radio cars, mixing with villains in their own haunts, its members became a legend of London life that a generation of novelists and script writers would have been forced to invent had it not been done for them. Criminals who had to live with their informal ways could have done quite nicely without them, however. The Flying Squad also became known as the Heavy Mob for the weightiness with which they bore down on their contacts. It could also have been because they took the law into their own heavy hands once or twice. But this time no matter how hard long or often The Sweeney applied their renowned gifts of persuasion, nothing came forth. Not a whisper. Not a hint. Nothing.

McArthur and Pritchard held endless conferences with Superintendent Fewtrell and the Buckinghamshire detectives, repeating the basic police exercise of trying to put themselves in the criminals' place. They debated the advantages of trying to stage a reconstruction of the attack but decided against it for fear of the ridicule and embarrassment it might generate. Anyway they already knew more or less exactly what had happened to and on the train.

If the robbers had been willing to risk venturing into less secluded surroundings with their sensitive cargo, they could quickly have reached the M1 Motorway which leads north to Birmingham and south to London. They would surely have known that the police were forbidden to road-block the unrestricted-speed highway and even without half the luck they had been enjoying they could dissolve unnoticed into the morning rush hour torrent.

But if they had not done that, then they must still be somewhere in the area, affluent as it was in abandoned farms, barges, barns and pits. Some of the callers who telephoned the Buckinghamshire headquarters reminded the detectives not to forget to look in the haystacks.

Less interested in who had taken the money than in what had been done with it were the insurance companies which for the modest premium of 1 shilling and 3 pence per 1,000 pounds (6 cents per $2,800) had now to cough up 2,131,100 pounds. When the total loss was worked out, the dazed loss adjusters realized that a reward of less than 200,000 pounds would simply be derisory. The shamefaced Midland Bank offered 10 percent of its uninsured 500,000 pounds and the Post Office tossed in a token 10,000 pounds, raising the amount that could be earned by the first person providing information that led to the arrest of the thieves *and* the recovery of at least part of the spoils to 260,000 pounds ($720,000).

The posting of such an impressive sum unveiled a far less appealing side of the national character than had emerged at the first news of the robbers' coup. Ordinary citizens by the hundreds began to think that there might be something in it for them and they force fed tittle-tattle about their neighbors on the telephone to Aylesbury and infiltrated the area to sleuth it up in person, outnumbering—but only just—the reporters.

Every passing hour added to the pressure on Fewtrell and his harassed colleagues. They tried yet another maxim policemen share with reporters. Always make the other fellow think you know more than you do. They announced—and the attendant press obligingly saw that it was printed and broadcasted—that the gang could have got no more than 30 minutes drive away from the scene of the robbery; that they were holed up and that phalanxes of police and tracker dogs were even then closing in on them.

Thirty minutes of driving on the different kinds of road was easily worked out and a ragged perimeter drawn around Bridego Bridge. The furthest that could be gone in any direction was 30 miles. Leatherslade fell within the area. But no one at search headquarters could see that. Although there had been buildings on the site for centuries, it was the only farm of any size not marked on the large scale survey map.

The robbers were there, all right, although the police were really only trying to appear more confident than they had any reason to be. They had covered the 20 miles from the now infamous stretch of track in 40 nerve-strumming minutes of careful driving through the dawn of the day before, fearful until the last turning that their way through the narrow lanes was about to be blocked by an early-rising farmer's tractor or a police patrol. But they met no one. They could not scatter until the next stage of the plan had been carried out, and the immense bulk of the loot counted and shared out. Only then would they split up, perhaps never to meet again, each man according to arrangements he had worked out for himself and submitted to the leaders for coordination. Impatiently, they had emptied the vehicles, ran them out of sight in the sheds and heaved the heavy bags into the roomy farm kitchen which, for all the fetid barrack-room air it had developed since they had been living there, now had the welcoming warmth of home.

Some of the thick bundles of notes in their wrappers were shaken out onto the floor and the men peeled off their Balaclavas and stared, abandoning themselves to the exuberance of a moment that neither they nor anyone else were ever likely to see repeated. Wilson launched into an exultant dance, chanting, "I like it. I like it!" Another man broke open a packet of crackling fivers, twisted one up and set it aflame from one of the candles they were using, rather than risk the noise of the diesel generator. They all crowded round to light their cigarettes, gleeful at the childish indulgence.

It took all the next day to divide the money. The bags were emptied in the small downstairs dining room of the farmhouse, the notes stripped of their wrappers and stacked as they were counted, not a job that could be done with gloves on, but some of the robbers intended to lie low for another three days until Sunday, and there would be time to remove their traces. Biggs worked with Roy James who, when they reached the first 1-million-pound mark said, "I suppose you all know that crime doesn't pay." They cracked a pipkin and drank to that bare-handed.

Even apart from the money Biggs was enraptured. Much as he had yearned to follow wherever Reynolds, his knowledgeable and worldly idol led, he had suffered considerable last-minute misgivings. His record was enough to make him liable to Preventitive Detention should he be convicted again, an indeterminate sentence that can be imposed on habitual offenders whatever the actual statutory penalty for their crime might be. But it was not that threat that had held him back when Reynolds offered him a place in the gang. It had been the thought of what Charmian, his strong-willed wife would say when she found out.

They did not need money. Playing the horses Biggs had won a double and collected 510 pounds. But the reward of this job was acceptance. It was an initiation. Rather than tell Charmian what he planned to do for those few days, Biggs made up a story about going timber-cutting in Wiltshire, the kind of thing he occasionally did. But he was certain there would be no recrimination when he came home with this lot. This was crime on the grand scale. They were rich.

"No more worries," Biggs told himself as he shuffled the notes with numbing fingers. "It's the good life all the way now." Sitting amid stacks of notes reaching higher than his head, he lunched lavishly off canned beans, splashing on extra ketchup from the abundant stock.

The money was divided evenly among the actual robbers with smaller sums going to helpers like their useless driver. Biggs's share was 158,000 pounds if you believe him, or 120,000 if you believe Charm—$442,400 or $336,000. But whatever it was the men of Leatherslade each took a fiver from his own pile and handed it to Biggs. It was his birthday.

5

One cannot hope to bribe or twist,
Thank God the British journalist.
But, seeing what the man will do
Unbribed, there's no occasion to.
Humbert Wolfe

•

Good news—which in Fleet Street may very well mean the worst possible kind of news for some poor soul somewhere—or the prospect of it blesses all it touches. The messenger who ultimately delivers it shares the warmth of its prosperous glow with everyone else who bore it for a while on the journey from wherever it was first plucked, squeezed or ground from its source, and a share of the credit for it accrues to all concerned. The fewer of those there are, the greater the share of glory for each, naturally. But the radiance given off by a successful story in the making draws claimstakers like a hip flask at a temperance funeral. This one generated so much heat that it almost burned Brian Vine's tongue as he hurried to tell the Editor. Assistant Editors do not need to knock. Vine was astonished to be received as though he was bringing word to the Shah of Persia that the Eskimos had just discovered how to extract premium crude from melted snow. But the word "exclusive" made the Editor wince. He could still feel the last one.

The island of Mull sulks in the icy sea off the charmless and inhospitable west coast of Scotland raising sheep and netting herring. Its population has never reached 2,000 and only one of them ever became the Editor of a national British newspaper. Ian McColl did not go directly from the island of Mull to Fleet Street, though. He paused for most of his professional life in Glasgow, the raw and cantankerous city that is Britain's third largest and where Lord Beaverbrook's wishes were promulgated by a mostly self-governing dependency consisting of a *Daily Express*, a *Sunday Express* and the *Evening Citizen*—all with strong local flavoring to them and all, for a very long time, vigorous and profitable.

It never did anyone any harm with the Beaver to be either Scottish or a product of one of the Imperial Dominions since he himself was both—the first at one remove. In much the same way that Howard Hughes entrusted his furtive affairs to Mormons did the Beaver strategically seed both editorial and business sides even of his London-based papers with loyal men of the North, schooled in the steely moral imperatives of the Kirk, the durability of a good bit of dark serge and the mystical properties of single malt whiskys. The Scotia Nostra. McColl did not completely fit the specifications when he first went to work for the Scottish *Daily Express* as a subeditor because he was a teetotaler. But he shared an unmatchable affinity with the Beaver himself. Both were sons of the Manse, their clergymen fathers custodians of the highly concentrated Presbyterian version of the Protestant ethic.

Vine, a portly man to whose imposing jowls a flush may readily be brought, left McColl's office indignant and trembling. On its threshold he encountered one of his own two principal subordinates, Brian Hitchen, the News Editor, whom he abruptly marched about and ushered down the corridor to his own office and confided to him, "I've just given that little bugger a story that could put three-quarters of a million on the figures tomorrow, and he won't listen to me."

It was not uncommon for complaints to be traded among McColl's executives. He had a talent for spreading exasperation in the higher ranks and providing amusement for the lower where a merciless sense of fun demanded constant nourishment. The remodeling job he had done on himself after bringing off the considerable leap across the ramparts of style and culture that walled off editorship in Glasgow from the life-sized, full-scaled original version in London had provided a dependable source of entertainment for the *Express* staff.

McColl had been a latecomer to the accepted pleasures of Fleet Street life. But he had caught up fast. In Scotland he had been not only a teetotaler but a bachelor until the age of fifty-three. But before his Great Leap South in 1970 he had married—as do many secluded and embattled men of power—the woman he knew best, his secretary. And he had gradually become adjusted to the privileges of his new status which included the regular consumption of fine vintages and good food eaten in the company of his peers.

His appearance too had been deeply affected by crossing the border. The *Daily Express* has always been noticeably conservative and conformist in dress, evolving in recent years by some communal instinct a house style similar to the mid-Atlantic rig Ian Fleming favored for himself when he worked at the *Sunday Times* and which he passed on to Commander James Bond—dark single-breasted suit, pastel shirt, black knit tie and moccasins. McColl remained true to the uniform. But his shirts were always a crisp blue that matched his clear and burning preacher's eye, and his shoes always gleamed with the glorious light of a freshly salvaged soul. The dutiful short-back-and-sides of Glasgow went under the trendy shears of John and Michael of Hatton Garden, and with his thick white hair theatrically cut and styled his rosy Highland cheeks well-scrubbed and his small, quick movements, he struck people like an actor turned floorwalker or like a brand new, fully wound walking doll.

One thing that remained unchanged from the manse at Mull, however, was a Calvinist caution to the tongue befitting the Elder of the Kirk which he had faithfully remained. To provide him with the punctuation and rhythm of everyday speech for which his colleagues relied on the practiced use of traditional expletives, McColl used a private vocabulary of onomatopoeic euphemisms. Where another man would say "fucking," he said "furstie." "The mon's a *furstie gink*," he would declare in piping Highland tones when sufficiently provoked, and add, with a coy glance at the company, "And ye know what ah mean by *that*, don't ye?"

So Hitchen was sympathetic but not deeply concerned about

Vine's complaint. He had troubles enough of his own, an entire clip-board full of them which he had to take up with McColl himself and which would be sure to collect their own share of rejections and rebuffs on the grounds of taste, economy or legal vulnerability. He wanted to get on with it. Vine did not tell him what the momentous proposal was that McColl had declined to take an interest in and Hitchen did not ask. He had no time to spare for dead ones.

If the *Daily Express* is one of Fleet Street's archetypal products, then Hitchen is another, and it is a mild wonder that they took so long to find each other. He had spent most of his career as a high-voltage by-line on the *Daily Mirror*, the tabloid bestseller among the nationals, putting in a stint in its New York bureau where he met Vine, then the *Express* bureau chief there. When both returned to London, Vine recruited him away from the deputy's chair on the *Mirror* newsdesk, and he came home in spirit to the huge jammed dilapidated Big Room of the *Express*, where the cast may not be what it was and the scenery needs repainting, but they still put on a stirring performance of The Front Page every night except Saturdays.

Hitchen had been a newspaperman since he was fifteen and at thirty-six could hardly be taken for anything else except, perhaps, because of his pink and white north-of-England skin and a tonsured semicircle of invincible hair, a recently defected, rather depraved friar. But that would necessitate ignoring the broken nose from his time in the Parachute Regiment and the overspill at his belt that commemorates years of dedicated expense account encounters in the pursuit of professional wisdom. Hitchen knew the reporter's arts as the friar would know his rosary. He knew who to call, when and where to call them and how to get them to say what he wanted to hear. He could talk into a telephone without being overheard by someone sitting three feet away and hold a conversation at a bar without having his lips read. He never forgot a name or a face and never threw away a telephone number. He always knew where a drink could be had, if necessary, in a place where no one knew what he did, or where they thought he was someone else—harmless misrepresentation being among the approved skills of the calling.

He had bartered with the nation's administrators and custodians and, on occasion, bribed them. His encounters with ordinary people had left them sometimes saddened, sometimes joyful or relieved, sometimes in terrible trouble. He had known long nights and cold doorsteps, and a lot of foul and makeshift food in his day. He was decent now and a good mentor to those he sent out to endure them in their turn. Wee Ian McColl was not, perhaps, the kind of editor he had hoped to find himself working for on this romantic paragon of a paper, but he liked him and was loyal. The Editor is the Editor.

The story that had left McColl so sensitive and suspicious was one that Hitchen was pleased to have had nothing to do with. It was a "foreign" story and they were normally under the care of Vine's lefthand man, the Foreign Editor, who controlled the paper's bureaus abroad and its dwindling band of foreign correspondents. In the heyday of the *Express*, an extensive and adventurous foreign staff had been the Beaver's personal pride and, not infrequently, the scourge which he capriciously ordered applied to the Foreign Office, the United Nations and whatever sovereign governments happened from time to time to merit his displeasure.

Front page "blurbs" boasting of its quality and alertness appeared regularly in the paper. The one for November 10, 1959, told the readers:

Throughout the world where there is news there is an *Express*man.

George Gale in India; Geoffrey Thursby in Beirut; Christopher Dobson, the only resident British newspaper reporter in Moscow . . .

Across the Atlantic: Ian Aitken, Henry Lowrie, and Ronald Singleton operate from New York, with Ross Mark heading the Washington bureau.

And daily, of course, Peter Chambers writes the famous *This Is America* column.

On again . . . across Europe . . .

Sydney Smith in Paris; Colin Lawson in Germany; Robin Stafford in Rome.

In the last financial year the cost of the Foreign Service was £356,000.

The Foreign Editor has at his disposal 169 staff reporters and correspondents permanently abroad.

By threadbare 1974, when the Beaver's egocentric policies had done their harm and the unimaginative stewardship of two generations of Scots accountants stood no chance of healing it, the exuberant foreign operation had been pared down to a sliver of the once lush whole. Jocelyn Stevens, unacquainted with the complexities of long distance news-gathering, and impatient with arguments that there could be any consideration beyond cost, declared it a dispensable luxury and McColl was under orders to throttle foreign coverage, following in any case, the instincts he had developed on the banks of the Clyde where even English news is treated much the same as anything filed from Ulan Bator.

McColl's misgivings about events in places he had never actually set foot in had been comprehensively vindicated only a few weeks earlier when he allowed himself to be convinced that the *Express* would be able to reveal the whereabouts of Martin Bormann, the fiendish Nazi still believed by many followers of that period to be alive if not so well (he would be seventy-five) in the jungles of South America. In the hope of an enviable coup, the *Express* had paid a generous bounty to Ladislas Farago, a literary adventurer of Hungarian origin, for an account of how Bormann had supposedly been tracked to his nest of retired stormtroopers. Despite the enormous panache with which it was presented and the plausible salesmanship that put it across, careful readers were left disappointed. After a couple of days of intriguing generalization and descriptions of the activities of many colorful subsidiary characters, they learned where Farago and Stewart Steven, a former *Express* Foreign Editor who became his collaborator, believed their evil quarry was skulking. But the authors, alas, had not actually seen or spoken to him. Nor did they offer convincing testimony by anyone who had. The main result of the articles was to cover the *Express* in ridicule and attract some hopeful lawsuits from Argentinian government officials who claimed to have been misquoted or wrongly identified in photographs. It was a fairly memorable disaster.

Not that things had not gone wrong occasionally back in the old days. The *Express* paid its men well, and when they did well, praised them extravagantly. But it also goaded them cruelly at times, and it took a sturdy will, particularly in faraway places, to resist the bait and show enough self-confidence to leave an impossible challenge go unanswered. The blurb of November 10, 1959, began with a proud salute to *Express*man Michael Cope.

The Paper That Is FIRST on the Spot, said the headline.
The *Daily Express* Foreign Service leads the field.
FIRST to get the pictures of the North Pole Kon-Tiki, the Russian ice-floe base.
FIRST to get a plane's eye-description of the Soviet ice station—from *Express*man Michael Cope.

In that early era of *détente* the previous year had been a United Nations Geophysical Year in which some hesitant Soviet–American scientific collaboration was achieved. It was already deep winter in the Arctic when word reached the *Daily Express* office in fogbound Fleet Street that the intrepid chief foreign correspondent of the *Daily Mail*, Noel Barber, was headed for the North Pole, and it was too late to organize a counter expedition. Barber's trip was an extravagant stunt more than anything else. Just the kind of thing, in fact, that the *Express* was accustomed to doing best itself. But Barber was headed for a double, having outfoxed the competition the year before by becoming the first reporter to reach the *South* Pole. Something had to be done this time to forestall the exclusive use of such a prestigious dateline by the *Express*'s chief rival and the Foreign Editor of the day, Norman Smart saw salvation in a report about the discovery in Canadian waters 300 miles from the North Pole of two Soviet ice stations that had been inspired by the Geophysical Year. He alerted his three most strategically placed correspondents. Which of them would be the one to add unforgettable luster to his reputation—and win the valuable esteem of Mr. Smart—by being the first reporter to set foot on one of these novel and intriguing islands of mystery?

In Washington, Ross Mark turned hopefully to the Pentagon contacts he had tended with expensive care for so long. Sure, they said. Sounds kinda like an interesting problem. Maybe they could get him somewhere close on a nuclear submarine. Fantastic! When? Oh, about April when the ice cap started to break up. Thanks, fellers.

In New York, Ian Aitken rummaged urgently through the possibilities of chartering one of the few types of aircraft that could make such a flight. Would the *Express* pay $10,000? Not if there was any other way.

In Moscow, Chris Dobson went to the expertly evasive Armenians, who ran the Ministry of Information like a branch of Lubjanka. Impossible. The bases were supplied from Siberian airfields. Everyone knew foreigners were not permitted in Siberia. Some tickets for the Bolshoi? Forlornly the correspondents searched on, for anyone who might be seduced or suborned into helping them but their efforts were cut short after a couple of days. Drop it, said the Foreign Room, skillfully allowing only a micro-edge of deprecation to show in the messages (you seasoned cosmopolitans have been outreached by a sturdy and enterprising backwoodsman). Cope of Toronto has discovered a Soviet polar station even the Canadian Air Force did not know about. He has flown over it and come back with not only a stirring and vivid account of his exploits but fascinating pictures as well. And there it was the next day on the front page, filed from Anchorage, Alaska, but carrying superimposed the tantalizing dateline, North Pole.

Ice-Floe Russians Bar My Plane, said the headline, a heroic picture of Cope in arctic glare-glasses beside it. And the story was in the classic *Express* I-witness tradition.

> I flew over North Pole station No. 8—the Russian Kon-Tiki on ice—in the heaving, crunching Arctic Ocean this morning.
> Twice we tried to land, but the Russians drove trucks and rolled oil drums on to their 6,000-foot landing strip to stop us. About 200 of them waved at us to go away.

Congratulations to him, said the others to the Foreign Room with deep insincerity. And afterward, as professional curiosity began to seep through their chagrin, how exactly did he do it? Our contacts would like a few technical details of this praiseworthy achievement, type of plane, exact location of the floe—that sort of thing. Asking Cope To Provide, said the Foreign Room, after a thoughtful pause.

Poor Cope. The rich and tempting bait had been more than he could resist. Blinded—even with dark glasses—by the glittering lure of the Big One he had hounded down his promise of glory not to the menacing edge of the far-off dayless white wastes but just to a Vancouver airport to borrow some charts from a pilot. On the basis of his studies, he stitched together a convincing story with the aid of the reports already published and sent it off to the *Express* with a batch of pictures of the genuine ice stations taken by the R.C.A.F. days before. As he had swallowed their bait, so the *Express* greedily gulped down his. But it is nature's law that the bigger fish will always win the last round. Good-bye Cope.

For all his prejudices and inclinations and his first reaction to the unwelcome tidings that Vine had brought him, Ian McColl knew that he would have to do something. There was nothing wrong with his instinct for appreciating the possibility of an important story in the offing, but his natural sense of caution had been strongly reinforced by recent events, and he was under constant pressure to save money. The probability of what Vine had told him turning out to be true was about as worthwhile as a bawbee's worth of good claret. But the risk of ignoring it would be enormous. Once something like that had come to light, another paper would hear of it soon enough if the *Express* did nothing. He brooded on it for four days, then during one of Hitchen's clipboard audiences, said to him, "Young Colin MacKenzie says he knows where to find Ronald Biggs."

"Does he, by Jesus," asked Hitchen. "Where?"

"He says he's not ready to tell anyone yet," answered McColl. "What do you think of that?"

"I think I'd better have a word with him," said Hitchen.

It did not sound right to Hitchen but even less than McColl was he prepared to ignore a lead of any kind on Biggs, no matter how unlikely. Apart from anything else he felt a particular and personal affinity for the Great Train Robbery. When one by one the telephones had begun to ring all across Buckinghamshire in that dawn, 11 years earlier, Hitchen's had rung too. He had been the district correspondent there for the *Daily Mirror*, and therefore an enthusiastic foot soldier in the army of reporters that fitted the fantastic story together.

For the first time, that is. For years afterward, the robbery and its motley band of begetters had kept on providing newspapers with highly nourishing fodder. A trial of unprecedented length and complexity had resulted in controversial sentences that were evaded in several cases by spectacular escapes ended in turn by spectacular recaptures. Of all the robbers ever identified only Biggs was still at large. And, since only four years earlier he had brought off a second magnificently impertinent and widely applauded bound to freedom, fresh word of him would be certain to find his same adoring public as intrigued as the powers that wanted him back in prison would be infuriated. The Great Train Robbery had always kept official tempers close to the boil for the excellent reason that although an eternity of prison sentences had been inflicted on those who had been arrested, only a tiny fraction of the money had ever been recovered.

However, there was a fundamental divergence in the attitudes of McColl and Hitchen. Where McColl was canny, pessimistic and reluctant, Hitchen's enthusiasm, once unleashed, would take him right up to the dangerous barbs that separated the merely venturesome from the reckless. He had been News Editor only nine months and already had a reputation for aggressive methods. He would be delighted if MacKenzie could tell him anything that carried a valid hope of finding Biggs. McColl, he knew, would be happier if he reported back that there was nothing worth following up. The Editor's last words as Hitchen had left his office had been, "We don't want another furstie Bormann story, mind."

Hitchen's preliminary misgivings did not stretch that far. He did not have an office of his own but operated from a high-backed leather chair at the head of the newsdesk that gave him a lordly view of the Big Room in which the controlled turmoil that would miraculously result in the production of the first edition was beginning to find its stride.

The men and women he surveyed were the usual contradictory Fleet Street mix. Some were confidants of people in surprisingly high places. Others could never get anyone to come to the phone for them. Some could have talked a bishop into making a blue movie; others could not even get a taxi to stop. There were those who would never come back from a job if they got offered a drink, and others who could only operate on a full head of Guinness. There were the ones people never noticed until they had slipped inside the front door and others who made better bodyguards than reporters. Some took down every word said to them in flawless Pitman's, others kept it all in their head and got it right just the same. Some got it wrong, whatever they did. Some could write 400 convincing words in 20 minutes on any subject mentioned to them. Some were as fluent in languages like Welsh and Greek as others were in their own. Some could be sent across the world at a moment's notice without a second's concern. Some could hardly be trusted to find their way to the office. Hitchen was confident by then that he knew the aptitudes of most of his staff as well as their vagaries and he was puzzled. Colin MacKenzie knew where Ronald Biggs was? Colin *MacKenzie*?

6

The legendary form of providence that supervises drunks and fools must do an occasional favor for the cops, too. At Leatherslade Farm the 30-mile hypothesis was heard on the radio, and someone went for the papers to see if it was being taken seriously. It was. In fact it was the only theory around. But no such fatherly providential surveillance was being kept over the robbers. Although the Fewtrell pronouncement did not cause a panic, it did bring about the first serious modification of the gang's plans. If there *had* been a mastermind his design was not meant to be tinkered with. The luck that had so far lubricated it ran out, and the delicately balanced mechanism of the plot began to falter.

Reynolds decreed that rather than wait until Sunday everyone should be on their various ways by nightfall that day, Friday. There was no argument. Everyone was edgy and anxious to bolt, now that the larcenous exuberance had subsided. Some had planned to leave well before the Sunday anyway, including the four leaders, Reynolds, Wilson, Edwards and Goody, their vast cut concealed in the false bottom of the Austin truck. But they had become nervous about using the vehicle, since the visit from their sightseeing neighbors, and they had no way of giving it a new numberplate. The three of them went off to London in one of the stand-by cars to gather together as many suitcases as they could get and to try to arrange transportation for others who would not be able to revise their own getaway arrangements by dark. Some of those who were left behind started painting the Austin yellow.

Goody was also appointed to make certain dispositions which had now become vital. Although the gang was making a fretful effort to clear up the farm and remove their traces, someone had to be found to do it for them properly after they had gone. A willing someone was found and paid a large amount of money to take mop, broom and swab to Leatherslade over the weekend. They christened him The Dustman.

Reynolds rendezvoused with a girlfriend and went to Chiswick to buy, for cash, a smart, black 1961 Austin Healey drophead. And he called in to his Knightsbridge shirtmaker to order half a dozen shirts in the finest poplin. When they got back to Leatherslade with two "clean" vehicles, Biggs was still counting. He had broken off to play Monopoly with one of the others, using real money instead of the make-believe scrip and occasionally he still lit a cigarette with a stray note, but always a 10-shilling one. He had begun to think that no matter how awesome his share seemed, sooner or later he might need every penny of it. The would-be racing driver Roy James, nicknamed the Weasel, was the first off the mark. Before he was whisked away into the night he gave the cats a last plate of scraps.

The others drifted on their chosen ways unhurriedly. There could be no question of a quick bolt abroad for any of them. Whatever arrangements had been made for the conversion or the safe-keeping of the bonanza, it could not be rushed. The underworld redistribution system could only digest so much richness at one sitting. It would have to swallow slowly like a python ingesting a prize bull.

Goody loaded his share in a van and drove it to the house of Brian Field, the solicitor's clerk, in a village called Pangborne on the Berkshire–Oxfordshire border. He was shown the way by Field's pretty German wife, Karin, driving ahead in a blue Jaguar and chatting to him by walkie-talkie. Welch and Wilson followed in a second van. Womenfolk were sent for after they had arrived safely and most of the weekend was partied rapturously away. When the others left on Sunday Karin who, according to a story she subsequently sold to the German magazine, *Der Stern*, had originally been pressed into service because her husband was too drunk on the Friday night to drive, took the mailbags that had been left behind in their pretentiously labeled house, "Kabri," and some axe handles to nearby Pangborne Wood and buried them. After all, gallant Gordon Goody had brought her a tribute of 30 yellow roses.

Some of the more unworldly of the remainder brazenly reappeared in their customary London preserves, places where they were an everyday sight and where they enjoyed the easygoing loyalty of other habitués who would never dare notice that they had been away. They saw their friends, some of whom had helped out with peripheral aspects of the robbery, some who knew no more about it than what they read in the papers or had gathered from the recent attentions of The Sweeney. Edwards, Reynolds and White went out a lot together with their wives and girl friends and in their usual opulent style. They saw the new film *Tom Jones* and joked quietly that soon they would be able to spread themselves about as uninhibitedly as its randy hero; they frugged tentatively to the songs that everyone was suddenly echoing back to four newborn pop stars with the faces of Victorian workhouse waifs.

I don't care too much for money. Money can't buy me love, sang the Beatles.

The *bon viveurs* kept their cool. They did not flash their fivers around like others, alas, felt compelled to. They were men already used to having money in their pockets. They knew exactly what it could buy.

Two days of that dreary summer's rain washed away the tracks of the armada of cars that had come and gone from Leatherslade Farm. The Sunday papers got their day, but with nothing to add to the devastating and eloquent facts already overexposed by the dailies they were forced back on conjecture of a highly competitive nature. Peter Gladstone-Smith of the *Sunday Telegraph* won easily with this authoritatively delivered corker.

Detectives investigating the Great Train Robbery know the identity of the criminal who masterminded the 2,631,784-pound raid.

He is a miser and lives alone in one room at Brighton. His home has been searched and he is being watched. There is not enough evidence yet to arrest him.

This man has a flair for the most ingenious type of crime. He works with infinite care and patience to prepare a plan which is perfect in every detail.

He never takes place in an operation himself. When his plan is complete he takes it to a master criminal well known in the Harrow Road area of London who carries it out with confederates.

The *People*, a larger circulation Sunday, was on far more realistic ground in raising for the first time the probability that the London airport raid of the previous November, in which 62,500 pounds had been grabbed by bandits anonymous in the commonplace British businessman's plumage of bowler hat, black jacket and striped trousers was pulled off simply to finance the Great Train Robbery. Other papers were hopefully in pursuit of a shady baronet and that perennial scourge, the Irish Republican Army—although the efficiency with which the robbery was accomplished tended to eliminate *them*.

The cumulative effect of the saturation coverage, however, and the confident reiteration by the police of the 30-mile theory finally induced a thirty-three-year-old farmhand named John Maris to wonder if there might not be something significant about the place a mile up the road from where he worked which had been, for the previous couple of weeks, the scene of such unusual comings and goings.

On Monday morning after he had milked the cows and had his breakfast he thought, in a way that is really far more typical of country folk than treating their neighbors with the indifference usually attributed to them, that he might go up there and nose around a bit. There was nothing discreet about the way he went. He clanked up on his tractor. And what he saw *was* suspicious. The windows of the farmhouse were covered with heavy fabric turned back at the corners to form peepholes. There was a bright yellow truck standing in an open shed and the garage, although locked with a new brass padlock, contained at least one other vehicle covered with a tarpaulin. There was nobody in sight, although he had no idea what might lie inside. Maris did something he had never in his innermost fantasies imagined himself doing. He chugged the tractor along to a call box, dialed Britain's universal emergency phone number 999, told the Buckingham police what he had observed, and awaited the dramatic outcome of his dutiful citizen's deed. Nothing happened.

Reynolds knew the man Goody had hired as The Dustman and did not trust him. But when Goody telephoned on Sunday night to check that all was well, Mop had assured him nobody would ever know they had been at Leatherslade. Reynolds, unconvinced and thorough, asked someone else to drive down for a look around. The four were appalled when it was reported back to them late on Monday night that from a quick look around the outside the place was still littered with debris, and it appeared that nothing had been touched. The Dustman did not answer his phone again.

Tuesday's papers were still reporting no progress. They also mentioned that hoaxers by the score were pouring unlikely stories into the ears of the overworked constabulary. John Maris took that personally. He dialed 999 again. "Look here," he said. "*I'm* not one of your hoaxers."

The Widow Nappin had also been slowly adding things up. She called as well. By mid-morning Police Constable Albert Woolley had climbed through a window of the main building at Leatherslade and unlocked the front door to let Sergeant Ron Blackman in. The two men stood overawed amidst the treasury of ruinous evidence. In London the four were arguing about who should go down to put The Dustman's double cross to rights when Reynolds's VHF radio, still tuned to the Buckinghamshire police wavelength, brought them the dreadful news. .

Fleet Street mounted a determined assault with air support on the farm and quickly forced Superintendent Fewtrell and his men to show the white flag. He agreed to allow heavily escorted reporters and photographers two hours in which to inspect the place in exchange for an agreement that they would not infiltrate while the scientific experts were at work later on. While they teemed in through the lanes every light plane within chartering distance buzzed the treetops, impetuous photographers straining from open cockpit doors and hurling empty film cans at the airborne opposition. *The Front Page Meets Dawn Patrol.*

The rustic constables, told to accompany the earthbound newsmen around, made them keep their hands in their pockets so they would not disturb vital signs or traces. That made the taking of notes or pictures a mite awkward but everyone was, nevertheless, profoundly intrigued by what they saw. They took in the half-finished meals, the unused beer supply, the sleeping arrangements, the enormous store of remaining food and concluded—wrongly but not unreasonably—that the gang had been holed up there for some time. From the games and the mounds of cigarette butts in the various rooms, they tried with the diligence of archaeologists to reconstruct the long, tense wait before the raid. They looked over the piles of abandoned army surplus gear, most thoughtfully the remains of some Balaclavas half-burned in a fire and the two Land Rovers which they were delighted to note bore the same license number, BMG 757 A. The theory of a military-minded mastermind moved sharply up the scale of popularity.

They climbed down into the farmhouse cellar full of mailbags deceptively stuffed with wrappers from their original contents but still containing, it turned out when they were emptied, 628 pounds of 10-shillings worth of notes which the robbers had wastefully overlooked. And they peered with particularly somber wonderment into a pit, dug in the clay near a bed of runner beans, that measured 6 feet long, $3\frac{1}{2}$ feet wide and 5 feet deep. The discredited train driver had worried about it too. But the robbers forgave him for bungling his job, gave him £20,000 and sent him on his way. The reporters were quite eager to leave when their time was up. There was many a colorful flag to be hoisted, many kites to be flown, lots of panting beasts of speculation to be unleashed to see where they might lead. As the newsmen swarmed down the hill in disorderly withdrawal toward the few scattered telephones in the district, Scotland Yard, having finally discerned where the main offensive must now take place was sending in the big battalions. Up the hill came their vanguard, the meticulous and scholarly men of C3, the unrivaled fingerprint department. If a single incriminating dab had not been found on the Up Special, it had been no fault of theirs and now their honor was at stake once more. They spread out watchfully through the new terrain, their heads bent low handling their aerosols of Ninhydrin confidently.

Reynolds, Wilson, Edwards and White—the latter enjoyed considerable standing in his own right as a safe and lock man—dropped out of sight with the aplomb of Mafia dons heading for the well-sprung mattresses. There was no need to warn the others with whom they were still in touch. They would realize from what was being said in the papers what must have happened. Only Goody was certain that nothing at Leatherslade Farm could incriminate him. He knew he had never taken his gloves off there without scrupulously wiping off the surfaces he touched nor had he left behind anything that could be traced to him. Besides, he had organized for himself an alibi in his native Ireland.

He had been charged and acquitted of taking part in the London airport raid, so it was only right and natural that the police would want to talk to him about this prestigious job. Goody decided on a double bluff. He made himself even more conspicuous and flamboyant than usual, switching his fleet of three flashy cars around, dropping in on everyone who knew him (by a surprising variety of names) and complaining rather proudly of the interest being shown in him by detectives and reporters. He moved out of the house he shared with his old mum in Putney so that she would no longer be bothered by the stream of callers and went to stay in a pub at the foot of Fleet Street, making himself accessible to a blatant degree by helping out behind the bar.

No such composure, however, was reflected in the behavior of the lower ranks, when the first touch of heat came on. Roger Cordrey, the key trainstopper, who was helplessly burdened with his share of 141,000 pounds, had linked up with a similarly technically-minded old friend called William Boal, who was the possessor of a criminal background as modest as his wits and who would have been painfully outclassed by the company Cordrey had just been keeping. Cordrey wanted to pay off a debt, which he did with substantial unsolicited interest, but when he showed Boal the money, he would not tell him at first where it had come from. "What you don't know you can't let drop," he said. But that expended the small stock of prudence they could raise between them and off they lurched on an exultant and haphazard toot.

First they rented a room in Oxford—which was not far from Leatherslade—then a flat; and then they bought a secondhand Rover. Boal returned to London to collect his wife and three children and, back in Oxford again, the Rover was loaded up with the family, several enormous suitcases packed solid with notes and some indiscriminately bought fishing gear. Camouflage. A holiday outing if any nosy copper wanted to know. They got as far as Bournemouth, a genteel watering place on the south coast, before they felt safe enough to dispense with the trappings and the rest of the Boals were packed off back to London by train. Once again the pair rented an apartment and this time a garage in which they parked the Rover. Then they bought a Ford Anglia and went out looking for somewhere to garage *that*. They found just what they needed advertised on a card in a news agent's window, offered for 10 shillings a week by Mrs. Emily Clark, age sixty-seven, of Tweedale Road, the recent widow, as Boal and Cordrey's bad luck would have it, of a police sergeant.

Mrs. Clark was properly impressed when Boal produced a wad of notes and paid her three-months rent in advance. But it was not the kind of thing people normally did in Bournemouth where there was a buyers' market in lock-up garages and years of living with her old man's constantly expressed doubts about human nature had trained her well. When Boal and Cordrey returned with yet a third vehicle they had bought, an Austin A35 van, Detective Sergeant Stanley Davies and Detective Constable Charles Case were only a couple of minutes behind them in answer to Mrs. Clark's telephone call.

"Help! Police!" shouted Cordrey, perceptively if pointlessly, and ran. Davies, a rugby player, brought him down with a flying tackle, and Case chased Boal across the road into another house where, cornered, he went strenuously berserk. The officers handcuffed the two together and drove them off to the station after congratulating Mrs. Clark on foiling a pair of obvious housebreakers. Only when Davies came back with Boal's keys and found 56,000 pounds in the Austin, did he realize it was a far more interesting matter than that.

"Fair enough," said Boal, for by then, of course, he knew. "It came from the train job."

The first public sight of the Great Train Robbery loot affected the populace at large like a school of piranha thrown a side of beef. That came on the ninth day after the robbery, when Superintendent Fewtrell had just returned to Aylesbury from Bournemouth, after collecting nearly the whole amount of Cordrey's share from the various flats and vehicles and was thinking that if the pair of sorry clowns he had just been questioning were typical of the gang, it would not be long before the entire haul was back in the banks. Ninety miles from Leatherslade and three counties away John Aherne, a factory clerk, was giving his workmate, Nina Hargreaves, a lift to the office on the pillion of his motorcycle when they stopped for a moment in a glade beside the road near Dorking. There they came upon the unexpected sight of an elegant leather briefcase, a plastic shopping bag and a well-cut zippered holdall posed on a grassy mound as though for a travel commercial. All were full of money which the couple instantly realized must have come from the robbery and which totaled—after police dogs had sniffed out another fashionable piece of luggage from the bushes—100,900 pounds.

"There is booty to be found in all sorts of places," proclaimed Fewtrell cheerfully, convinced that the robbers, intimidated by the size of their swag, had panicked and abandoned it. That Friday, the police officially appealed for public help in finding more of the money and over the weekend thousands of people conducted a frenzied treasure hunt. Skindivers hurled themselves into flooded quarries, courting couples were stalked deep into leafy woods and farmers digging holes to transplant trees found that their work attracted unsettling scrutiny at close quarters.

But the next cache was discovered the following Tuesday by an eagle-eyed copper strolling through a trailer park near Dorking. When the outside panels that had seemed to him to be such a bad fit were taken off one little house on wheels just vacated by a couple with a baby and a white poodle, the entire thing turned out to be insulated with bundles of fivers. Thirty thousand pounds.

Something else, too, had come to light by then. Although most of the notes taken from the High Value Coach were completely untraceable, it had been the custom in some banks for clerks to note a couple of serial numbers at random from every bundle of fivers. The police had collected the numbers of about 15,000 notes and circulated them. One had been found to be part of the payment for a black Austin Healey bought at the Chequered Flag Garage in Chiswick. The salesman picked Reynolds's picture out as the person who paid him and the car had been discovered at a garage near London Airport dropped off by the man in the same picture who said he would be back for it next month.

On Thursday, August 22, a description of Reynolds was issued and one of White. The poodle with White was named Gigi, the police noted solemnly. But what really made the day a mournful milestone for the gang was that Wilson was arrested. "I don't see how you can make it stick without the poppy," he said to Detective Chief Superintendent Tommy Butler, the top Scotland Yard man now on the investigation. "And you won't find that."

Apart from providing fashionable vocabularies with a welcome morsel of argot, all of this put the police clearly on top for the first time since Driver Mills, had applied the brakes. Not even a whopping tactical blunder the following day dislodged them. They added James's name to the wanted-to-assist-police-in-their-inquiries list when only the day after that he would have been on the point of realizing his life's ambition. He was down to roar off the mark as favorite in the News of the World Junior Formula race at Goodwood, having qualified with a record lap time of 95.57 m.p.h. in his new 1098 c.c. blue and white Brabham Ford. If The Sweeney had only waited until August 24, all they would have had to do was to stroll down to the pits and flag him in.

Goody chose that grim weekend to go courting in Leicester where the object of his attentions, nineteen-year-old Margaret Perkins, had just been awarded the title of Miss Midlands, winning, among other trophies, a mink-covered settee valued at 2,250 pounds. When he appeared in the Grand Hotel (booked in for the occasion under the name of Alexander), a florist in the lobby took a close look at the sharply dressed stranger escorting the glossy new local celebrity and came to the bizarre and wholly illogical conclusion that he was Reynolds whose picture by then had been on television and in the newspapers for several hours but who resembled Goody in no way whatsoever. The local police got him out of bed at 2 A.M. and telephoned Butler at the Yard. Miss Perkins, called at home by other officers, was questioned most pointedly about the settee.

Goody had to be let go that time, however. There was nothing on which to hold him. But the incident caused huge and widespread amusement, and a good deal of thoroughly unfeeling fun was poked at the police and their ponderous ways, especially by the sharp tongues of the new breed of satirists blossoming forth in London's trendy dens. In fact the inexorable though undramatic routine of investigation was producing results more often than not. Apart from the combined Buckinghamshire–Yard detective force, only the West German Federal police had yet been told that the lining of the holdall found in the forest glade yielded a bill from the Sonnenbichl Hotel in Hindelang, Bavaria, made out in February that year to Herr and Frau Field. The Germans obligingly sent back a description of the blue Jaguar the Fields had driven during their holiday.

Tediously, a thousand pipkins, the entire day's production of July 23 at the Friary Meux brewery at Guildford, had been traced to equate the ten bought in Bicester with those found at Leatherslade, one of which carried the palm print of Robert Welch, the first loser to be fingered by the dreaded Central Records Office, Scotland Yard's nemesistic storehouse of criminal pasts. Gallons of Ninhydrin spray had brought up dabs in the most unlikely places. Wilson's had been on a large drum of salt. Thomas Wisbey, a cheerful lefthanded bookmaker with fastidious personal habits, had left his on the hand rail by the bath. James Hussey, a housepainter, had been careless in letting down the tailboard of the Austin. James's were on the cats' dish.

They got around to Biggs on August 24. He was waiting for them listlessly, not having been able to organize a useful move. He had got home to Redhill in Surrey from Leatherslade bearing his 158,000-pounds worth of tribute in two huge bulging kitbags and lain it before Charmian. "Oh my God!" she said. "Where have you been?" Money had been on her mind while he was away since she had managed to get through most of the 510 pounds he had won at the races, but this was preposterous.

"I've been chopping down trees in Wiltshire, haven't I?" said Biggs, elated to the verge of mania, bumptious and preening.

Charmian told him. His brother had died on the first night he had stayed at Leatherslade. She had gone to the local police and asked them to get the Wiltshire Constabulary to find her Ronald. They had obligingly looked for him on the site at which he had told Charmian he would be working. When they did not find him there the police, doing their best to be helpful, had checked out every other woodcutting site around. No Biggs. No alibi now either.

"What will we do?"

"Hide this lot and hope for the best."

When the warrant for Biggs's arrest was granted, the magistrate asked the detective sergeant swearing it out what the evidence against him consisted of.

"We do not believe, Your Worship, that he will be able to explain how his fingerprints came to be on the Monopoly board at Leatherslade Farm and on a tomato ketchup bottle," said Jack Slipper.

7

Ronald Biggs has very little chance of avoiding being sent back to Britain to serve out the remaining 28 years of his sentence for the Great Train Robbery.

The best he can expect is to stay on in Brazil for 90 days—in the hands of the Ministry of Justice.

Colin MacKenzie, the *Daily Express,*
February 7, 1974

Before Hitchen had a chance to send for him Colin MacKenzie appeared, a dark-haired young man whose blue-eyed good looks usually reflected a genuine good nature and readiness to please. He was at that moment jumpy, distracted and apologetic. He wished, he announced, to resign in order to pursue the momentous opportunity that had come his way. Hitchen had possibly heard of his amazing piece of good fortune?

Properly speaking, MacKenzie should have come to Hitchen in the first place instead of going over his head to Vine. But the deviation from protocol was understandable. He and Vine were old friends. When Vine had been in charge of the prickly and snobbish *Express* gossip column by-lined William Hickey (the *nom de guerre* it took from a rakish 18th-century chronicler who would *never* have been given a job by Lord Beaverbrook) MacKenzie had been one of his assistants. They were also partners in an engrossing private venture, the ownership of a racehorse called Overall in which, up until he had grasped the full implications of his present position, MacKenzie's best hope of prosperity seemed to lie. The anonymous legmanship of the Hickey column had marked the high point of his time on the *Express*. He had an impeccable background for writing gossip. He had been the Head Boy of a prestigious public school, Malvern, and had a respectable Oxford degree. He had distinguished himself in the energetic arts of tennis and squash. He had expected that the *Express* would offer him rapid promotion and development for he needed more money than he had so far earned at twenty-eight to support the way of life for which his background had prepared him.

But his feet had remained firmly planted on the lower rungs of the ladder. From the Hickey column he had transferred to the job of Deputy Education Correspondent, an undistinguished specialization that practically petered out when student issues faded as national news in the early seventies. On the general staff he had been given a few foreign assignments, for he spoke some languages, and carried out one of them brilliantly, snatching a young English woman doctor with Palestine Liberation Organization connections from the opposition in Paris. But still his career did not take off. MacKenzie could see that he was getting nowhere as an *Express*-man. He had decided to go back to gossip. He had applied for the job of second in charge of the gossip column on the *Express*'s principal rival, the *Daily Mail*.

Hitchen listened sympathetically or so it must have seemed. It was his first chance to find out exactly what MacKenzie did know about the man he assumed to be Biggs and how he came to know it. In making a case for being released without serving out notice, MacKenzie found himself going into rather more detail than he had intended. But for all Hitchen's adroit pressure, it remained a frustratingly unfleshed tale.

A man MacKenzie knew slightly had returned to Britain after a stay abroad and told of meeting an exiled Englishman known to everyone as Michael Haynes, who had one day confided that he was actually the notorious Ronald Biggs. The name had been totally unfamiliar to MacKenzie's young and unworldly friend, to whom the Great Train Robbery was just another elders' legend, but

Haynes had been delighted to recount the details. And Haynes—or Biggs—had tired of life in other peoples' countries. He yearned to see green old England again. He understood there had been some changes in the British legal system since last it had dealt with him so rigorously, and he believed it might be possible, were he willing to speak to the police about certain matters on which up until then all of the robbers had remained silent, to be granted a new trial and receive a lighter sentence. He could even expect in a few years to be paroled.

MacKenzie had spoken to Haynes by telephone and as a result was convinced that he was indeed Biggs. Convinced enough, he now told Hitchen, since he had done his duty by the *Express* and offered them the story which they were apparently not willing to pursue, to be ready to gamble his future upon it.

"Look, Brian," he said to Hitchen. "I know I'm never going to get anywhere here. This is the only chance I might ever have of making any real money and getting my wife and kids out of that dump in Battersea. Writing a book with Biggs could make me 100,000 pounds."

Battersea a South London district of Victorian working class cottages in the shadow of an enormous power station that is being nibbled at by the impecunious middle class looking for cheap housing was where MacKenzie and his family lived. A couple of days reflection at home there had helped him work out the proposition he was now putting to Hitchen.

"I can see that there might be ethical difficulties in the paper getting itself involved with a crook on the run. But if I can go and do it by myself—after parting from the *Express*—I could give you first bid on the British rights of the story."

MacKenzie did have a point worth bargaining over because if he had really found Biggs, it was the preraid Up Special to a policeman's whistle that someone would soon raise the subject of a large sum of money. As the result of an accumulation of embarrassing publicity and some admirable revision of older Fleet Street values, the ancient custom of checkbook journalism had all but expired, at least when the checks were to be made out to criminals.

Paying some villain or his family for a firsthand story of the crime that had got him where he was—in the nick or on the way to the gallows—had once been the shortest cut of all to exclusivity and only deplored by rivals whose offers had not been high enough. A slightly self-righteous consensus arrived at a few years earlier among the newspaper managements to stop subsidizing successful crime in that way had been departed from, interestingly enough, only when the same Ronald Biggs while in hiding sent a written account of some of his adventures to be auctioned off by a lawyer. They were bought, to the envious disapproval of every other paper, by *The Sun*, who paid 20,000 pounds for it in such a way that "only his three innocent children will benefit."

Hitchen, however, was less worried about crossing a bridge so far along the road from his meeting with MacKenzie than in how they were to negotiate the first bend. And he was beginning to think that MacKenzie, for all that he was an unexpected source for a story of such grandeur, might really be on to something. The actual evidence itself was infuriatingly scant and frail. All it meant was that someone, somewhere wanted someone to believe that he was Biggs and there were nuts galore who would lust after the fleeting attention that that could win them. Hoaxers plague newspapers, so Hitchen was appalled by the readiness with which MacKenzie had accepted everything he had been told. Some intensive testing would have to be carried out before he was prepared to show any degree of enthusiasm himself.

But the improbable tale with its motive thread of half-grasped exercise-yard lawyering, which Hitchen had pried from MacKenzie as delicately as a battlefield surgeon removing a live mortar shell from a body cavity, did have the random, uncontrived feel of the possible to it, which the seasoned stalker of the heights knows he can ignore only at some peril. The worst of avalanches gives the least warning before the snow begins to slide underfoot. It was a good time to keep an unswerving eye on the obvious.

So Hitchen was mischievously gratified to note MacKenzie's reaction to finding himself the sole proprietor of such a potentially valuable property. There was nothing, really, anyone could do to stop him if he decided at that moment to take off after the big prize by himself. All he had to lose was a few weeks salary. But there was no flicker of the irritating though convincing self-assurance of a reporter firmly clutching the key to a safely locked-up scoop that was about to transform his life. He was scared stiff.

"I've already told two of you," MacKenzie complained. "I can't afford to have any of this leak. I have to think of what could happen if the police get on to it. And Biggs must have plenty of friends left in London. I've got my family to think of."

The idea that Biggs might be in a position to arrange any harm at a distance sounded quite ludicrous to Hitchen. But if it would help keep MacKenzie's own mouth shut and make him think that the world outside was going to be inhospitable and dangerous, he was delighted to encourage it. And if, against all odds, they did find themselves making some progress, leaks would be a grave hazard. It was harder for a newspaper to keep its own secrets than it was to keep the petty cash in the Night News Editor's float. The omens were not too bad, Hitchen decided, that if Biggs was really ready to be found then it would, after all, be the *Express*—and only the *Express*—that found him. Unobtrusively MacKenzie was being measured up by Hitchen's shrewd eye for the puppet strings which would help guide his movements in the busy days that, with luck, lay ahead.

"I think we'll be able to work something out, Colin," said Hitchen, the sympathetic editorial puppetmaster. "Let me talk to the Editor and later on we'll go and have a drink."

Hitchen went off to see McColl brooding lightly on the cosmic injustice of such a prodigiously covetable story going in search of an author and stumbling over Colin MacKenzie. He did not know MacKenzie well, but he was already worried that he would not have either the instinct or the experience to see a testing situation like that through to the end. MacKenzie was an admirable and well-brought up young chap, thought Hitchen, with a self-made newspaperman's condescending mistrust of a privileged latecomer to the game, but he might lack a certain professional savagery. Hitchen would have been more unhappy still had he not managed like a retired pickpocket keeping his hand in with a charity performance, to extract a useful clue during their conversation to the sanctuary that MacKenzie would not name without his victim feeling a thing.

What Hitchen would really like to have done was to get out from behind his desk and take the story on himself. But he could not do that. Nor could he assign a less miscast reporter to it even when he had all the facts he needed. MacKenzie had brought in the tip and MacKenzie—if he could be conned or coerced into staying with the *Express*—would do the story. That was The Code Of The Street.

Poor MacKenzie would certainly have been even more unhappy if Hitchen had told him what had happened after his first conversation with McColl. When they had finished their discussion the Editor had sent for his deputy John McDonald and the paper's Legal Manager, Andrew Edwards, a barrister in charge of the staff of lawyers, who, in keeping with the general Fleet Street practice, read all the copy that was prepared for publication and advised on the possibility of libel or contempt of court, the gravest nuisances that British newspaper editors suffer. The reaction of the two men to what they were told of MacKenzie's claim froze Wig and Pen into their classic opposing postures.

McDonald, the journalist, veteran of 20 years on the Back Bench, the editorial table where the front page and the other key sections of the paper are assembled every night, saw instantly what the outcome would be of ensnaring someone who was, in effect, one of Fleet Street's heraldic beasts, and he saw it, naturally enough, in the largest and blackest typeface the house could supply.

"Fantastic," he said cautiously. "Sensational. The greatest."

From the convoluted position into which he had to force himself in his dual role as defender of the *Express* from legal error and a friend and sworn officer of the Royal Courts, Edwards got a different view.

"I am afraid," he said to McColl, "that your position is perfectly clear. If you or anyone else on the staff knows the whereabouts of Biggs, who is an absconded felon, you have no choice in the matter. The police must be told at once."

Hitchen and McDonald were scandalized at the thought and said so. Hitchen pointed out forcefully that they had little enough of a stake in the matter as it was, since MacKenzie was still the only person who knew where his man was and to bring in Scotland Yard would lose them even that advantage. Besides, like any criminal—so long as he was not a demented mass murderer or a depraved child molester—Biggs was entitled to assume, at least for the time they had his proposal under consideration, that he could trust them with his liberty. It was not a very highly polished moral argument. But it had been applied to many a workaday journalistic situation down the years and was fairly generally accepted even by most policemen. The journalists understood that Edwards was duty bound to give McColl the advice that statute and his professional devotion dictated. McColl, if he wished to be guided primarily by journalistic values, was entitled to ignore it or accept it as he pleased. The exchange of opinions concluded, they all arranged to meet again later in the day. Everyone agreed that they must keep everything to themselves until Hitchen had been able to run an assay on the data available and report back. They promised to speak to no one.

"Especially not MacKenzie," said Hitchen, "or we'll never see the bugger again."

When the conclave resumed McColl was positively and uncharacteristically enthusiastic. He had decided, he told them after hearing Hitchen out, that he coveted Biggs for the *Express* very badly indeed. He would not consider MacKenzie's proposal to resort to private enterprise not only for the sound reason that a reporter ought not be allowed to switch off his professional obligations when it suited him to profit by them elsewhere but for the same credulous fears that Hitchen had just heard expressed by MacKenzie.

"We can't have young MacKenzie wandering around the underworld by himself," said McColl, adding with the wisdom gleaned from years of reading his own newspapers, "He might be Bumped Off."

Hitchen, considerably heartened, said he would immediately begin trying to convert MacKenzie to their point of view. But McColl had something more to tell them which he did, managing to sound grave and sententious, his fluting Highland tones notwithstanding.

"I have decided that my duty is clear," he said, sinless blue eyes aglitter. "I am going to inform Scotland Yard."

The journalists, shocked, protested in as much wrathful detail as the pecking order permitted. They had not taken the possibility seriously before.

"We don't know if it's really him yet," said Hitchen. "Let alone where to even start looking for him."

But McColl was already at his private phone, dialing 230-1212 and asking to speak to Deputy Commissioner Colin Woods whom he had met only a few days before at a Saints and Sinners lunch at the Grosvenor House Hotel. Edwards, a wiry gaunt-faced man with, as a rule, a relaxed and gregarious manner, shuffled his papers in a businesslike fashion. The other two sat enshrouded in a disillusioned and reproachful silence. This was *not* The Code Of The Street.

They heard McColl greeting Woods as though he had been a repentant sinner returning to the Kirk.

"It's not what *you* can do for *us*, Colin," he said. "It's what *we* can do for *you*."

In time-honored style he added, "I can't mention names over the phone. But it's a big one."

Then, perhaps feeling he was overdoing the mystery, he fell back on a habit that often confused his staff, "We're talking about *R.B.*," he said, confidentially.

Woods could have had no idea whatever whose initials they could be. But he obviously decided that a call from the Editor of a great national newspaper deserved a response of approximately equal magnitude.

"He said he'd send his best man down right away," announced McColl to his unhappy company. "We'll all wait here the while."

Until that moment keeping the developments to themselves had not really gone beyond the bounds of normal discretion. But waiting in McColl's office for their eminent copper to arrive, the four between them established the standard for the truly impressive level of secrecy that they managed to sustain right to the end of the operation. McColl sent his secretary, Christine Wallace, away from her desk so that she could not see who came in. Edwards went down to the building's front hall—a superb 1930s period piece—to intercept their visitor and personally escort him up. The others kept up a desultory respectful bickering with McColl, but the damage was already done. In less than 20 minutes Edwards was back with a young man, evidently trying with commendable success, to avoid looking like a detective sergeant in purplish jeans and a scruffy leather jacket and his superior, a man who would never, no matter what he wore or how he acted, stand much of a chance of being taken for anything other than himself—Slipper of the Yard.

McColl made the expository remarks. Just as Hitchen was wondering how he was going to get Slipper to believe that they really did not have the slightest real reason to think the man they were talking about was Biggs, let alone know where to find him, he heard himself being asked to do it.

"You know the details better than I do," said McColl. And as he ran grudgingly through the scantest possible outline of the developments up to then, Hitchen began to see that there was a strong possibility that all was not yet lost. In the first place, it was far from a convincing story, and in the second, he thought that he detected sympathetic echoes from Slipper when he told him frankly that he had not agreed with the Editor's decision to call the Yard in. Not that Hitchen was fool enough to trust a policeman who agreed with him.

"A detective would not go on getting much information if he turned in everyone who came to him with something," said Hitchen, stating his own stand. A few feet away the Editor's chair squeaked uneasily, guiltily.

But in the third place, Hitchen was now also stubbornly resolved to get Biggs if he was to be got. And if, since McColl had "shopped" them—before they even knew where the poor sod was—and they had to go ahead manacled to the Yard, then they would do it that way and make the best of it.

He found Slipper's skepticism comforting.

"Are you in touch with this man now?"

"MacKenzie is, no one else."

"Can *we* establish contact with him?"

"*You* can't. We can."

"Should we talk to MacKenzie?"

"The whole thing will collapse if you do. That's just what he is most afraid of."

"I'm sure there's a lot you're not telling me," said Slipper.

Hitchen wished there was a lot *more* that he was not telling him.

They arranged that Hitchen would go to work on MacKenzie as strongly as he could and that Slipper would be kept in close touch.

Before he left—the outer office cleared once again and the silent, seedy sergeant sent out alone—Slipper gave Hitchen a list of numbers where he could be called.

"We get dozens of reports about this bloke," he said. "There's not much real chance of it being him. But see if you can get him to give you the answers to these questions."

Hitchen wrote them down, and Slipper made his own ostentatiously furtive departure.

"Have you really got no idea at all where MacKenzie rang the gink up, Brian?" asked McColl, more puzzled than ruffled at the unexpected rapport that Hitchen seemed to have struck up with Slipper.

"I picked up from MacKenzie that it's somewhere with a four-hour time difference from here, and that there are long delays in getting calls through," said Hitchen. "And he was last in Australia. Indonesia?"

MacKenzie never really had a chance. But he put up an admirable defense for a couple of days while Hitchen abandoned the newsdesk and took him through some classic nice-guy, tough-guy routines, switching between the parts himself when McColl was not around to act as his foil. First came the hard line appeal to conscience and principle, hammered home amidst the imposing leatheriness of the Editor's office, unattainable territory to MacKenzie until then. With McColl's worrisome magisterial presence backing him up, Hitchen gravely told MacKenzie that it was unthinkable he should walk out on them with a story that really meant something to the paper. That would be against all the rules of the game in which up until now he had played a fairly inconspicuous part, but for which he had regularly drawn an ungrudged if not perhaps conspicuous salary. Call it settling time if that might appeal to MacKenzie's punter's sense of honor, but he had a clear and inescapable obligation to the *Express*.

Hitchen told him confidentially that something like this had happened to him early in his own career. While working for the *Mirror*, he had been the reporter who first levered open the Christine Keeler story. Naturally, he had been tempted to forget his allegiance to the paper and collaborate with her on a most rewarding set of literary rights. But in the end, of course, he had been faithful to his trust. That bond between a reporter and his paper stretched far beyond the considerations of an ordinary job, argued Hitchen. Fulfilling it—and in return feeling it fulfilled—was an important element in the vocation. Duty. Dedication. Commitment.

"Perhaps you made the wrong decision about Keeler," said MacKenzie.

The softer sell worked better, for in addition to relentless application of his formidable powers of persuasion and flattery, Hitchen promised MacKenzie that he would be free to make any deal he wanted to with Biggs about a book just so long as the *Express* got a very large first bite at him. MacKenzie knew when he was finally licked. He consented to telephone the object of their joint desire and put to him the questions that Hitchen would provide.

"I'll have to call from home," said MacKenzie. "It could take as long as eight hours to get the call."

"I'll sleep at your place," said Hitchen.

The working arrangement they eventually concluded was hardly one of mutual trust. MacKenzie would still not reveal the country he planned to call; not even the continent. They decided, after a while, against going to Battersea—MacKenzie because he was still nervous at being in some way compromised and Hitchen because he preferred to keep the operation on ground where his writ would be hard to challenge even though he was not letting it show. He put MacKenzie in a borrowed office, next to the editorial floor men's room, with a direct dial telephone not connected to the switchboard and, by agreement, waited outside while the call was placed so that he could not tell where it was being made to. Then, he went in and sat down. Periodically, Hitchen would leave the room while MacKenzie checked with the operator, but the circuits to their objective were booked solid. They waited all that day together— creating enormous puzzlement and speculation among the staff— until, late in the afternoon, the phone rang. Hitchen left the office again to let MacKenzie establish his link. Reentering as soon as he could within the etiquette of their compact, he overheard a second number being passed to the operator which he stacked away in his mind until there was a chance to write it down. Two clues.

Michael was not at home, said a girl far away. It was Constantine's friend calling, MacKenzie told her. The girl would arrange for Michael to be at that number the following day if he could call back.

The following day began for Hitchen and MacKenzie at 6 A.M. in the same office. The call was placed by the same routine. There was no answer. All day they waited once again. If MacKenzie went to the toilet Hitchen left the office with him in case the phone rang while he was alone. When the phone did ring Hitchen left the room. Not until early evening did MacKenzie get an assurance from an operator that he could have a connection at 11 P.M. An office car took them for a strained and impatient dinner at Angelo's, a fashionable basement in Mayfair, strategically far removed from the pale of Fleet Street, and they returned to their provocative isolation. It was shattered by the promising squeal of the telephone right on the minute of the hour. Bursting back into the office Hitchen clamped his ear to the other side of the receiver that MacKenzie was gripping like a pistol butt in his strong, flat-nailed, tennis player's fingers and heard across an echoing satellite beam a cheerful South London voice demanding to know what the weather was like.

The answers MacKenzie noted down to the questions Hitchen had briefed him with were given readily and at length. MacKenzie had never shown any curiosity about the origin of the questions Slipper had provided and Hitchen, who had no way of confidently judging the accuracy of the replies, simply pocketed them noncommittally. But MacKenzie suddenly demonstrated that he had not, after all, been totally guileless in his earlier contacts. ·

"Michael," he asked the man on the other end of the mortifyingly enigmatic connection. "Did you send me that letter?" Yes, he nodded to Hitchen's wryly inquiring eyebrows.

Neither did Slipper like to talk too much on his own telephones Hitchen found when he called him the next day. He preferred the vigorously informal atmosphere of a dreadful pub called The Pill Box, a den of cops and robbers, near the Elephant and Castle. When they rendezvoused there, it turned out that the voice on the phone had indeed been able to name the day on which Bigg's brother had so fatefully passed on, knew the birthdates of the three Biggs children on which Biggs was known to dote, gave accurate details of the landlord (a retired police inspector), the rent at the house at Redhill and related some quite lyrical recollections of the roses that grew around the coal shed in which, for several days, the 141,000 pounds of the Up Special booty had been stashed.

Compelling as this was, if not conclusive, it was rendered obsolete even while Slipper was still chewing it over. When Hitchen got back to the *Express* MacKenzie showed him a sheet of paper he had received in the mail that morning. At its head had been drawn the circle and rays of the sun and at its foot a childish caricature of an old-fashioned locomotive and a pair of coaches. Framed between them was a complete lefthanded set of fingerprints in brownish ink. Hitchen—unknown to MacKenzie, who still had no inkling that the police were involved—smuggled them out of the office later that day to be copied and compared with the originals at Scotland Yard. They could only have been those of Ronald Arthur Biggs and no other.

8

"Biggs, it is my unpleasant duty to inform you that your
earliest possible date of release is January 12, 1984."
Commander Cooke,
Governor of Lincoln Prison

A nation totally captivated by the Great Train Robbery was
desperately keen to make celebrities out of the men who had done
it just as soon as they could be found. The pacing of the arrests and
the sporadic emergence in unlikely places of jettisoned bundles of
overheated loot kept up the suspense admirably. But pathetic Boal
and ridiculous Cordrey were not quite what everyone had been
hoping for. Wilson was a good deal better. But Biggs, when he
appeared in Aylesbury police headquarters via Scotland Yard,
looked like an irresistibly classical personification; the man of
humble origin but native courage compelled to risk anything to
prove himself to the woman he had married beyond his lowly
station. That was more like it. In the earliest days of the frantic and
unremitting raids that The Sweeney was making to try to haul in
everyone on the fast unfurling list of suspects, Biggs shone forth
with particular brightness, but a good deal of the tawdry gleam
in which he stood illuminated was reflected from his singular
wife.

Charmian Biggs had been called Powell when they married exactly three years earlier at Reigate Register Office not far from where they lived in Redhill. Her parents were respectable schoolteachers—her father a headmaster—and apart from her being only eighteen when she first ran off with Biggs, they had something quite different in mind for a son-in-law than a thief so unsuccessful that he had spent seven of the last ten of his thirty-four years in some kind of detention. They were mortified when Charm herself was locked up for eight weeks after Biggs took her for a spin in a car he had stolen for the occasion. They were unrelenting when they found she had kept in touch with him during the two-and-a-half stretch that followed the escapade and, incidentally, qualified him to be treated in the case of any future offense as "an incorrigible rogue." But Charm was hooked. As soon as Biggs was released the impetuous young couple overrode the parental objections to marriage in a forthright and practical fashion and five months after the ceremony a son, Nicholas, was born.

Charm settled down to dedicate herself to her husband's career. Biggs could earn a modest livelihood as a carpenter, having learned the rudiments of the trade while serving a previous sentence at Lewes Prison. But, although he expanded into contracting in a casual way, he remained at heart a dedicated and unregenerate thief. All that worried Charm about that was he might get caught. The bars behind which she had spent such a relatively brief time had scarred her soul as a hot grill burns into the skin of a fish.

He really ought not to have told her that nonsense about going to Wiltshire to chop down trees. She guessed what he had been doing as soon as she heard about the Train Robbery.

But everyone still believed that The Dustman was on his way to Leatherslade to wipe out the recent past, and days were to pass before the first description of a suspect would be issued. Biggs and Charm went to bed more mettlesome and carefree than ever. The following day they took a handful of fivers and drove to London to dine by expensive candlelight.

On the Monday, like any prudent couple blessed by a windfall, they went to the local Barclays Bank and paid off their 200 pounds overdraft. And when, toward the end of the week, Detective Inspector Basil Morris of Reigate C.I.D. dropped in as a matter of course to ask when they had last seen their old chum, Reynolds, whose picture by then was making regular appearances on television, Charm invited him to stay to tea. The money was still buried in the coal shed then, but it was quickly "banked" in the care of faithful family friends. When Biggs was picked up the account was automatically transferred to Charm.

Once Biggs had actually been charged (robbery while being armed with an offensive weapon) the severe strictures of British court procedure, intended to guarantee that potential jurors would not be exposed to information that might prejudice them for or against an accused person, made it impossible for newspapers to publish anything but the barest and most innocuous facts about him. And, of course, he could not have been interviewed for publication even if he had been allowed bail.

By the same rules neither could Charm's views on him or on anything connected with the robbery be reported. Nonetheless, with an eye to the end of the trial journalists tried persistently to ingratiate themselves with her. Soon her photograph became familiar to newspaper readers, a sizable, well-rounded young redhead with a soft chin and rosebud mouth, always lip-glossed, eye-lined and hair-sprayed to brittle suburban perfection and dressed in faultless mail-order taste. Nothing came through in the pictures of the profane and versatile vocabulary she had acquired from Biggs and the extrovert ruffians to whose company he had introduced her and which she frequently employed on the photographers. Nor did even the most perceptive of the reporters who dealt with her in the ample pink and white flesh get any real idea of the savage, possessive and enduring passion which bound her to her blundering husband.

By December 2, when 18 men and women assembled in the makeshift dock built in the Aylesbury Rural District Council Chamber, the antics of The Sweeney had practically paralyzed the ordinary course of crime in the great metropolis of London and in most provincial centers as well, where normally it would have been flourishing boldly in the pre-Christmas season. No workaday villain dared leave his own doorstep for fear of being scooped up and questioned with severity.

The regular magistrate's court at Linsdale had had to be abandoned since the dock there had never been planned to hold more than a brace of poachers and the Council Chamber, a poem of municipal architecture in blonde wood paneling and plate glass, which had only just been completed, precipitately requisitioned. The main trial eventually took place there as well as the preliminary hearings, but the councillors never forgave their dispossession. When it was all over they voted 18 to 10 against the installation of a plaque to commemorate the event.

But when all was just beginning with the Great Train Robbery, safely established for all time as organized crime's most illustrious landmark, everyone was breaking into the act.

Life magazine had planned on an elaborate pictorial reconstruction. However, finding British Rail understandably uncooperative in the way of loaning them a Model 1B locomotive and a couple of mail coaches—let alone allowing them to be stopped at Sears Crossing—London Editor Tim Green was compelled to run through the events with less authentic but far more picturesque rolling stock borrowed from the Bluebell Line, a group of steam-crazed amateur railwaymen in Sussex, and a gang of office boys to play the robbers.

Back in the United States the advertising agency that handled the Land Rover account also seized the possibilities offered by the gang's choice of transport.

"We are strictly on the side of law and order," the copy read. "But can you blame us for feeling a certain warm glow when we read that the perpetrators of England's greatest robbery also chose a Land Rover to do the job?"

Bernard Rixon, the owner of Leatherslade Farm, had repossessed it after the uncompleted sale and was charging sightseers half a crown admission, including a peek into the cellar. Children half-price.

Charm brought Biggs the story that had everyone they knew outside in stitches. Reynolds and his pretty Irish wife Frances had been hiding out in a London flat and somone, presumably an underworld opportunist, thinking there might be some easy pickings there, tried to break in. The burglar was disturbed by a neighbor who to the considerable consternation of the occupants called the police before telling them about it. With the law already hammering on the door, Reynolds had torn off his clothes and jumped into bed leaving Frances in an entirely unsimulated state of terror and distress to explain that she was entertaining a lover in the absence of her husband. The worldly and understanding coppers withdrew, pausing only to note the name that Reynolds mumbled from beneath the sheets. By the time they returned in force, having checked it out as false and been struck by some second thoughts, the couple were on their way. Reynolds was never knowingly seen again until he was arrested five years later living comfortably in the estimable south coast resort of Torquay. That was the last laugh before the 18 were committed for trial at the next sitting of the county assizes court the following month. The 12 of them who had been ordered to be kept in custody were driven in a wary police convoy from the jail where they had first been gathered together at Bedford while the specially isolated and heavily secured hospital wing of Aylesbury Prison was being prepared for them, with admirers, especially young women, waving them on their way. Charm had long since brought Biggs word, gleaned from a girlfriend who had a fiancé at Scotland Yard, that the main evidence against those who had actually ripped off the train was the best that a British court could be expected to find convincing. Fingerprints.

"Impossible," said Biggs. Superintendent Butler, who had greeted him at the Yard, had not told him what the case against him depended on, and the police were not obliged to go into details of their evidence at the preliminary hearings in the magistrates' court. He thought he had cleaned up his own dabs. And none of the men inside knew anything about the defection of The Dustman until Brian Field arrived to join them. When Field had been arrested he was asked how much money he had on him, and he replied, "About 35 pounds." There were 110 pounds in his wallet. In fivers.

Goody, too, caught up with them at Bedford. He had been grumbling two weeks earlier to Ian Buchan, a *Daily Express* reporter, with whom he had become friendly, about the frequency with which the police had been taking him in for questioning.

"Either they charge me today or they get off my back," he said. It seemed that he had indeed succeeded in not leaving a fingerprint at Leatherslade. But on a pair of suede shoes the police had taken from under his bed at The Windmill pub there was yellow paint that appeared to be similar to the stuff used on Land Rovers and on the Austin truck. Unhappily, said Goody, what the other prisoners had been told about the Dustman's dereliction, and therefore, presumably, about prints, was absolutely correct.

"We've got to get out of here," said Biggs.

A final flurry of impudent entertainment was provided by Roy James, who since leading the exodus from Leatherslade had been sought and not found in no fewer than 76 countries. Someone he trusted had shopped him and Tommy Butler, now acclaimed by every crime reporter in town as the Scourge of the Train Gang led 30 heavies to the door of a mews cottage in seemly St. John's Wood less than three miles from the Yard's front door, No. 14 Ryder's Terrace.

No one answered his knock, but a face was spotted peering through the upstairs curtains. Two detectives swarmed up onto a balcony and broke in. But their man had taken to the rooftops, dancing along the top of the little row of houses clutching a leather overnight bag. When he got to some adjacent buildings which actually stand in Blenheim Terrace, he dropped into the grounds of No. 40 and, as so often seems to happen, almost into the arms of a pair of coppers.

Butler had thoughtfully stationed them there and they had been watching James's airy progress with great enjoyment. The bag he carried contained 12,041 pounds and there was 131 pounds in his pocket, two of them Up Special fivers whose numbers had been jotted down by a bank clerk in Inverness. The same night 47,245 pounds was found in a pair of sacks left in a south London telephone booth. They had spent some time underground and had presumably been dumped by whoever had tipped off the Yard about Ryder's Terrace. Butler said to James, "You took a chance running around three storeys up. Didn't you know there was concrete underneath?"

"Was it, guv?" said James bitterly. "I thought it was grass."

The neighbors said he had lived in the house for six months which would have put him there two months before the robbery. But at that same time James had kept a flat in a shadily fashionable block of flats in Chelsea favored by costly call girls. For that was where Biggs, taken there by Reynolds at about the time James began going to No. 14, had first met the rest of the gang.

The money that had been buried in the sacks was the last substantial part of the Up Special loot ever to be recovered. Still missing is 2,300,000 pounds and only four of the men—18 or 11, depending on who you believe—have ever accounted for their shares. Long after the robbers—those who were caught—had been sent to prison, the dream lived on in many a good citizen's heart of stumbling across a treasure trove of fivers or of somehow collecting the reward. And by the hundred they continued to obediently inform on the suspicious behavior of their fellow countrymen.

This national characteristic, so lamentably easy to stimulate, has since inspired a weekly television program in Britain called "Police Five," on which appeals are made for information about unsolved crimes and descriptions given of stolen property or wanted persons. As well as inspiring a weird national network of amateur stoolies, it has become indispensable to thieves and receivers who rely on it to authenticate goods that have come into their possession.

While the vicarious venality was at its height, *The Times* assigned its learned financial staff to explore the most likely ways the robbers might use to recirculate their takings. After allowing for the far less likely possibility that the loot had been got as far as Africa or the United States, they wrote:

> As far as Europe is concerned, the Swiss banks are without doubt the most genuinely free-thinking establishments of their kind. Yet it is doubtful whether today any one of the leading institutions would readily accept, say, anything more than 1,000 pounds in notes.
>
> Some, it is thought, might not shrink at 5,000 pounds, but even such an amount would at once arouse suspicion after the theft and all the publicity it has received the world over.
>
> Certainly anything like one million pounds or more in notes, offered suddenly anywhere on the Continent, would have an immediate impact on the note rate even if such an amount is small in relation to the genuine dealings on the foreign

exchange market which run into many millions a day but are largely done on the telegraphic transfer system.

Conclusion: "In fact, a once-and-for-all exchange of a large amount of Sterling notes is not thought to be a practical proposition on the Continent."

Diligently, the writers explored the robbers' options.

"Another possible way towards quick exchange could lead via the gambling halls of Europe. Quite large amounts, say, at least 1,000 pounds at a time, might be quite readily acceptable in the big casinos of Cannes, Monte Carlo, Le Touquet and Baden-Baden."

They explained to their intrigued though upright readers how such a thing might be done.

"The cash would be changed into chips; if the gangster is lucky, he will double his money with a coup or two and walk out with twice as much in the native currency. But the casinos know their large gamblers, and really big amounts exchanged by anyone not known as a habitué would arouse suspicion."

Judiciously, the experts concluded, "There is no easy way out, it seems, except for the robbers to sit on their hoard and use the money or exchange it only as required for normal living."

Any of the robbers who reached a similar conclusion and decided to, as it were, simply live off their capital must be serving out their sentences in bitter frustration. Robbery money that was simply hidden or "banked" with friends has long since ceased to be legal tender. The old white fivers were already on the way out and the first series of blue notes issued to replace them were withdrawn from circulation a few months after the robbery—and partly because of it. Their only value now would be the current price of two tons of waste paper.

As the lengthy work-up to the sentimental British Christmas began to get into its open-handed stride, the prisoners of Aylesbury enjoyed some dividends from their notoriety. And their prosperity. The authorities at first showed an uneasy respect for their organizing ability by keeping them separated and by guarding them with warders conscripted from all over the country who were rotated every two weeks as insurance against their developing too close a bond with their charges. Exercise was limited and searches frequent. But this unusually severe treatment of unconvicted men was soon reported to the press by families or friends and, once it had been mentioned in print, dropped.

Innocent men were still entitled to innocent pleasures. They kept their expensive new clothes. Meals could be sent in from a decent hotel, and they were permitted reasonable amounts of beer and wine to have with it. Their relatives seemed to have no trouble coming up with money. Biggs always ordered Portuguese *rosé*. He had just been learning how to live a little.

But man does not live by wine alone. Charm brought him the only consolation she could offer in the circumstances, magazines with inspirational erotic pictures concealed between their pages.

Running tirelessly over the sparse permutations of the situation open to them until the trial began, reporters even managed to unearth an angle that rewarded their readers with another all time public favorite, The Animal Story. Goody owned an Alsatian bitch named Sheena, who had been pining for him. A deeply concerned nation was comforted to learn that the governor of Aylesbury Prison had been sufficiently moved by the spirit of the season and the incessant bedevilment of the press to waive the rules for a reunion between dog and master to take place in one of the visiting rooms.

Not that the robbers got all the adulation. The organizers of a rather garish charity proclaimed Driver Mills one of the country's Men of the Year and made the confused old man the main feature at their annual lunch at the Savoy Hotel. With wondrous insensitivity British Rail pressed upon him the maximum reward for exceptional service that the regulations permitted for his "courage and resourcefulness." Twenty-five pounds. Suggestions that it seemed a less than generous gesture were turned away with the explanation that in addition Mills was being kept on full pay even though he had not been fit to work since the hold-up.

The warm glow generated by all this good will, however, faded out in Aylesbury when a transistor radio battery was found hidden in a roast chicken being sent in to one of the men. Seized by the fear of a breakout assisted by walkie-talkies and similar technical aids of which the prisoners had already made such infamous use, the prison staff cracked down again and the robbers went back to the nauseating official menu for Christmas. And to their worries.

Among the flow of essential supplies, like Havana cigars, had come a copy of Archbold's *Criminal Law and Practice*, the indispensable guide of bewigged judge and jailhouse lawyer alike in establishing who can be given how much for what. The principal charge all of them faced was robbery with aggravated assault for which the sentence could be life imprisonment. At that time in Britain "life" was established at 15 years which, with remission for good behavior, could be reduced to ten and perhaps even eight years. To sturdy old lags, as most of the robbers were, that was a surmountable length of time considering the profit they still expected to make; they could never earn as much in a lifetime honestly. But what worried Briggs was that there appeared to be no maximum sentence prescribed for the other main charge against them, the amorphous and unnerving one of conspiracy—in this case conspiracy to rob.

Goody was optimistic that the evidence against him would turn out to be inadequate. Jim Hussey, whose palm print could have found its way on to the Austin anywhere and Bob Welch, who felt the same about his on the pipkin. were prepared to take their chances with a jury. But the others, especially Cordrey and Boal, who had been charged with receiving money as well, were becoming very thoughtful. They were beginning to get the idea that their punishment might be scaled to fit not the crime so much as its proceeds.

Biggs calculated that he had two chances of avoiding far more time in prison than he could possibly bear to spend. He needed to contrive an acceptable explanation for his fingerprints being found on the sauce bottle and the Monopoly set that did not necessarily connect him to the actual robbery, and he worked out the possible ones. A: He had been among the men recruited to clear up Leatherslade Farm after the gang had gone. B: He had been summoned down there to take part but after hearing what the gang was planning to do had left. Pretty thin.

The only practical solution was the one he had instinctively blurted out as soon as he heard about the fingerprints. Escape. After her every visit to Aylesbury Prison, Charmian found herself sent on an ever-widening round of friends and acquaintances collecting advice. She also had to go repeatedly to their bank, paying interest on every withdrawal. Biggs, drinking prison tea in his basement cell thought wistfully of clever Reynolds, Edwards and White safely away somewhere where the *rosé* flowed, no doubt, and plotted away the days until he would be back in the mock-dock of the Rural District Council offices, swamped among all these people whose company he was already beginning to find an affliction.

But Biggs's standing as an individual was to be dramatically reinforced when the robbers made their definitive public appearance. He went on trial all by himself.

9

"It would seem from admittedly a considerable distance that
the circumstances reveal either that the police are incom-
petent or that there was some collusion between them and
the *Daily Express*."

Mr. Ray Carter M.P.
for Birmingham Northfield,
February 5, 1974

•

Slipper, invincibly suspicious, had been more interested than
impressed at having the correct answers come back from MacKenzie's telephone call. It was conceivable, if unlikely, that a painstak-
ing impersonator could have gone thoroughly enough into Biggs's
background to be able to produce them. But once shown a
fingerprint the distant clanging of cell doors began to sound in his
ear. When Hitchen met him and Jones once more in The Pill Box to
hear that the prints had been authenticated—Biggs in his innocence
of a world he had always had to deal with at a distance apparently
imagined that newspapers had their own facilities—the two Sweeneys greeted him with a triumphant little jig across the well-stomped
bar carpet before they remembered where they were.

Hitchen never understood why they persisted in using such a pub
for their conspiratorial encounters unless they were making a

deliberate effort to convince the milieu that they were not up to anything more than just chatting up a contact. The gaudy orange and purple cornerless bar—true to its name, The Pill Box was octagonal—was always crowded with plainclothesmen and their equally inquisitive contacts. For the instincts of a chicken-sexer to tell them apart; every time the door opened hooded glances raked it in short bursts. When Hitchen had first arrived there with the Biggs answers scrawled on an *Express* page-layout sheet, he had found Slipper tranquilly sucking away at half a pint of Guinness and sharing a plate of sausages and ham sandwiches with Jones. The two distinctive customers drew themselves around him like a gendarme's cloak while they read what he had brought, walling off the rest of the room and thus insuring the unabridged attention of everyone else in it.

There was always a possibility, of course, that the eavesdroppers were hoping to pick up one of the enchanting malapropisms with which Slipper sometimes confounded his interlocutors.

"Gawd," he would say, expansively reaching for the first Guinness, "am I hydraulicked!" He meant dehydrated. When Slipper joined, it had been a one-syllable police force.

This time Hitchen was astonished to find that after that one forgetful burst of elation, the detectives' second reaction to the fateful news was trepidation and despair amounting to only a shade short of panic. What worried them, Hitchen was fascinated to discover, was the illicit early warning system, operated within Britain's prestigious crime-busting apparatus, by a small but ineradicable network of expediently placed "bent" coppers. A matter as sensitive as the possibility of nabbing Biggs, Slipper explained, could be entrusted to only a carefully selected few of his colleagues, right at the summit of the Yard's hierarchy. Which was why he had taken the precaution of asking the head of the fingerprint section to check the Biggs prints himself and mention it to no one.

What could happen, Slipper and Jones confided with many an embarrassed wink and a whisper, was that if a long dormant file was removed from the Central Records Office or some other form of interest shown in a "client" of one of the few perfidious record-keepers, a silent arrow of alarm could go winging out of the building, to land . . . ? Where? That was the interesting thing in this case, wasn't it, Brian? The time had come, said Slipper to Hitchen rather forcefully, for a little straight talking.

A distinctly introspective mood prevailed as Hitchen was delivered back to Fleet Street in Slipper's car, a Rover 3500 of finely calculated anonymity driven by a silent, broad-shouldered plain-clothesman named Ken. Just as Slipper's practical considerations had been swept aside by the fingerprints, so were Hitchen's moral qualms evaporating. With the knowledge that the man MacKenzie was in touch with really was Biggs, mere covetousness for a fine story had been transformed into commitment, although not without a final tingle—if not much more—of conscience on behalf of the poor fool who was so incautiously delivering himself up.

Hitchen felt worse about Biggs than about MacKenzie, since the rules would have to be changed slightly now that the game was to be played for real. The chance of a lifetime it might be, but in the end it was the lifetime of the *Daily Express* that mattered. There could be even less question than before of letting MacKenzie go solo on such a story. And none whatever of allowing Slipper to straight talk himself into the vital information and gain the initiative. The only hope of sustaining the bloom of exclusivity lay in keeping Slipper convinced that he would get his man only if he did things the way the *Express* wanted them. The greatest danger Hitchen feared was that hands far heavier than his own would make a grab for the strings he was so far manipulating success with and that MacKenzie, spooked beyond endurance, would never tell anyone anything.

However, Hitchen's delicate task of keeping MacKenzie under his control and out of Slipper's reach while at the same time squeezing out of him Biggs's exact whereabouts was quite enjoyable by comparison with what Slipper now had to do. *He* had to go back to the Yard and sheepishly break it to his superiors that the *Express* had certain information that might lead to the apprehension of the nation's most notorious fugitive but that they flatly refused to give it to him. Unless the Yard played ball. Sir.

The law gives no protection for a British journalist who withholds information from the police, irrespective of what he might get away with by long-established custom, so long as the matter does not get as far as a courtroom. Andrew Edwards's counsel to McColl had been faultless on that point. Slipper's chiefs would be bound to inquire of him with some heat why this should not be brought home to the scoundrelly scribblers concerned in a manner likely to make a lasting impression on them.

Almost the last thing Hitchen had been prepared for was that Slipper, after a few more surreptitious encounters and telephone conversations, would request a meeting with McColl and jauntily announce, "All right then. It's on. But remember this. We've *got* to get him."

It was too easy. Trade relations with the British police always leave Fleet Street with an unbridgeable deficit—all the papers getting in return a good deal less than they give. To anyone resigned to the shabby conventions of highly individual, unpredictable and extremely limited relationships between reporters and policemen that kind of gracious surrender with official approval was as uncharacteristic of Scotland Yard as the public at large would imagine, say, phone-tapping was. Mindful of the curious echo that had developed in the last few days on both his home phone and his confidential office number, Hitchen wondered what really had happened up at the Yard when Slipper explained his predicament to Commander Ernie Bond who, as Deputy Commissioner, would be the source of most of his orders. But while waiting for the bottom line to come into sight, there could be no harm in pressing his luck.

"No, Jack," said Hitchen, dropping into the bantering, though far from disrespectful, manner he had found to work best with Slipper. "*We've* got to get him. *We've* done all the work and *we* want first bite at the cherry. In fact we want the *whole* cherry. You can have the stalk."

"Any way you like," said Slipper, still most uncharacteristically deferential. "We'll play it any way you like. Just as long as we catch him in the end."

"All right then," said Hitchen, generously. "We'll see what we can do."

Slipper leaned forward, close to him, a powerful man and an imposing one, even to anyone ignorant of his well-deserved reputation for being ready to resort to severe measures in the interests of justice. His clear blue eyes, worn flat and sharp by the many a terrible sight in the line of duty zoomed into close focus as he sized Hitchen up as expertly and carefully as a hangman squinting through the peephole of a cell.

"Brian," he said, his lugubrious style of delivery not in the least detracting from the earnestness of his question, "you wouldn't be holding out on me, would you?"

"Of course not, Jack," replied Hitchen, although not as truthfully as he would once have been able to.

"Are you sure MacKenzie's the only one in the know?"

"That's right."

"Then," said Slipper, "I'm afraid that the time has come for me to have a word with Mr. MacKenzie up at—" and he paused, to weigh the pronouncement with a practiced old one-two—"the Yard."

MacKenzie came into the Editor's office as breezily as Slipper had left it. Everything that had been said to him and whatever had been craftily allowed to remain unsaid had left him with the happy impression that his arguments and his strategy had won converts. Biggs would be his, the *Express* was going to give him leave to write an enriching and transfiguring book and would be happy to settle for the serial version of it that he would provide. Battersea would soon be far behind. And he would never have to be a gossip columnist again.

Hitchen gave him the chair in which he usually sat himself, a few feet away from McColl, but he took another from which he could get a clear view of MacKenzie's face. It was going to be a bad moment. Unhesitatingly McColl unsheathed the cold claymore of self-righteousness and plunged it in. On legal advice he had been obliged to inform Scotland Yard of the discussions they had had. The *Express* would now be cooperating with the police in bringing Biggs back to Britain. Sorry, Colin.

MacKenzie turned as pale as Biggs's remaining chances. His well-turned jaw sagged. He rose off the quilted black leather, the tension and suspense built up through the previous few days bursting forth in an explosion of fear, shame and umbrage. They had, said MacKenzie angrily, turned him into a Judas. Yes, a Judas.

He would be betraying not only Biggs but the intermediary who had brought the story to him. To *them*.

Not necessarily, said Hitchen and McColl. Wait a minute. Biggs, after all, was a convicted criminal.

"That's another thing," said MacKenzie. "You have not only impugned my professional honor, you have exposed me to danger. You have exposed my family to danger—Biggs may have dangerous friends in London."

"Where was your professional honor?" asked McColl and Hitchen, "when you wanted the story all for yourself?"

"That's different," said MacKenzie.

And precisely because this could be such a risky business, the partners in persuasion said, each with his own purpose in mind, is all the more reason for you to put your faith in the not inconsiderable resources of the *Daily Express* and your trust in the police. "You must," answered MacKenzie bitterly and brokenly, "be joking."

But he knew that he was beaten, even though his last suspenseful card still lay face down on the table and no hand had reached out for it. MacKenzie gave himself up at last to the consolations of corporate planning and the comfort of realizing that others far more hardened and experienced than himself appeared to share his sage regard for the long arm of the outlaw they were dealing with.

"What," he asked meekly at last, "do you want me to do now?"

"Come with me," said Hitchen, who had already told Slipper what time to expect them at the Yard.

Although he was fairly sure he had Slipper convinced that a wrong move would instantly unravel the whole flimsy web of intrigue, Hitchen was far from happy about what could happen once they delivered MacKenzie up on The Sweeney's own turf. He took Andrew Edwards along for reassurance. And when they got to the awful new building in Victoria that is now Scotland Yard (the picturesque older one in Whitehall having been, in some kind of metaphor, turned into offices for Members of Parliament), traveling for the sake of discretion in MacKenzie's red Fiat, an elaborate performance was called for. When Slipper came down to sign them in, nicely turned self-made introductions had to be exchanged all round so that MacKenzie would not suspect that the other three had ever met before. The production was nudged perilously close to a farce, however, by the impromptu entrance of an infuriated elderly doorkeeper cop who pursued them down the ominous vinyl-lined corridors, complaining relentlessly to Slipper that the Fiat had been left in forbidden territory.

"Jesus Christ," grumbled Hitchen, "we're going to fix them up with the biggest comeback of a condemned man since the Resurrection and they want to give us a bloody parking ticket."

But MacKenzie was too far gone to raise a giggle or a grimace. Shaky and doom-ridden he shuffled into the office of Commander John Lock, chief of the Flying Squad, whose cordially extended hand he took as he did that offered by Commander Bond, the man with whom it had all begun. One twist of that arm instead of a handshake, thought Hitchen, and he might spill the lot. If only they knew it. But by then Edwards's briefcase contained the original folio of the Biggs prints, which MacKenzie had been talked into handing over on the way down. The law might very well carry off his reporter there and then. But Hitchen wanted to make sure that he would not lose anything else that mattered.

As it happened, though, the same warm and friendly spirit Slipper had shown—and a similarly praiseworthy standard of acting, for Bond knew Hitchen—was displayed by his two superiors until MacKenzie, who was expected home to baby-sit while his wife went away for the weekend, had to leave. It was Friday, January 25, and Slipper said, "We'll all have the weekend off and make the final arrangements on Monday."

"You'll be around, won't you Colin?" asked Bond, the meaning not entirely absent from his voice.

"Oh, yes," said MacKenzie, sadly. "I'll be around."

A secure meeting place had now to be found in which the ultimate piece of outflankery could be worked out in detail. It would require too lengthy and detailed a session for The Pill Box, but the trio of top coppers had been adamant in their distrust of the Yard's security. Anywhere, they had warned, but there.

The *Express* office, however, would have been even worse. Gossip is the food of Fleet Street's soul (if not its drink) and the movements and absences of everyone concerned in the secretive machinations of the past few days had already generated a colorful crop of speculation and rumor, immeasurably wide of the nearest mark. What had to be prevented even at far beyond the usual cost was the escape into circulation of a single virulent fact.

The various editorial, circulation and advertising offices in Fleet Street are all linked by informal but extremely sensitive espionage networks, the busiest of which keeps the *Express* and the *Mail*, the two most dedicated rivals, fairly well informed about developments in each other's headquarters. Similarly, direct lines of communication are kept up between other more or less matched competitors, the *Daily Mirror*, and *The Sun*, *The Times*, and the *Daily Telegraph*, *The Observer* and the *Sunday Times*, which have developed in much the same way. Although most news editors have one or two outright turncoats on their confidential payroll list, information is mainly exchanged on a purely amateur basis between people who have worked with or for each other in the past and are always aware that they may find themselves doing so again. And there are always those who are extreme examples of the general journalistic compulsion to spread the word widely.

That seems to be in total contradiction to the loyalty syndrome which results in the potent and propulsive *esprit de corps*, so frequently demonstrated. But it illustrates another guiding truth about the personal psychology of newspapermen. They are often as strongly bound by a horizontal craft loyalty to other fellow-practitioners—irrespective of who works where—as they are to the vertical allegiance their individual newspaper commands; the "us" of the reporters helplessly enthralled by whatever they have been witnesses to, opposed to the calculating "them" of remote editors, managers and proprietors. But whichever motivation applied, Hitchen knew that if as few as half a dozen more people got to know of what was being hatched, someone in *some* other office would know something about it within hours.

Andrew Edwards's flat near Olympia, the great exhibition hall, was commandeered. Edwards was a newspaper lawyer, and a good one, whose job was to find ways of getting difficult stories into the paper rather than keeping them out. No editor was obliged to take his advice. And once it had been given he was as keen as any of the other schemers to see Biggs landed to the credit of the *Express*.

Again, Hitchen put MacKenzie under escort and marched him out of the office. He would not have been completely surprised if he had had to go looking for him that Monday. On the Saturday MacKenzie had called Hitchen at home from a public telephone—his own phone was manifesting a certain numbness of tone and other telling symptoms of interference—to mount his last obstruction. Pointing out that they would not keep many secrets with only one unbugged phone Hitchen plucked up the name of an obscure *Express* executive to call, phoned the man himself and apologizing rather than explaining, asked him to pass on to MacKenzie the number of a fourth party to whose house he drove and from where he could be sure of talking to MacKenzie on a safe line. For nearly half an hour, praise, promises and persuasion flowed silkily from Buckinghamshire to Battersea. The story stayed intact for a while longer.

But by Monday, the treatment had to be renewed once again, although it was a far easier task to perform in person and with the help available of a traditional sedative, in MacKenzie's case, vodka. Three large doses were administered in the Albion, a pub near Edwards's place before the final rendezvous took place.

Peter Jones was back by Slipper's side in the Edwards's dining room. He had not been in on the Yard negotiations, but from then on the two Sweeneys were never to part company. He was an unobtrusive, smartly dressed man with none of Slipper's bluster, bravado and size who, after a distinguished career at the head of the Pickpocket Squad, had just passed his examination for Detective Inspector. Slipper, who had worked with him before, wanted a trustworthy assistant for the historic exploit that was about to be added to the annals, and Jones wanted very much to meet Ronald Biggs. Wherever he was.

Yet again, Slipper went through the story he had heard in all but a couple of details at the Yard, painstakingly writing down the critical points in his notebook. The *Express* in turn took Slipper through his pledges. MacKenzie would have time to milk Biggs dry. MacKenzie's middleman, Benckendorff, would not be molested. Neither side would admit this deal had been made. Agreement reached, the terms of the transaction clear to all, it seemed, Slipper then launched himself on a rehearsal of the actual denouement. Swinging around on Hitchen he promised, with a robust and malevolent chuckle, "I'll give young Colin a right seeing to when I get in there. When I nick Biggs I'll make his bleeding ears burn. Because I'll probably have to arrest him as well."

MacKenzie's eyebrows tightened sharply. The tennis knuckles whitened.

"Hang on," said Hitchen swiftly, "*that's* not part of the deal. If you arrest MacKenzie how the hell is he going to file the story?"

"Well," said Slipper, puzzled, "he'll have it all sewn up by then, won't he?"

The arrangement they had come to was that before Biggs was arrested MacKenzie was to have him to himself for 72 hours so that he could thoroughly debrief him for their book. He had wanted a week but the extra days had to be bargained away against the promise from Slipper that he would leave Benckendorff untouched.

"Not with the story I want, he won't," said Hitchen. The story of the actual arrest of Biggs was the one that was going to sell the *Daily Express*. And it had to be filed on the unbeatable instant with its events choreographed to fit a demanding timetable.

"If there's any suggestion MacKenzie's going to be arrested, even to make things *look* good," said Hitchen, "the deal is off."

"You can't do that," said Slipper, threateningly.

"Easily," said Hitchen. "You still don't know *where* Biggs is."

"Oh," said Slipper with a show of his endearing capacity for overlooking details he had not committed to writing. "Christ Almighty!" That was, as he said himself, the dil*ee*ma.

Hitchen felt understandably smug. For the question that had tantalized him for days as well had been answered only that morning. Trying to keep MacKenzie's mind off the cheerless preoccupations absorbing him, Hitchen had chatted as they walked through the lobby of the *Express* building about preparations that would have to be made for the expedition that was obviously shaping up. Plane tickets, visas, traveler's checks, maps.

"Maps?" asked MacKenzie blankly.

When he had made an expediently premature return to the borrowed office by the gents, during one of the attempts to raise Biggs, Hitchen had overheard MacKenzie using a few words to the operator in a language he did not recognize but which he realized was neither Italian nor Spanish, although it resembled both. It had to be Portuguese. In addition to Portugal itself, Portuguese was spoken, he knew, in the African colonies of Mozambique, Angola and Guinea. The three-hour time difference, however, did not fit any of those. Nor would it qualify Macao, near Hong Kong, where Portuguese is also spoken. Nor Timor which, in any case, could not be raised on the telephone in a wait of 24 *weeks*. Portuguese was not, he must admit, spoken in Indonesia. So that really left only one possibility. A large and very likely one.

"Colin," he said, "I know it's Brazil."

"They won't need any maps," said MacKenzie, relieved to let the burden fall at last. "It's Rio."

"It's Rio," they told Slipper and Jones when the order of ceremony for the arrest of Biggs agreed by all had been clearly noted down in Slipper's notebook.

"Gawd!" breathed Slipper, taking out his moustache comb for a reflective stroke or two. "How are we going to get *there*?"

Normally, arrangements for *Daily Express* travel would be made by the Foreign Desk which controls all operations abroad. But that was one of the departments of the paper most susceptible to leaks. And Hitchen had no intention of going anywhere near it. He telephoned his own secretary, Joan Fenton, and had her book three seats on a flight the following day to Rio de Janeiro from Madrid and another three with a different airline on a London–Madrid flight. A routine European destination would not attract undue attention. The second seat was for William Lovelace, the paper's top photographer. The third was for Constantine Benckendorff, the Brazilian Connection.

McColl himself briefed Lovelace in the theatrical secrecy that had now become habitual to all involved. It was arranged that after he had left the country Lovelace's wife would telephone the Picture Editor, his departmental boss, and say that he would be ill for a few days. MacKenzie was keeping another urgent appointment. He was deep in opposition territory being interviewed by David English, editor of the *Daily Mail*, about the gossip column job.

Joan Fenton also made reservations for Slipper and Jones on the only flight going to Rio on the day after. They too had arranged to take leave—as soon as they had discreetly drawn their travel allowances—so that no one at the Yard would realize they were going anywhere.

Later in the day Hitchen went out by himself to a travel agent, picked at random, and paid cash for the MacKenzie, Lovelace and Benckendorff tickets. First Class. The Sweeneys picked up their tickets for which the Yard had to pay. Economy.

After the *Express* party had left on Tuesday, Hitchen met Slipper and Jones for a farewell drink in The Pill Box where, to his utter horror, they insisted on describing in rash and uproarious detail the shopping spree they had just been on. Proudly, they ticked everything off on the back of an envelope. Lightweight suits from Austin Reed at 60 pounds each. Tropical shirts, shoes, sandals— and everything else an unseasoned traveler might need in the tropics.

"Just as well we'll still be stretching this out longer than 48 hours, Brian," said Slipper, as every extensile ear in the pub strained to hear. If the job lasted less than that it appeared regulations required that they cough up the cost of the clothes themselves. The money issued them for the trip was safe in Jones's pocket, $2,000 in traveler's checks. But Slipper kept frowning anxiously at the list. He knew there was something he had forgotten. "I know what we haven't got, Peter," he announced at last. "We haven't got a pair of bleeding handcuffs. How are we going to nick him without handcuffs?"

The Sweeneys also had something far more disturbing to report. The News Bureau of the Yard, the official spokesman's office, which Slipper regarded in much the same light as Hitchen did the *Express*'s Foreign Desk, had received a call from a reporter at *The Sun* asking if it were true that there was some activity over long lost Ronald Biggs. And because the Biggs file was logged out to Slipper—he having been unable or unwilling in the end to do without it despite his own admonitions—the inquiry was channeled to him. He had dismissed it with bland and accomplished duplicity, saying that he had investigated a totally discredited report that Biggs had been sighted aboard a slow boat to Africa. But it had rattled him. He wanted to bring the *coup de grace* forward 48 hours and take Biggs on the Friday rather than, as they had arranged with MacKenzie, on the Sunday.

The news rattled Hitchen, too. *The Sun* was the Fleet Street flagship of News Limited of Australia, an aggressive fast-moving group with a particular interest in Biggs ever since he had so narrowly missed being nabbed on their own doorstep in Melbourne in 1970. *The Sun* had snapped up the story of his escape when half the coppers on earth were looking for him. The copy had been sent around in a perfectly businesslike fashion from a local solicitor's office. Hitchen pondered the opposed perils, the possibility that *The Sun* was on to anything against the risk of pushing MacKenzie too fast. "All right," he said, "Friday it is."

There was a last obstacle to be overcome before Slipper and Jones could be sent winging on their way to Rio and the dazzling exploits that awaited them there. Not all the journalists in Britain are in print or broadcasting. A surprisingly large number work more or less successfully as freelancers or in agencies, news-gathering microcosms that usually specialize in a region or a particular sphere of interest. London Airport is covered by an old-established agency named Brennards manned by 20 reporters and photographers who provide dozens of clients with all kinds of stories gleaned from their teeming parish, arrivals and departures, industrial disputes and crime. They do not miss much. They would very likely not miss Jack Slipper, who was fairly noticeable, and in any case a well-known figure even outside the immediate circles in which he moved. The least alert Brennards reporter would want to know why such a heavy copper was making such a trip.

The day before, Hitchen had telephoned Brennards in his capacity as a valued patron. It had been a long time since he had covered a story out that way, he said, lightly. Ha ha. There must be a lot of new faces on the beat and now that he had settled in as News Editor perhaps it would be a good idea if he was able to match them to the voices he heard every day on the phone. It so happened that he would be out their way on Wednesday evening. Could he buy them all a drink in one of the airport clubs? The Brennards people were delighted. Attention like that from the power houses of Fleet Street was damned rare.

"Get as many people together as you can," said Hitchen. He knew there would be a full house. Sooner or later ambitious youngsters who start out in agencies shoal toward Fleet Street. None of them would miss a chance to meet one of the men on whose door they might one day have to knock. And the older ones knew the value of knowing the face of a man who knew their name on a piece of copy.

Slipper and Jones said good-bye to their families and Ken the driver picked them up to take them to the airport. Ken had solved the embarrassing problem of the handcuffs. Since neither of the two had signed out on leave, they couldn't very well go back to the Yard to pick up a pair nor risk drawing attention to themselves by turning up at a strange police station to borrow some. Therefore, Ken had searched out a parked and deserted police car and discreetly lifted the cuffs he knew he would find in the glove box.

It was 5:30 P.M. on Wednesday evening when Hitchen strolled into his warm welcome by the boys and girls at Brennards and ordered the first of many rounds. Slipper and Jones were due to check in at 6 P.M. Outside Fleet Street journalists are beer drinkers and pint followed pint at the generous expense of the *Express*, catalyzing the flow of flattering attention in which the earnest airport specialists felt themselves enveloped. The agreeable session never faltered until Hitchen looked for a last time at the hefty and grandiose Rolex he kept as a trophy from his foreign correspondent days and politely mentioned his next appointment. It was 7:30 P.M. A photographer and a young woman reporter walked with him to his car. "What would you normally be doing at this time?" he asked them. "Over in Number Three Terminal," they replied pointing to the huge, well-lit building across the field. "Checking out any interesting departures."

Out at the end of the runway where the reeking jets sat nose to tail waiting their turn for take-off, Slipper was uncomfortably crammed into a tourist-class seat aboard Aerolineas Argentinas Flight 133. Beside him, a rather better fit for the accommodation, was the faithful Jones and at his feet a briefcase containing a photocopy of the warrant for the arrest of Ronald Arthur Biggs that he had sworn out in his sergeancy so long ago.

The briefcase contained quite a thick wad of documents. For Slipper had belatedly been apprised of something that the *Express* had known all along but not bothered to mention. There was no extradition treaty with Brazil. And the Yard, not trusting even the Foreign Office to be leak-tight, had decided against seeking a diplomatic solution. Slipper had been told to take with him the photostats of Biggs's records and a polite letter explaining how badly Britain wanted him back, and the rest would be up to him.

"We're counting on you, Jack."

10

"There are those who speak and write as though the sole object of punishment is the reformation of the accused. I think this is so exceptionally benevolent as to be capable of being positively mischievous."

Mr. Justice Edmund Davies,
addressing the Magistrate's Association

•

Despite the acute—and never relieved—shortage of actual evidence, there was never much doubt that the men accused of the Great Train Robbery were going to be convicted. The good people of Buckinghamshire had been a captive audience to the highly publicized investigation that finally brought 20 people together in the improvised dock, and they felt a proprietary interest in the matter. Their county had provided the setting for the Crime of the Century. They were now proud to be accommodating the Longest Trial in Living Memory—in the Council office—and the jury drawn from among them knew its duty.

Attempts to avoid local prejudice by transferring the proceedings to the Old Bailey had come to nothing. There must have been around the olde-worlde market town of Aylesbury some residents of roughly the same background as the jurors who were unconvinced of the robbers' guilt until the evidence had all been given and the arguments heard, but none of the reporters who clattered into town like a troop of hussars and billeted themselves in the Bull's Head, a hostelry of picturesque, low-beamed interiors, had an easy time finding one. They felt much the same way themselves having looked over Leatherslade and (even if the rules of contempt prevented them from printing the result) talked to some of the accused and the important witnesses.

Once its ranks were thinned by the anticlimactic routine that follows the first days of every trial, the press of about 60-strong were fairly evenly matched in numbers by the Bar. Between them prosecution and defense were represented by nearly 40 barristers, including a dozen Queen's Counsel, senior advocates whose elevation entitles them to wear a silk robe (suitably tattered) and multiply their fees outrageously, together with the inseparable entourage of solicitors and their clerks. The crucial distinction between barristers and solicitors is that only barristers may be trial lawyers and argue cases in court. They may not be engaged directly by a layman but must be "briefed" by a solicitor with the "instructions" of a client. There are only about 2,000 barristers in all of England and Wales and fewer than half of those earn an enviable income. The trial represented an upsurge in living standards for them as dramatic as the robbery had provided for the prisoners for the retainers and "refreshers" were being promptly paid. And they were going to have a far better chance of spending the money. The lawyers settled down comfortably in a hotel called the Bell at nearby Aston Clinton run by a retired solicitor who did his considerable best to make them at home and prepared for a long, congenial and profitable stay. Their host had a good nose for wine and kept a celebrated table to quite the equal of the standard established by the robbers in the hospital wing at Aylesbury.

There were 206 witnesses down to be heard, among them 58 Scottish bank clerks ready to testify that they had put their marks on some of the recovered fivers. But the problems of proving the theft of money that had never been found so daunted the prosecution that instead of being accused of stealing the unique and astronomic sum that they had really got away with, the robbers were charged with stealing the mailbags that contained it.

Something else made it an even more unconventional trial. The

Council offices were ringed with uniformed policemen and the mile and a half route of the Black Maria that had delivered the occupants of the hospital wing had also been guarded. The vehicle itself was led by a police car, flanked by motor cyclists and followed by a van full of police dogs and handlers. These were sensational precautions for a country which if not exactly law abiding was accustomed to manage its criminal affairs with unobtrusive good taste and moderation. But men who could treat Her Majesty's mails with such efficient disrespect were obviously capable of anything.

Her Majesty's judge in this case was Mr. Justice Edmund Davies, a small, neat man who had been something of a terror as a defense counsel when he had been a barrister himself and whose probable performance had been the subject of vigorous debate in both the sitting room of the Bell and the hospital wing. Alarming rumors had reached the robbers that they could expect to find one Mr. Justice Hinchcliffe on the bench, a man with a fearsome reputation for handing out severe sentences where violence had been employed, and they had seriously discussed going on strike and refusing to go to court. If taken there forcibly, they could lie down in the dock and remain mute. But in the end they decided it would be better to try to escape. Charm was given a shopping list and the "banker" paid out another 1,500 pounds.

British judicial proceedings operate with surprising speed. There are rarely any of the delays, detours and repetition endemic to American or Continental trials. In the heyday of the hangman (capital punishment was abolished in 1965) a murderer who timed his crime to avoid the Law Vacation could reasonably expect to arrive at the gallows within two to three months of committing it, even counting time for an appeal. In one of the more deplorable cases that took place in the final flurry of judicial slaughter before the noose was unknotted for good, that of Derek Bentley, a moronic nineteen-year-old accomplice to a murderer, exactly 86 days elapsed from the fatal gunshot to the drop. Jury challenges are rare, though permitted, the assumption being that an accused is just as likely to benefit by the jurors' personal inclinations as he is to suffer from them.

By the afternoon of January 20, 1964, the proceedings were under way. Three of the original jurors had been excused because of the long haul it was certain to be; eight prisoners had pleaded guilty, mostly to lesser charges of receiving and had been remanded for sentence. Mr. Davies had briskly defused a suggestion someone was supposed to have made to Karen Field about the possibility of bribing the jury to her husband's benefit which, had it been taken seriously, would have added the doughty though rare old offense of embracery to a trial that already seemed to have everything.

The 12 conspirators left in the dock spaced themselves out comfortably in two rows. Biggs sat in the back one, smiling amiably, taller than most of the others at six feet and well filled out by the months of good eating and leisure in prison. James was on one side of him, a tiny man just the right size for squeezing into a racing car cockpit, and on the other, Goody, a sardonic and appealing villain, by far the most interesting of all in appearance. The other three were Brian Field, the solicitor's clerk, and Wheater, his boss, an uncomfortable example to the lawyers beyond the rather utilitarian black iron spikes with which the dock had been traditionally furbished, and the other Field, Lennie, a part-time deckhand whom the gang had roped in as front man for the purchase of Leatherslade.

In the front row were Welch, the club owner, Hussey, the painter and decorator, Wilson and Wisbey, the two bookmakers, an antique dealer named Daly, and Boal, red-faced and bewildered—the one man that the guilty robbers knew had never been anywhere near the train or Leatherslade. Even Superintendent Fewtrell did not believe he should be tried on equal terms with the others, although his chum, Cordrey, had pleaded guilty and been taken back to prison.

They looked, the dozen of them, completely interchangeable with the jury that faced them: a printer, an insurance salesman, a shop assistant, an architect, a jeweler, a sales manager, an engineer, a factory foreman and a municipal clerk. They all were being supplied with maps, photographs and magnifying glasses to inspect them better and notebooks in which to record their conclusions. If anything, the robbers were rather more expensively turned out than either the jurors, the large force of plainclothesmen and some of the learned counsel, under their gowns. Goody had paid for a new suit for Boal, who was broke, just as he had subsidized his food and drink bills so that he would not have to eat prison rations while the others had everything they wanted. The defendants had done an accomplished job of managing to look like anything but the team of lawless visionaries that had captured the country's imagination so completely along with the money. Nor were they, strictly speaking. There was still plenty of room in the improvised dock for Reynolds, Edwards and White. And for the other three major participants that Biggs—still the only member of the gang ever to give any information at all about the actual robbery—claimed, in the set of titillating newspaper articles that he sold to *The Sun* had never even been suspected. Who, according to Biggs, had, like Goody, the sense to keep their gloves on all the time they were at Leatherslade and have stayed free to enjoy their share.

The trial proper opened after a decent lunch for everyone—except the reporters who had engaged themselves in their first major competitive struggle against the antiquated, inadequate long-distance telephones—with an address by the leader of the four counsels retained by the Crown, Mr. Arthur James Q.C., that was a model of the precision and lucidity for which British advocacy so often claims renown while so rarely delivering the goods. It lasted for ten hours, and he was well into it on the second day before he succumbed to temptation and wrote himself a headline. Linking the clue of the yellow paint on the brown suede shoes to their owner, he called him playfully: "*Goody Two-Shoes.*" A sigh of appreciation swept the press benches.

Not until the third day was the first witness heard. The driver, Mills, pale and inaudible, was allowed to sit beside the witness box rather than stand in it while he told his story. But he could not identify any of the men in the dock as the ones who had tumbled up onto his footplate five months earlier. Nor in the entire 51-day course of the trial could anyone else.

Among the scores of prison officers who had taken turns guarding the hospital wing, there had to be some who could be bought and Biggs found one. He tested him out by getting him to bring in a transistor radio for 5 pounds, and then he got him to smuggle the breakout kit that Charm had helped get together—files, chisels, small crowbars, hacksaw blades and watches by which movements could be coordinated when the time came. That earned him 200 pounds.

Biggs, Goody, Wilson and Cordrey were the three most active plotters. But they found a vigorous ally in Boal, the pathetic latecomer who had become determined to get out because he was afraid his children would not be looked after properly if he were given a long sentence. At that stage nobody expected Boal to do more than five years "porridge." He could hardly hope to get off since Cordrey, by throwing away his own chance for acquittal, had also sunk his old chum's. Biggs was beginning to think that he would draw 15 himself, of which he might have to serve the lot, if the dormant specter of preventive detention were invoked. The schemers planned to make a master key to the hospital block and, while the others kept the guards turned the right way by talking or asking for things, Goody sketched out a perfectly gauged pattern of the keys that hung from their belts. The robbers were confident that with this as a blueprint they could turn out an effective key with the hacksaws and files. They put in an order, through Charm, for a suitable blank and waited.

There were not too many dull moments in the early days. If the witnesses were boring, the interested spectator could browse over the exhibits collection which under the conscientious curatorship of Detective Constable Milner had grown to 613 fascinating items from an instructional pamphlet on how to use the handcuffs that had pinioned Mills and Fireman Whitby to the fateful Monopoly board. Everything, including the recovered cash, was laid out like a flea market stall in a corner of the courtroom. Certain police witnesses made it plain, however, when giving their evidence, that not all the official preparation of the case had been as meticulous. The boys in the dock particularly enjoyed those moments.

Detective Sergeant John Swain of Scotland Yard won the first reproof on Day Six. After Goody had emerged as a suspect and had moved out to the pub in town, Swain had turned up at his home in Putney. Goody's mother invited him in, he said in the witness box, and he made a thorough search. Yes, sir, he responded to the eminent counsel Goody had retained, Mr. Sebag Shaw Q.C., he had told Mrs. Goody that he had a search warrant. No, sir, he had not actually had one. He had *thought* he had.

"Did you lie to this elderly woman?" asked Shaw Q.C., disdain-fully.

"It was a mistake, not a lie," said Swain. "I had other warrants to search other houses on me, and then I was told to go to Goody's home."

"See that it never happens again," the judge told him sharply. It would be up to the discretion of the judge to admit evidence obtained by such doubtful means. But in this instance there was no evidence to admit.

Even though the search had produced nothing, Shaw Q.C. made a point with the jury while the going was good. "There was no warrant," he said, "because there was no reason for searching the house at that time."

Mr. Davies also had some sharp words for the Scotland Yard men who appeared to have questioned Wilson *after* he had been taken into custody.

When something like that was going on, the dock was astir with lifted eyebrows and knowingly pursed lips. It was swept with unrestrained titters when one of the mail sorters told of the precipitate entry of the first masked bandit—Goody, had he known it—into the High Value Coach and how he had stood there growling.

"Growling?" inquired the prosecuting counsel, solicitously.

"Growling," repeated the witness. "*GrrrrrGrrrrrrrr.*"

But the 12 were intrigued and rightly appalled at the perfection-ism the gatherers of scientific evidence seemed to have brought to their jobs. There were no smiles, even when they heard that a meticulous check of 12 dozen eggs had not produced any finger-prints. Enough had been found elsewhere.

It was on Day Fourteen of the trial when Inspector Morris of the Buckinghamshire C.I.D., the detective who had gone to Redhill to ask Biggs when he had last seen Reynolds, entered the witness box.

Morris was an avuncular man with the kind of dabbed on black moustache that used to be worn unfailingly by provincial detectives and regular army sergeants. Biggs was quite pleased by the sight of an old friend and looked forward with interest to hearing what he had to say. One of the prosecuting team—there are no permanently appointed prosecutors in Britain apart from the barrister–bureaucrats of the offices of the Attorney General and the Director of Public Prosecutions; a counsel who defends today may be engaged to prosecute tomorrow—asked him about the visit. Morris said that when he questioned Biggs the reply had been, "I knew Reynolds some years ago. We were doing time together."

A pained silence settled on the court, heavier than the pall of afternoon digestion. Every lawyer there realized what had happened and so did the more artful defendants. The forlorn expression shaping itself around Morris's moustache reflected the toothmarks in his tongue. By mentioning that Biggs had been in prison he had told the jury something that British court procedures are specifically designed to keep from it—the criminal past of an accused person, should they have one, for fear that it might influence its judgment in the case being considered. It could be grounds for a retrial, bringing an end to the complicated proceedings in mid-stride, the summoning of a fresh jury and the waste of two enormously expensive weeks. Mr. Justice Davies, his face tight, leaned toward Biggs's counsel, Mr. Wilfred Fordham, who had been on his feet before Morris's words reached the back of the room.

"There is a matter which I think I ought to invite your Lordship to consider at some convenient moment," said Fordham with the casual urbanity by which the most feral events become tamed and domesticated in British courtrooms. If the jury had not grasped the significance of what they heard, their attention must not be drawn to it. What passed between judge and advocate could not be reported by the goggling press since it took place after the jury had been led out. Mr. Davies agreed that the remark had been prejudicial.

"That the Inspector who of necessity must be a man of great experience," he said, "should have so far forgotten his duties as to bring in a phrase of that kind quite gratuitously is grossly improper and cannot be too strongly condemned."

"But what was to be done?" asked Fordham. "If it were an individual on trial I would have no hesitation as to the way my duty lay. But in a case like this, with so many accused and a multiplicity of witnesses, I think I must take instructions."

Biggs, always delighted to be the center of attention, was taken from the dock for a consultation and, under the guise of giving Mr. Fordham his "instructions," accepted the most practical solution.

Mr. Fordham returned to apply for a new—and separate—trial for his client which Mr. Davies immediately granted, and Biggs was taken back to the grey stone hospital wing while the mystified jurors, told only of an "irregularity," continued hearing the case against the others. Sensation in court.

Despite the tactical advantage fortune had thus awarded him, Biggs was still heading over the wall. The key blank had arrived and Goody worked on it with the contraband tools night after night until, after trying it out on several of the cell doors, he was sure it could be relied on. The following Saturday night was chosen as the time to go because the escapers would be less conspicuous in the late night weekend traffic. Their transportation had been arranged and skilled hands carrying Charmian's blessing would be ready to heave up a rope from outside. Before the plot gathered its final momentum, Welch, Hussey and Wisbey, who thought they stood a good chance of acquittal, backed out. But the four left were sure they could bring it off.

By then Wilson was cooking for the warders so the unsubtle idea of lacing their soup with chloral hydrate got some brief consideration. But in the end it was decided that Wilson and Goody would unlock their cells after they had been "slammed up" for the night and grab the lone officer who patrolled the block every hour. First, however, the barred door to their floor had to be sawn through and for this they relied on Boal, the engineer.

But it had been wrong to rely on Boal, the criminal and the Train Robbers' friend. Not only did his nerve fail him totally when the time came but after the desperately frustrating night of wasted preparation—Biggs had heard the getaway car pull up outside—he became so unraveled that he was taken for a medical examination. That Sunday morning a horde of prison officers swept through the two-storied building and plundered its every hiding place. The bent one later reported that everything had been found, even the transistor. Said Goody, "That Boal can eat porridge for the rest of his miserable fucking life."

Stifled by the fervent security onslaught that followed, Biggs went back to perfecting the story that was now his only remaining hope. He was soon appreciably heartened when on Day Seventeen the prosecution rested its case and one by one his accomplices' counsel ritually submitted that no case had been made against their clients. Mr. Davies agreed with one of them, Mr. Walter Raeburn, and ordered his client, Daly, discharged. Sensation again, followed by hectic press pursuit of the first man out of Aylesbury Prison. The *Daily Sketch* got there first with the check book. It seemed to Biggs that the evidence against Daly had been precisely similar in nature to the evidence against him if slightly lesser in degree. A fingerprint on the Monopoly set.

The 18th-century Assizes Court in Aylesbury's old Market Square is a dark and menacing, carved and paneled grotto—a shrine to dreadful things done in the name of the law in times not so long gone by. There had been something everyday and commonplace about the incongruous dispositions in the District Council offices but with the court back in its own somber abode, now that only one robber remained to be tried, Mr. Justice Davies's scarlet robes glowed with unattainable remoteness against the aged wood beneath the cypher and sword and the shade of many a hanged, racked or banished soul shared the dock with Ronald Arthur Biggs when, panting slightly, he climbed the ladder through its floor on April 8.

Biggs had put on 30 pounds since his arrest. Charm had had to buy new clothes for his solo appearance; cavalry twill trousers, a Harris tweed jacket, a gate-check shirt—gentleman farmer's gear—just right for Aylesbury. The new jurors listened solemnly while Mr. Davies charged them with the impossible task of putting out of their minds everything that they had heard about the earlier trial.

Every man, woman and child in the land with normal vision and hearing knew by then that the other robbers had been found guilty and would be sentenced as soon as Biggs's fate had been decided. In their defense some had simply argued through counsel that the facts did not prove them guilty of the charges; others had gone into the witness box themselves and told a series of inspired and beautifully adumbrated tales, mostly involved with the innocent delivery of groceries, of how their fingerprints had come to be found at Leatherslade.

Goody had given evidence himself in support of his contention that the police, desperate for something to connect him with the robbery, had faked the evidence of the yellow paint. But the jury had not been swayed—or not at any rate capsized—by the interesting fact that the police did not remove the paint tin from Leatherslade until they had spent three weeks trying to find some other evidence against him. Nor did the dozen good Buckinghamshiremen heed his convincing assertion, as he sat there in an immaculate suit and flaunting a Royal Artillery tie, that no one as fastidious in dress as he would keep around a pair of shoes with paint on them. Long after it could do him any good, Goody insisted that those suede shoes had never been anywhere near Leatherslade.

It was already being argued by devoted followers of the saga that the verdicts might have been different had the men not all been tried together and thus provided a constant reminder for the jury of a single entity. In individual trials there might have been room for more doubt because of the complete absence of any identification or other connection with the Up Special itself, or because of the total lack of any admissions or—except in the case of Cordrey and James Boal—any sign of the spoils. More weight might have been given to the fact that all the prints found at Leatherslade, except those of Wisbey and Wilson, were on portable objects and therefore conceivably could have got on to them while the things were somewhere else.

The men still in prison or freshly paroled have never given any information about the robbery, its planning or—except for Cordrey and the ones who were not arrested until after the main trial—its profits. The only detailed accounts, apart from what has been gleaned from the supporting cast, have come, at the gain to themselves of about a quarter of a million dollars, from the Biggs family's literary offerings.

But, in reality the outcome would not have been altered, considering what happened to the one lone defendant. The jurors of the main trial spent 66 hours and 24 minutes—another record—in melodramatic seclusion to reach their verdicts. But the second lot, who heard out Biggs's hopeful fantasy about having been invited to the farm in advance of the robbery to take part in a caper that was being planned but then being frightened off by the sight of the army uniforms and leaving again, took only 90 minutes to register their emphatic disbelief. Guilty on both counts, armed robbery and conspiracy to rob the Up Special.

As drama, the sentencing of the robbers in the forbidding Assizes Court lacked absolutely nothing. It took place on the day after Biggs had been dealt with, a grey squally Thursday. The courtroom was packed inside and out with detectives, some of whom, the press whispered among themselves, were armed. The police had never quite lost their fear that the robbers had an organization on the outside capable of mounting an assault to free them, and the reporters never gave up hope that the police were right.

All the counsel were arrayed together before the bench, a murky sea of surging black gowns crested with plaited horsehair. The agreeable fraternal evenings in the Bell were over, but a significant number of new cars sparkled in the barristers' parking lot.

On the raised Bench the judge's grave eminence had been reinforced by the presence of the Sheriff togged up like a playing card to personify the county as ostentatiously as his companion in the full-bottomed wig sat there for the Queen herself. And in the first row of the privileged spectators' seats, in the well of the court rather than in the gallery above, was the sorry but self-important figure of the only physical victim of the crime, Driver Mills.

In the three weeks he had been studying the criminal records of the main batch—only Brian Field and Wheater lacked them—and hearing submissions on their behalf, Mr. Justice Davies had not found much to persuade him that they were suitable cases for considerate treatment.

"You are the first to be sentenced out of 11 greedy men," he said to Cordrey and, after a speech in which he said he was taking into consideration his prompt admission of guilt, sentenced him to 20 years imprisonment. A low, soft grunt rippled across the court as though the audience had just seen someone stabbed.

"Jesus Christ," they said on the press benches, "twenty years on a *guilty* plea! That means 30 for the rest. Incredible!"

They were right, so far as the other robbers were concerned. The two Fields got 25 years, Boal 24 and Wheater was let off with 3. But the other seven were given 30 years, shocking sentences in a country without a parole system and where time could be shortened only by good behavior and then merely by one-third. Well-man-nered moans and sobs poured briefly from relatives in the public gallery, but there was only one real outcry. Leonard Field's mother shouted, "He's innocent! Justice is not right!"

And in the only exclamation from the dock, Field called back pathetically, "Don't worry, mother. I'm still young."

To Biggs, standing pale and heavy behind the spikes, the judge said tersely, "Your learned counsel has urged that you had no special talent and you were plainly not an originator of the conspiracy. Those and all other submissions I bear in mind, but the truth is that I do not know when you entered the conspiracy or what part you played. What I do know is that you are a specious and facile liar and you have this week in this court perjured yourself time and again."

When sentence was pronounced Biggs took a deep breath and turned the best smile he could manage up to the public gallery where, beside the clock that marked the beginning of his terrible future, Charm, the inadvertent alibi-despoiler, sat, tears eroding her dainty make-up.

The savage sentences caused as much of an uproar as the Great Train Robbery itself, instantly restoring the gang to public esteem. The only longer term ever inflicted had been on George Blake, a particularly industrious though unglamorous spy, who got 41 years.

"People everywhere are puzzled by one glaring contrast," said a *Daily Mail* editorial. "It is this—an evildoer convicted of conspiracy and robbery as in the Train Case can be sentenced to 30 years which, with normal remission, means serving 20 years in prison. But an evildoer convicted of murder and jailed for life is unlikely to serve more than 15 years.

"Does this mean that stealing banknotes is regarded as being more wicked than murdering somebody?"

There was only one possible meaning to it when Biggs and Charm met fleetingly in the cells below the dock before he was taken back to the hospital wing to await assignment to a permanent prison.

"Promise me you'll get out," she said, urgently. "I'll help."

The *Express*, however, found itself in agreement not only with the judge's conclusions but with his crisp, Beaver-like delivery. Its editorial said:

In terse phrases Mr. Justice Edmund Davies cuts the "Great Train Robbery" down to size.

If anyone thought of this theft in romantic terms—for example as a brilliantly organized coup—they now know better.

It would have been an affront, as the judge said, if the criminals were at liberty in the near future to enjoy their ill-gotten gains.

In his epic summing up Mr. Justice Davies had mentioned—among other things since he took 11 hours—the matter of the "guns" that had been referred to when the robbers first stormed the High Value Coach. Even if none had been found, he said, that did not mean there had not been any.

Even if they had been asked, the members of the gang who had gone into the witness box to testify in their own defense would have been too polite to clear things up by explaining that what was actually shouted out, when someone saw that the sorters were trying to lock the doors, was not "Get the guns!" but "Get the cunts!" Accents, in a country as rich in them as Britain, can be a problem.

Brian Vine. Assistant Editor (News) of the *Daily Express*. Colin MacKenzie brought him the Biggs story first.

Brian Hitchen. News Editor of the *Daily Express*. To him a story would always mean more than a reporter. (London *Daily Express*)

Ronald Biggs. Above, in 1963. (London *Daily Mirror*)
Below, at time of his arrest.

Anthea Disney.

Dermot Purgavie.

Michael Brennan.

Bill Lovelace.

Derryn Hinch.

Colin MacKenzie and Raimunda de Castro. Trying to evade other reporters. (Mike Brennan, London *Daily Mirror*)

MacKenzie and Raimunda outside Catete. (Eric Piper, London *Daily Mirror*)

MacKenzie and Raimunda driving away from the siege. (Eric Piper, London *Daily Mirror*)

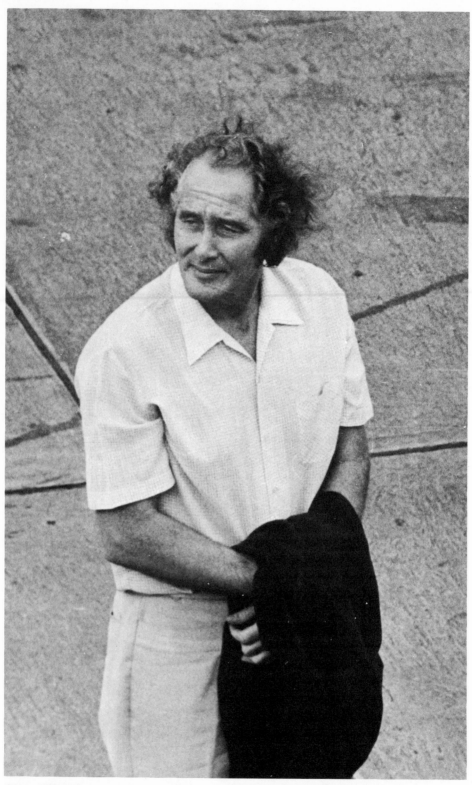

Biggs. When he arrived at Brasilia Airport he shouted to the reporters, "I was under great pressure."

Biggs (center). "The Animal" (right).

Charmian and Biggs. When the reporters burst into the detention center in Brasilia, she cried, "Why can't you leave us alone?"

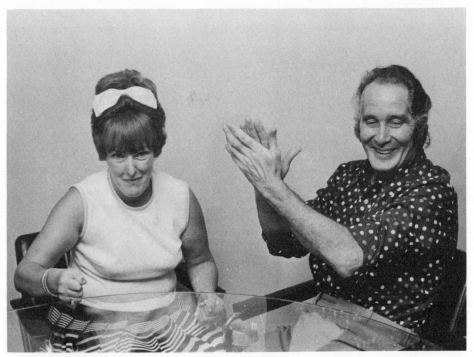

Charmian and Biggs. But after they had spent some time with each other they could not stop talking.

Mike Brunson. Independent Television News reporter gives Biggs a copy of *The Odessa File. The Day of the Jackal* had inspired Charmian to suggest some tricks to Biggs.

Charmian and MacKenzie. En route from Brasilia to Rio on her way back to Australia. (Mike Brennan, London *Daily Mail*)

Biggs and his son Michael. (London *Daily Mirror*)

The empty seat. Slipper on the flight back from Rio. (Mike Brennan, London *Daily Mail*)

11

As well as holding the obvious in high regard, newspapermen share a healthy respect for the power of coincidence, having usually learned the hard way that it plays a far larger part in matters of fact than it is ever permitted to in those of fiction. Rio de Janeiro, for instance, is slightly off the tracks that Fleet Street beats with frequency in the endless quest for exotica. Teeming, storied, and alluringly carnal it might be, the cynosure of the most dynamic nation in Latin America; but that whole continent is rather lost to English eyes these days even though a lot of mercantile adventuring went on there in the past and durable fortunes were made in coffee, sugar, cattle, chemicals and railways. Some connections linger, however. MacKenzie, who had never exactly been flung far afield by the *Express* up until that moment, was quite at home there. By completely unqualified coincidence his father had worked much of his life in Brazil in the service of a mighty meatpacker and MacKenzie had learned as a boy to know the country and something of its language.

But even before the three furtive travelers reached their first staging point, they were shaken rigid by a far less welcome coincidence. If Lovelace, before he left London, had been asked to name the one person he would least wish to meet before getting such a delicate job safely in the bag, there would have been plenty to choose from. But only one final choice by whatever means he reached it. And there the bloody man was, taking down his camera case from the overhead locker as the *Express* party filed out through the economy section—Hitchen had bought them first-class seats as a morale boost—of the plane in Madrid. Tall, sharp-featured, sharp-voiced and sharper-eyed Harry Benson.

Benson had worked for the *Express* himself until *Life* magazine, that exclusive news photographers' dude ranch, gave him a membership card not long, alas, before it was compelled to convert itself from a weekly to an occasional.

But Benson had gone on working for *Life* after its death. And he was still exactly what he had been in his Fleet Street days—a crack camera handler and a wily adversary, rightly feared for his aggressiveness, persistence and wiliness.

The two old colleagues greeted each other with spurious warmth and sly questioning, possible explanations for the other's presence rattling through their minds like a motor-driven film shift. "We're both going on the Big One," said Benson, playfully probing Lovelace's discomfort. But by the time they got to the terminal, hasty bluntness had set in. Lovelace said, "Well, Harry, it's quite simple. You tell us what *you're* doing here, and I'll tell you what *we're* doing."

Faced with an offer he had to refuse, Benson, buying time with a show of good fellowship, said, "Let's share a taxi into town."

"Sure," said Lovelace, maneuvering to give the impression that they also were ending their journey in Madrid, although there was dangerously little time to make the connection to their far more conspicuous and significant destination. Murmuring to MacKenzie and Benckendorff, he marshaled them into a passport line a little longer than the one that Benson had joined. As Benson, his passport stamped, went through into the baggage claim area, Lovelace called to him, "Get the taxi, Harry, we left something on the plane." And once Benson was unsuspectingly out of sight the three turned from the passport desk—through which there was no reason for them to go since they were transit passengers—and hustled off to catch their Varig flight. Adios, Harry. A Latin American job, Benson realized instantly. That would be the only reason for changing planes in Madrid. He was going that way himself the following day to Cuba, something he would no more have told Lovelace than Lovelace in turn would have dropped a single word of his own destination.

There had to be a photographer, of course, even though Biggs was only expecting to receive Benckendorff and MacKenzie. A story like that without pictures would be unthinkable. Apart from their entertainment value they would provide the final proof. Biggs would be seen to have been found. They were also a vital element in the budgeting of an expensive adventure of that kind. Exclusive pictures sold to other publications throughout the world through the paper's syndication department could bring in many times the cost of getting them. And it could hardly be any other photographer than Lovelace.

Not because there were no others on the 22-strong force in the *Express*'s London office who could take pictures of equal quality—although he had just won the Photographer of the Year award for his unforgettable and endlessly reproduced pictures of Bangladesh irregulars cold-bloodedly bayoneting their captive countrymen.

Nor because no one else would be as reliable or as ingenious in getting the pictures back to the office. Away from home a photographer's duties and difficulties are only half over when the films are taken out of his battery of Nikkons. But a dozen other men working for the picture desk could transform any hotel bathroom into a photolab as deftly and speedily as Lovelace, develop a dozen films in the bidet, make prints on their miniature folding enlarger and, unhampered by the telecommunications code of whatever country they might be in, patch their portable wire-photo machine into the nearest dialable telephone and transmit the result to London.

It was bound from the outset to be Lovelace because the kind of tactical ingenuity he had shown when confronted with the unnerving figure of Harry Benson came instinctively to him and unfailingly. In the 19 years he had been practicing his complex and peculiar arts, Lovelace had played a productive part in high-intensity *Express* plots and intrigues more often than MacKenzie had been out to lunch. In addition, he was wholly and unswervingly loyal to the paper, the only one he had ever worked for since leaving the Royal Air Force at the age of twenty-six. And, more, although he was a relaxed and equable man, he had big hands and powerful shoulders which he did not in the least mind using if it became necessary. The story was a good deal less likely to stray from MacKenzie's grasp with Lovelace there beside him. Nor would MacKenzie himself be likely to stray.

The assignment of Lovelace was actually welcome reassurance to MacKenzie. When MacKenzie had distinguished himself in the affair of the lady doctor it had been Lovelace who had actually found the plane that she was taking, the vital link in making contact with her.

On the long flight Lovelace settled down to find out from the other two exactly what he might expect when they reached Rio. Nothing he had heard up until then convinced him that they really were going to find Biggs—much as he would love to—least of all the confident assurances of the Editor when he had told him where he was going.

When McColl had finished briefing him, Lovelace had said cheerfully, if not quite tactfully, "Well, I hope it's not another Martin Bormann job."

"No," snapped McColl. "It's not another furstie Bormann."

But McColl had told Lovelace only as much as he wanted him to know. He did not tell him about the deal with Slipper. Nor, as they chatted and dozed their way across the South Atlantic, did MacKenzie.

While MacKenzie, Edwards and Hitchen had been having their meeting at the Yard on the previous Friday, Brian Vine had embarked on a long promised treat. He had taken himself off to New York to see the Muhammed Ali–Joe Frazier fight billed for Madison Square Garden on the night MacKenzie and the others left London. And, since he was on vacation, he had arranged to finance the trip by a little bit of business.

Vine was a man with a certain standard of living to maintain, and if the horses were misbehaving it sometimes took a bit of doing. He leaned toward ventures into private enterprise that were more colorful and imaginative as a rule than they were practicable, such as the importing of air-conditioned umbrellas from Hong Kong, little oriental parasols with battery-powered fans built in. This time it was commemorative plaques of the big fight itself that he was hoping to sell. They were the idea of a man he knew in London and Vine took samples with him, one in gold and one in silver. He had many friends in New York where his stint as bureau chief had only ended less than two years before and was looking forward keenly to seeing them all again as indeed they were to seeing him. A boisterous round of celebrations had been arranged to begin the moment that he checked into the Waldorf Astoria.

Vine had been peeved and mystified by McColl's attitude since he had first gone to him with MacKenzie's story. After his initial display of consternation at having been approached at all ("I'm afraid you've told me too much already," McColl had said when Vine had finished), the Editor had excluded him from the small circle within which it was further discussed. Vine had offered his advice about what should be done, which was first to establish beyond doubt that they really were dealing with Biggs and if so to try to persuade him to surrender to the *Daily Express*. That would not have involved them in any ethical transgressions and it would have ensured the utmost exploitation. But McColl, apparently afraid that Vine might tell MacKenzie about the negotiations with the Yard were he to be let in on them, refused to include him among the plotters. After Slipper had been brought in McColl mentioned the subject to Vine only once and then during an accidental encounter in a corridor. "You've got to let me do this in my own way, Brian," McColl said mysteriously and strutted busily on.

MacKenzie kept Vine up to date to the limited extent that he knew himself what was going on. Hitchen, embarrassed by McColl's exclusion order avoided the subject as much as possible when they were together. But Vine too had been working hard to convince MacKenzie that he—and therefore the story—belonged to the *Express*. As MacKenzie's mentor Vine knew of his job negotiations with the *Mail* and he was just as apprehensive that the Biggs story might be used as a bargaining factor in those as he was that MacKenzie would decide to go it alone.

And Vine, although MacKenzie had no idea of it, was the only other person in London apart from Benckendorff who knew from the beginning where the trial was leading. When MacKenzie had first sought him out Vine, who knew his old partner in horseflesh to be chronically broke and in any case rather parsimonious, had guessed that he was unlikely to be making any expensive overseas calls on his own phone. So he simply went through the log of the *Express* switchboard until he found the record of the numbers in Rio that MacKenzie had been driving secretly into the office to call in the early hours of the morning.

With Slipper and Jones airborne the only men in London outside Scotland Yard who knew what was going to happen in Rio were McColl, his deputy McDonald, Hitchen, Edwards the lawyer and Jocelyn Stevens. Stevens had shown a stylish gambler's faith in the venture from the start, personally signing the check which Hitchen had cashed to get MacKenzie, Lovelace and Benckendorff on the way to avoid explanations to accountants. Hitchen and McColl had gone together to collect it. "I hope it's not another furstie Bormann," muttered McColl as they left.

"Don't worry," said Hitchen. "It's him."

Within the remaining 48 hours a few others would have to be included, at least partially, but for the moment everyone in the know accepted the awkward obligation of preparing the paper for the story of its lifetime without telling anyone else what it was going to be. The strain and the suspense stretched their nerves as taut and thin as the endless ribbons of newsprint running through the giant rotary presses beneath their feet. When Hitchen came back from the airport after arranging his diversion his doubts had to be voiced. He said to McColl, "Once MacKenzie hears that Slipper is going in early he could easily fall apart. Why don't I call Vine?"

To Lovelace what he was told on the plane by Benckendorff was a horror story. It would have been to any Fleet Street man accustomed, as they are, to measure the value of an event by the length of time it might take to get it into the paper. But a sense of time was not a dominant factor in Benckendorff's life. Nor, it seemed was curiosity. Biggs could have looked under every umbrella on Copacabana Beach and continued along the golden strand of Ipanema, Leblon, Gavea and headed on down to Tierra del Fuega without finding a less likely envoy to have sent out into the world with his ingenuous appeal for help and understanding.

Benckendorff, a large young hedonist, had been searching not too energetically for a suitable way of life since his time on the playing fields of Eton had run out some two or three years earlier. That inimitable English background had been wished upon him by his father, Count Benckendorff, a minor White Russian nobleman who had settled in Britain after a prior sojourn in Brazil during which Constantine had been born. It was while visiting relatives in Rio some six months earlier and fastidiously exploring the possibilities of livelihood there that Benckendorff came across personable Michael Haynes who, although he had been there three and a half years was still far from settled himself. In an amazingly short space of time the gregarious Englishman had disclosed his true identity—which meant absolutely nothing to twenty-year-old Benckendorff—and entrusted him with the task of finding him a suitable journalist champion back home.

When Benckendorff did return to London he did not actually forget what he had been asked to do. He just did not seem to know any journalists. And a chap couldn't go and knock on the door of any old newspaper could he? So it was time for yet another flash of that unjustly discredited phenomenon. His mother the countess now lived in Battersea—doing property values a power of good when she moved there—and who should be living a couple of doors up the street but her new friend Colin MacKenzie whom he discovered worked for the *Express*. Coincidence, what? Three months after his return to Britain Benckendorff got around to mentioning the odd encounter in Rio.

"Good God Almighty," said Lovelace reaching weakly for the Varig champagne. "You mean to tell me you had the greatest story I'll ever work on in your head all that time and you didn't say anything to anyone? It's enough to make me airsick."

Even then Benckendorff had forgotten something. Haynes's final admonishment when they had parted in Rio so long before.

"Don't go near the *Daily Express*," Haynes told him. "They're a treacherous lot of bastards there. They did a hatchet job on Charlie Wilson."

Hitchen had already telephoned Vine in New York once on the Sunday to tell him that things were on the move and to alert him that he might be pressed into service. To get a line he could be sure was unmolested he had got his local pub in Buckinghamshire, the Wagon and Horses, to let him in during closed hours to use their coin phone.

Needing another secure line on the Tuesday, he went to Vine's home in Islington, a restored Victorian enclave near Fleet Street greatly favored by fashionable communicators, and told his wife Beverley that her husband would be coming back the long way around. She gave him a drink while he put a call through to Vine who was visiting the *Express*'s New York Bureau in the *Daily News* Building to ask him to get to Rio as quickly as he could to reinforce MacKenzie, reassure Slipper and Jones and, above all see that the story, when the swoop actually did take place on the Friday, was filed in full and on time.

Vine had no such fascinated audience as Hitchen was enjoying in Beverley. When he had heard that Hitchen was coming on the phone he had hung up, cleared the outraged New York staff out, and called Hitchen back so that they could talk securely.

Getting away from New York without attracting attention, especially to where he was going, was Vine's next problem. Yvonne Dunleavy the winsome and astute amanuensis of Xaviera Hollander and Fanne Fox was giving a party for him that night and all the British newspaper correspondents in New York would be there expecting to see him. But in his haste and given the distraction of redeeming his valuable samples of merchandise from the manager's safe at the Waldorf he had no time to work up a creative excuse. Taxi!

By Thursday afternoon Hitchen could be set leaping about wild-eyed by the clang of a paperclip on a desktop or worse the mere sight of his own silent telephone. Although, known only to the cleaners and the switchboard, he had begun sleeping in Vine's office at night he had by then returned to his usual center-stage location in the Big Room for the first time in more than a week. But the scent of intrigue and suspense that had come to permeate the higher executive retreats clung to him. The reporters, already inflamed with curiosity, picked it up unfailingly, chattering out the message through every corner of the editorial jungle, watching for the first sign of the great beast of revelation they sensed stalking in the corridors. They ducked and darted and sidestepped to avoid being picked for assignments. If there was a big kill coming off they wanted to be around for it. What was unstringing Hitchen was that there had been no word from Rio. None.

Slipper and Jones felt much the same as Hitchen. They had been all business when they hit Copacabana Beach in the dazzling 8 A.M. sunshine that morning. They checked into the hotel the *Express* had booked for them, the Metropole and—carefully attired for the climate in their new tropical kit the better to blend with the scenery—set forth in that fabled realm of samba, soccer and The String to give the place a good butcher's. Butcher's hook. Look.

Oblivious to such distractions as the vivid paper kites fluttering over the beach, the bloodthirsty traffic, the blatant theatricality of Sugar Loaf Mountain and the compelling deportment of the local womenfolk, the two Sweeneys strode resolutely through the rising temperature and the heady vapors of coffee and orange peel to the Copacabana Palace Hotel where, Hitchen had assured them, MacKenzie, Benckendorff and Lovelace would be registered. But they were not. Therefore there was no way to get to Biggs. Foul play was immediately suspected.

Vine too had developed grave misgivings. His flight had arrived soon after the coppers' rather lengthier one. He had no trouble in finding *them*. Indeed by then it was becoming difficult for Slipper and Jones to move from their hotel since the first symptoms had appeared of the traditional hazard of the inexperienced traveler and they were having to spend more and more time in the bathroom of the room the two of them under the pressures of *carnaval* were sharing.

But Vine had no more idea than they did what might have happened to the others. He had never shared MacKenzie's nervousness back in London. But now it seemed to Vine that far from protecting its reporter the *Express*, by virtually forcing him to collaborate with Scotland Yard, could have exposed him to a considerable amount of peril once the whistle had been blown on poor old Biggs. Who was to know what kind of unpredictable friends their victim might have surrounded himself with in Brazil? Time and again as Vine kept on coming up with confident and plausible suggestions of where MacKenzie might be, he saw

Slipper's doubting eye turn to the shiny new handcuffs on the dressing table.

By the time the *Express* flight had got to Rio, Lovelace was a good deal more optimistic that Michael Haynes would really turn out to be Biggs than he had been when they set out. Benckendorff's disarming insouciance had affected him in much the same way that Hitchen had responded to MacKenzie's impetuous conclusions. He had started to plan his moves, though in terms of limited achievements rather than a long-term outcome. Time for that later.

The proposal, as Lovelace had come to understand it, was that Biggs was ready to surface in order to collaborate on *what* he wanted to have written about himself and would afterward disappear again or not, depending on the outcome. He said to MacKenzie, "If we are going to have a week or two to work on this Colin we should settle in somewhere. Perhaps we could take a house down by the sea."

"Good idea," said MacKenzie.

But first they went to the Copacabana Palace, the hotel where Hitchen had asked the travel agent to book them. Many regrets, said the reception clerk, the hotel is full. Had you forgotten that it was *carnaval?* And so it was, or nearly, the first stirring of that world-renowned and awe-inspiring sensual cataclysm was already exciting the air.

A few hundred yards down the swirling mosaic pavements of the Avenida Atlantica they found rooms at the Trocadero at least for a night or two. Lovelace and MacKenzie's rooms were on the sixth floor. Benckendorff's was 909.

It was understandable that MacKenzie in his distraction did not tell London that they were not where they were supposed to be. Normally it would be the first thing Lovelace, like any other veteran, would do. But there was not, so far as he knew, any urgency. And anyway first he wanted to meet the object of the expedition whom Benckendorff telephoned as soon as they arrived and who came around to the Trocadero soon afterward with a lovely dark-haired girl named Lucia; a fleshy but impressive man just over six feet tall, with snappy good-natured blue eyes and long wavy hair that was just beginning to give out in the middle. He looked nothing like the old photographs Lovelace had by then grafted onto his mind's eye. But it was Biggs and both *Express*men knew it with certainty on the instant.

"Hello Colin. Hello Bill."

"Hello . . . . . er, Michael."

By Thursday night Hitchen was gradually faltering under the weight of the dread and despair that had been accumulating since he discovered that his men had not checked into the Copacabana Palace. He cared less about what might happen to MacKenzie once Biggs had been collared than about yesterday's newspaper. But if something had happened to him beforehand it meant no collar. Far worse, no story.

Had the Yard leaked? Even if that was it, Slipper would be back to carry out the amiable threat he had made before they parted. "You know Brian if anything does go wrong you are the one that'll be left holding the can." Too bad.

Had the *Express* leaked? Astonishing as it might be, that seemed far less likely. None of the knowledgeable hypotheses other fascinated and curious *Express*men tried out on Hitchen half a dozen times a day to explain the electric atmosphere of the office came anywhere near the target.

Had MacKenzie defected after all? All Hitchen could do was put his faith in Bill Lovelace and get on with briefing the Editor about certain critical and precise arrangements that had to be made even farther from home than Rio.

In Wellington, New Zealand, about as far from Rio de Janeiro as Rio is from London and about as far away in terms of the human spirit as the mind can grasp, the Royal Yacht *Britannia* lay alongside, gorgeous with flags and bunting, her decks scrubbed, her dark blue paintwork gleaming. The Queen and Prince Philip were visiting the most distant of her realms to bestow their gracious patronage on the Commonwealth Games that were being held there and it was the day of the Press Reception that is traditionally given at such times. A couple of hundred of her subjects from newspapers, radio and television were about to come aboard for gin-and-tonics and a brief brush of the royal fingertips. Assistant Press Secretary Laurie Bryant—the Royal Family runs a businesslike and purposeful P.R. operation—was expecting a full house. Most of those to whom the richly engraved invitations had gone were sports writers and photographers. But there were a few foreign correspondents of rather less impressionable caliber gathered in Wellington too because it was the starting point of a lengthy tour of the South Seas the Queen was to make and about which they would be reporting.

One of them John Monks, the Southern Hemisphere correspondent of the *Daily Express*, took Bryant aside as soon as he arrived on board and, with as graceful an apology as he could manage, said he had been recalled to his base in Sydney, Australia.

"Will you be coming back?" asked Bryant, surprised because the *Express*'s interest in royalty is intensive if inconsistent. The Royals feel the same way about the *Express*. "Picking us up somewhere?"

"Don't know," said Monks, disappearing down the gangway with Albert McCabe the photographer assigned with him. Nor did he. In London, McColl had given the Foreign Editor John Ellison no explanation for the instructions he had told him to pass on to Monks and Monks and McCabe had no idea what to make of them. Go straight to Melbourne. Book into a particular hotel. Wait for a call.

Monks was beyond being surprised at anything he was told to do. In the previous few weeks the *Express* had been trying to decide whether to shut down his post in the pressing interests of economy and he had been trying to make up his mind whether to quit. He was beginning to feel at the mercy of an undirected and malignant force capable of any caprice and folly. But whatever awaited had to be better than another day in Wellington.

Giving the orders to a sulky and aggrieved Ellison, McColl had been struck by another thought. Was there not a faithful member of Scotia Nostra in those parts? Aye, there was. Jim Sanderson, a sports writer who had gone out to the Games on a suitably parsimonious charter flight. Get him to Melbourne too. They might be glad of a Glasgow laddie if things got really tough.

"No doubt," said Ellison, starchily. What things for God's sake?

The *Express* switchboard told Hitchen that there was a Mr. Watkins waiting to speak to him from Edinburgh. By then, well into

Thursday afternoon in London, Hitchen had all but forgotten the comprehensive code in which the plotters had agreed to conduct all their communications. MacKenzie had taken a copy with him and it had been dictated to Vine in New York. Lovelace, on the inspiration of the soul singer, had been labeled Watkins. And in order to keep the geographical references well within the grasp of all concerned Rio became Edinburgh and Brazil, Scotland.

Hitchen picked up the phone in the drab little office by the men's room that had been his operational headquarters for so many days. And when he put it down again the dull ochre walls seemed aglow with the golden light of the south and echoing to the stirring off-beat cadenzas of Bossa Nova bands. Hanlon was safe with Betchworth. MacKenzie had begged to be known as Betchworth because he had grown up there and Hanlon, of course, was Haynes. Haynes, Hell! Biggs. Biggs!

"Get around to the Trocadero," Hitchen told Lovelace after some carefully limited recriminations over the cruel silence. "Vine is there. He has some news for you."

"Vine?" said Lovelace. He knew it had been too easy up until now. "What's he here for?"

"He'll tell you," said Hitchen. "And by the way, from now on we'll use his code name. It's Gout." Vine could take a joke.

When, having slipped away from his relaxed and cheerful companions at the Trocadero, Lovelace arrived in the room at the Metropole to which Hitchen had directed him, he was not entirely surprised to find Slipper and Jones—or, as they were known to possessors of the code, Bluenose One and Bluenose Two. Old *Express* hands are hard to surprise. But when Vine told him what MacKenzie had not, that the time he had to work on Biggs would come to an abrupt end at eleven o'clock the following day, Lovelace replied with the traditional lament of his tribe. "You can't nick him tomorrow," he protested. "I haven't got enough pictures yet."

In fact Lovelace had a bagful of devastatingly eloquent pictures, taken that lunchtime when Biggs and Lucia, a deep-bosomed and toothy twenty-two-year-old, necked fondly in a restaurant, and, warm with Chilean wine, frolicked later on Benckendorff's bed at the Trocadero. They had made him understandably greedy for more.

But there was a less professional reason why he wanted to see his subject remain free. The two of them had taken to each other almost on sight. Not immediately. Biggs had needed a little while to accept the idea of a third man in the deal. But it was soon apparent that he felt more at ease with Lovelace, an unaffected fellow South Londoner, than with MacKenzie whose university mannerisms he found uncomfortably superior, or even with his old chum Benckendorff.

Lovelace, who had been ready to keep his cameras out of sight until a dependable bond of confidence had been established, knew the value of such an advantage. Subtly he began giving elementary lessons in how they would best achieve what Biggs wanted done.

"It's different for the writer," said Lovelace. "He can catch up with the moment after it's passed. People can tell him about it. The pictures never happen again. I can see pictures happening all the time now that are lost and gone forever. Beautiful pictures."

"You'd better start taking them, then," said Biggs.

The debate that got under way when Lovelace joined Vine and the two Sweeneys at the Trocadero was heated and at times hostile. Now that he was within striking distance Slipper had begun to chaff sulkily under the restraints of the scenario, even though he still did not know exactly where Biggs was. When Lovelace began to press his objections to the ambush that was shaping up with himself as one of the lures, Slipper started looking at the handcuffs again. There was another call to Hitchen, and at an astronomical number of *cruzeiros*-a-minute Slipper bawled his own complaints across the Atlantic. When he had finished there was no room left for argument.

Vine pulled his rank. What had up until now been suggestions and guidelines, he told the mutinous Lovelace, were now clear and undefiable orders. Pass the word to MacKenzie that it has to be tomorrow.

Lovelace's report to Vine on the picture sessions he had so far had with Biggs and Lucia had done nothing to cheer up Slipper either. Where, he demanded, had all this taken place anyway? Why just a block away, Lovelace told him. Just down the road at the Trocadero Hotel. They were still there.

Slipper reared to his feet spluttering duty-free whisky indignantly about him. He had taken off most of his clothes because of the unaccustomed heat and to facilitate his frequent trips to the bathroom and in his underwear he resembled a great animal dressed for someone's cruel amusement, a tall and sinewy dancing bear perhaps, shackled and goaded beyond tolerance.

"Just down the road!" he bellowed. "Just down the bleeding road! Why Ernie Bond'd have me pensioned off if he knew that there was Ronnie Biggs with a bird in a bedroom just down the road and me sitting here being dictated to by the bleeding *Daily Express*."

12

"All proper steps were taken to ensure Wilson's safe custody on the assumption that the integrity of the staff could be relied upon."

The Chief Director
of the Prison Department

•

The first suggestion Charm brought Biggs after he had been transferred to Lincoln Prison was that they should hire a helicopter to winch him up from the exercise yard. Although he was quite ready to think big it was a little more flamboyant an idea than he thought they really needed and so was the price quoted by the willing but deranged pilot: 2,500 pounds. Also Biggs had in mind that since the prison authorities seemed to be taking their duties so seriously they may have issued the wall guards rifles and one could take a shot at him while he was twirling slowly in the rotor wash.

While they were waiting for their appeals to be heard the gang was moved around the prison system like the pea in the shell game, ending up in London's sullen Brixton during the hearings at which the two Fields had their sentences reduced to five years, Cordrey and Boal got theirs chopped down to fourteen and everyone else's were resoundingly confirmed. Having exhausted the legal possibilities of deliverance they were then redistributed to high security establishments throughout the country. Biggs was sent to another London nick, the shamefully antiquated and decrepit Wandsworth where, surely not by chance, he was put to work sewing. Mailbags. He was still there, living in Cell Number 18 on the second floor of D Hall when, on August 12, 1974 just over a year after the robbery, Charlie Wilson got himself and everyone else concerned spectacularly back in the news by an audacious and beautifully organized leap over the wall of Winson Green Prison, Birmingham.

Some of the choicer details of the Wilson escape did not reach the general public until an inquiry had been held under the august chairmanship of Lord Louis Mountbatten, the Queen's uncle and the last Viceroy of India. But everything that mattered was broadcast the same day through the insidious and stealthy communications network that linked Lincoln Prison not only to Winson Green but to various nicks where the other robbers now lay in well-disseminated isolation: Wormwood Scrubbs, Wandsworth, Liverpool, Manchester, Leicester, Bedford, Oxford, Shrewsbury.

Wilson had inherited his cell from the spy Gordon Lonsdale whose record sentence ended abruptly when he was traded with Russia for one of Britain's own hard luck intelligence cases. Apart from that he was not difficult to locate should anyone go looking for him. Since he was on the Escape List he had to put his clothes outside each night and they stayed neatly but conspicuously piled by the door. Three daring but confident men using ladders and a plank scaled the two outside walls at 3 A.M. and let themselves into the cell block with two pass keys made from soap impressions of the originals. They knocked out a patrolling guard and tied him up, unlocked Wilson's cell, handed him the change of clothes they had brought and helped him to leave as they had come in. It took 15 minutes. What went over particularly well down the penitentiary grapevine was that when the police arrived at Winson Green they had to wait outside in the rain. The warders who called them, not knowing what was going on, had locked themselves in an office and were sitting tight.

The thought of Wilson on the Outside made life Inside more intolerable than ever for Biggs. On Charm's next visit he told her how to get in touch with the "firm" that had organized the Winson Green exercise and, disgusted with the time he had wasted and his overweight slothfulness, went into training for his own big event. As well as taking advantage of every minute allowed for exercise he took out a slenderizing volume on yoga from the prison library and, while bent on self-improvement, some travel books to help him decide where to go once he got out. But the professionals who had sprung Wilson had decided to quit while they were winning. No more contracts were being accepted.

With the engaging aptitude he has always shown for getting others to take a fatal interest in his problems, Biggs enlisted the help of a fellow convict, veteran escape artist and beggar for punishment Paul Seabourne who had once got ten people besides himself out of that very same Wandsworth, and was just finishing off the four and a half year sentence it had earned him. Daily in the mailbag shop they discussed between stitches the possibilities—which were considerably complicated by the extra precautions being taken with Biggs since Wilson's escape—surprise cell changes, the replacement of all keys and a guard outside his door all night. But by the time Seabourne was discharged in May 1965 they had a plan put together. And Charm had drawn 16,000 pounds from her bank to finance it.

On July 8 she drove to Whipsnade Zoo with her two children in the new Rover 2000 she had bought—to the anguish of the insurance adjusters still taking an interest in the womenfolk of all the robbers—and got a car park ticket time-stamped 2:30 P.M. Alibi.

So improbable and presumptuous was the Biggs breakout that it would never have played in Hollywood—or even in Howard Hunt circles. At three o'clock, just as Charm and the kids got to the giraffes, the uncertain throbbing of a well-worn motor sounded faintly through the thick stone walls of Exercise Yard D. Inside Biggs and an old friend Eric Flower with whom he had become re-united and had invited to join in the little frolic that he was arranging were strolling soberly around at the beginning of their precious daily hour in the open air. They had expected to reach that stage two days previously, but it had rained. In order to prevent exactly the kind of thing that was about to happen from happening the guards made Biggs exercise in a different yard each day. But he and Seabourne had worked out the sequence in which the changes were rung and Seabourne's iron-bar intuition told him which wall to park when he arrived outside a second time.

Right behind Biggs ambled two convicts who had been promised 500 pounds each for their help.

Over the wall and clattering down into the yard came two metal-runged rope ladders. Biggs and Flower whirled, ran and leaped for them, the two men at the rear earning their money by dancing heftily into the way of the warders on duty in the yard as they pounded across trying to yell and blow their whistles at the same time.

The vehicle Biggs had heard outside was an old furniture van. Cunning hands had removed its roof which could not, of course, be seen from normal eye level and built inside it a platform to be raised and lowered by pulleys. A man borne up on the makeshift lift as it rose had no difficulty heaving the ladders over the 25 foot wall. As the two intrepid escapees teetered on the stone lip a masked and overalled figure on the platform wagged the ugly double muzzle of a sawn-off shotgun downward like a traffic cop's finger and ordered, "Don't hang about mate. JUMP!" They dropped past the ingenious apparatus and landed, winded, on a pile of old mattresses laid on the floor of the van. Another thump followed as the shotgunner from the platform dived after them and then, unexpectedly there were two more. Another pair of time-servers had not been able to resist the opportunity.

"Over here," yelled Seabourne, waiting by the getaway car with another shotgun bearer. And away they all went in a considerably crowded Ford Zephyr, leaving the van there as a reminder of the kind of polished lark the public thought the robbers owed them.

Charm heard on her car radio that the break had come off. But it was days before she managed even to speak to Biggs by keeping a phone booth rendezvous at a prearranged time after first shaking off detectives who were keeping her under surveillance; and well into September before she got a message to go to Victoria, near one of London's main-line stations, and wait outside the Bertasso Hotel. Sentimental to a fault, her Ron. That was where they had spent their first night together when she was only eighteen and she had taken him up to London to the annual dance given by the company that employed her as a 7 pound 50 pence a week clerk. Then, he had not even been interested that it was a bullion firm.

A man in a taxi gave her a train ticket, a front-door key and an address. At midnight she let herself into a nondescript house in the suburbs of Bognor Regis, a seedy resort on the South Coast, and impatiently shook awake the man for whom she had hungered for two years.

Charm and Biggs found little time to discuss the future during the two weeks they spent together then, but by the time she made another visit with the children he told her he had decided to strike out for Australia the sunlit land of opportunity in the sixties for thousands of British emigrants every year. A consultation had been arranged with the man who had, or said he had, made travel arrangements for Wilson and Buster Edwards.

It was a classic pulp-fiction episode brought to vigorous life by a large injection of money. Any other carpenter who wanted to migrate to Australia could go there for ten pounds; the Australian government would pay the rest of his fare. It cost Biggs 20,000 pounds for himself and eventually another 6,250 pounds to get his family out there.

Bigg's first fake passport called him Gerald King. But no one asked to see it as he and Eric Flower, who had been with him all the time, were smuggled aboard a small steamer in Tilbury Docks. A conspiratorial sailor hid them in the hold until they were landed, seasick and miserable, in Antwerp. True to style and script a car materialized with their own luggage in its trunk. Later, separated into two cars, they were driven across the frontier between Belgium and France accompanied by girls whose looks were calculated to distract the negligent attentions of the border guards; and in Paris, installed in a garish flat near the *Opéra* belonging, they were assured, to a starlet-moll who had been shipped off to the Riviera to make room for them. Her patron it seemed, was the Continental representative of the travel agent they were doing business with. Even in Pigalle it would hardly play.

After a few days of traditional Parisian pleasures laid on by their considerate host, Biggs had his nose neatly broken by a stainless steel hammer. The heavy aggressive hook that Charm had always fancied so much became a narrow ski-jump. Plastic surgery had been included in the pricey package deal Biggs had agreed to and the rest of it, a jowl-paring facelift, was done a few days later just in time for a visit from the family. Charm still recognized him although he frightened the children. They had a couple of weeks together packed with their own traditional pleasures and on December 29, having changed his passport for another in the name of Terence Furminger, Biggs flew to Zurich and switched to a BOAC flight for Sydney. On the way he sat next to a retired judge who gave it as his considered opinion that the sentences handed out to the train robbers had been far too severe.

Criminals are as vain as debutantes and as indefatigably fascinated by each other's exploits. Biggs and Charm, once she had joined him, lapped up every word they could find in the Australian papers on the robbery and the robbers and pestered friends at home with whom they were still in touch to send out clippings from the British ones. Much of what they read sounded pretty hilarious at that distance, particularly the items speculating on where Biggs might be.

Eighteen months passed before Charm got there. And just before she left Britain James White the trailer enthusiast was arrested in the small Kent town of Littlestone-on-Sea where he had been known to all as Bob Lane a jolly, friendly dealer in boats and trailers and a volunteer member of the local lifeboat crew. He had been shopped, and a detective posing as a barman collected his beer glass from a pub one night and sent it, fingerprints and all, to Scotland Yard.

"How was it you only found 30,000 quid in that caravan?" White asked the coppers who were asking *him* a lot of questions. "Is it still around?" It was. "Look behind the insulation panel over the stove," he said. There was another 4,800 pounds.

Soon after Charmian arrived in Australia, White was sentenced to eighteen years having pleaded guilty and, through the offices of none other than Biggs's old defender Mr. Wilfred Fordham, unfolded a sad and cautionary tale. He could account for about 50,000 pounds of his 130,000 share but the rest of it had been the price of silence and refuge paid out on the installment plan, sometimes at the rate of a 1,000 pounds a day. Biggs could sympathize with that. Poor old Jim. But at least it was not poor old Ronnie. Terry, rather.

Wilson the pacesetting wall-jumper went next. In January 1968 while Charm was enjoying her second upside-down Australian summer. Where Wilson was, in a bedroom community called Rigaud, forty miles west of Montreal, Canada, the snow lay deep. And it registered the small but remorseless footsteps of Detective Chief Superintendent Tommy Butler, a man who had reduced the romantic science of crime detection to methodical ploddery.

Once the robbery investigation had passed out of the provincial environs of Buckinghamshire, Butler as head of the Flying Squad had the job of keeping it alive. He had turned it into a fanatical personal crusade. Despite what Biggs or anyone else said about three never-identified participants, Butler was convinced that there had only been fifteen men originally and having masterminded the arrests of so many of them he literally devoted the rest of his life to getting the others—or getting them back.

He was a very odd little man. He looked like a bad-tempered gnome with a high bald dome of a head and large hairy ears, the impression fortified by a long ill-fitting leather overcoat he usually wore. He was fifty-five, retiring age, but after being a policeman for 34 years he just could not stop. He talked the Yard into giving him a year's extension so that he could bring in the last of the train robbers.

For three years he had haunted the lives of anyone who knew anything about the missing men, White, Wilson, Reynolds and of course Biggs. He thought of nothing and nobody else except, perhaps, the aged mother with whom he lived and with whom he shared his only diversion—watching Westerns. He even took his annual leave in spots that he thought free-spending Robbers might fancy, crawling uncomfortably about Riviera beaches with a pair of binoculars, risking arrest and the *voyeur's* lot of wrath and ridicule.

This year he had gone to Canada for his holidays. He had an address given to him by a man who had received a letter and who badly needed some consideration extended to him. A silverware salesman whose Rigaud neighbors had always thought of as a pillar of the community and whose hobby was embroidery was driving his children to school the morning that Butler, in the front seat of a Quebec Provincial Police car down the road said, "That's him all right." Pull over, Monseiur.

When he had arrived in Canada in 1966 just like any bona fide landed immigrant Wilson's passport certified that he was Ronald Alloway. His wife kept her own first name Pat, and their three daughters Lianne 4, Tracy 9 and Sheryl 11, kept theirs.

Wilson's credentials were convincing enough for him to meet the stiff requirements of the national Central Mortgage and Housing Corporation which loaned him $18,000 to add to $24,000 he put up in cash to build the five bedroom house of native stone on a lot that he purchased for $4,000.

In Rigaud the Wilsons lived a life of blameless ease that any British immigrant struggling to set themselves up might have envied. In addition to the Pontiac the police flagged down, the garage of the two-storied home held a Volkswagen. Wilson-Alloway let it be known to the friends he made in the local Civitan Club and the golf club that he had kept on some real estate interests in Britain and that his salesman's work was more in the nature of a hobby. The real reason he had left the Old Country he told them was that there were too many damned niggers there these days. And if there was one thing that still annoyed him it was the difficulty the exchange control regulations created in getting money out of Britain. And the devaluation was dastardly.

Ron and Charm would have sympathized. But Wilson had done better than they appeared to have. When the mixed force of local Provincial, Montreal City and Royal Canadian Mounted police which Butler had gathered around him during the week he had kept his prey under surveillance went through the house they found 20,000 Bahamian dollars in $100 bills, $14,000 U.S. and a respectable nest-egg of Canadian currency as well. They also noted that the house had been thoughtfully built 1,000 yards from its nearest neighbor and that the Wilsons kept two Great Danes that appeared to be less than good-natured.

Butler's productive stalking set off a classical press tournament. The taking of White had had its own particular elegance but since he had never stood trial he had been quarantined by all the precautionary apparatus of British courts. No such inhibition applied to Wilson an already convicted absconder. Reporters *could* talk to him—if they could get past Butler and the Royal Canadian Mounted Police to whom Wilson was eventually awarded and who were fairly evenly matched with the old bloodhound in their resentment and dislike of the press. And the reporters could print what they were told without fear that they or their editors would go to prison for contempt of court.

British newsmen shivered into Montreal, mainly correspondents from New York, but a couple flown over from London. They were surprised and disappointed to discover that the Mounties were square-jawed, tight-lipped well-cropped men in tweedy plain-clothes. They had been looking forward to something a little more colorful and, you know, traditional. During the few days it took for the cooperative Canadians to arrange a hearing to order Wilson deported as an illegal immigrant they got only the most perfunctory attention from Butler, but they were patient. They booked seats on all the likely flights out. If Wilson was going back, so were they. And they would be hard to avoid in mid-air.

There were some bad moments when they had to board the plane with only a stony official assurance that Wilson and Butler would be getting on at the last moment. Disturbing visions blossomed in their minds of a tribe of shamefaced hot-shot reporters tumbling out at London Airport while the object of their expensive attentions was still languishing in Montreal. So preparations were made to storm the emergency exits. But they need not have worried. Butler smiled more on the seven hour trip than he had during his entire career in The Sweeney and Wilson, wry and forbearing, gave gratifying interviews. When Butler offered a stewardess a pound note to pay for a drink his prisoner said to her, "Better check the serial number."

Wilson got a pretty good press even in the *Express*, despite Biggs's parting admonition to Benckendorff in Rio six years later. Perhaps Biggs thought it unsporting that in order to make sure they got the greater part of the prisoner's attention—and the only photograph of him in Butler's gratified custody—the *Express* took the care to send a photographer, Terry Fincher, who had been at school with Wilson. Or perhaps what Biggs had not liked was the way the story seemed to dwell on the 28 years that Wilson had waiting for him rather than the three and a half years that he had been out.

By the time Butler went to get Reynolds, Biggs's sponsor in the robbery gang, Charm had had a third child, they had changed their name yet again—to Cook—and moved from Adelaide, where they had first settled, to Melbourne. They had received a message from London that the Yard knew about the passports in the name of Furminger, the name they had used before they became the Kings.

Bruce Reynolds whose *protégé* Biggs had been was the only one of the robbers to realize the fevered dream of luxury that all of them had shared. He and his wife and their son Nicky, named after the first Biggs baby, lived the life of the idle rich in just the kind of places Butler had been working his way around before they decided that home was best. The Riviera. The Costa Brava. Paris, Rome, Madrid.

The Reynolds came back to Britain in 1967 and rented a comfortable furnished house with a well-kept garden in Torbay on the West of England Riviera. They lived there for nearly a year before Butler came calling just as the afternoon gin-and-limes had been poured out. And with shattering suddenness Reynolds—they had changed only their first names—made his long-awaited appearance in the Buckinghamshire Assizes Court. Twenty-five years. He took it well.

"The kind of life I was leading," he said, "was just like serving your time on the outside."

As a story the Great Train Robbery simply would not lie down. With Biggs the only man knowingly left at large yet another generous airing in newspapers the world over was inevitable even in such an unlikely forum as the Australian *Women's Weekly*, a national magazine. In June 1969 Charm had given a copy to Nicky then aged seven and Chris, her second son, four, before looking at it herself. They came across a pre-plastic surgery picture of Biggs. "Look," said Nicky happily, "it's our daddy."

In Adelaide a man called Max Phillips saw the same article. "Look," he said, "that's Terry King." He said it again to the police who had no difficulty finding plenty of more recent pictures on which the scars of the Parisian surgeon's knife that Biggs had always explained away as a mastoid operation showed up clearly. Ron and Charm were the kind of people who enjoyed having their pictures taken in a nightclub when they were out on the town.

The photographs that went up on the wanted notices showed a classical Australian suburban couple. He smiling modestly for the camera; well-pressed dark suit, narrow tie, white handkerchief in breast pocket, short sideburns. She in sleeveless little black dress with plunging neckline, fringe combed down her forehead, fall of false hair tumbling behind. On the table between them was the debris of an expensive meal, wine bottles prominent.

It took time for notes to be compared between the various state police forces in Australia and Butler poised and predatory in London. But gradually detail was piled upon weighty detail. The police in Melbourne were told that Biggs was thought to be in their city working—as indeed he was for 60 pounds a week—as a carpenter. Then the names and descriptions of all the family were distributed. By October Biggs's picture was being shown on television. It was time for him to go.

During the months of dreadful suspense Biggs's chief concern had been that one of the quite extensive circle of people he had encumbered with revelations about his past might not be able to resist mentioning it and putting the finger directly on him. That none did was typical of the loyalty that Biggs with his disarming and guileless ways often managed to inculcate in people with whom he became friendly. He had to rely on a lot of them in Australia, most of whom were straight and upright taxpayers, to help him get out of the country again. The police arrived at the door of the house in Hibiscus Road, Blackburn only two hours after Biggs had left. Once again front pages everywhere blazed with the ever-gripping saga. Would it ever end?

Biggs had a plan. What he needed was rather more money than he had been able to get together. Before he had left London he had deposited 32,000 pounds with various "bankers" including the one that had delivered Charm her allowance of 200 pounds a month at a regular rendezvous in the pets' department at Harrods. She had spent 15,000 on herself and on Biggs's luxuries apart from the cost of the breakout and they had gladhanded away 13,000. Another 10,000 had been paid out as commission on trading in 40,000 pounds worth of the old white fivers for new ones.

After Biggs arrived in Australia the bankers as arranged sent him a few hundred pounds concealed in rolled up magazines or simply marked as "Printed Papers" and posted. But after that, guessing that he was out of reach for good, they raised the interest rate to 100 percent and pocketed the lot. Charm had brought 7,000 pounds with her when she came but that was long since gone. All they had apart from the small escape fund Biggs took with him was what they earned.

Left alone with three children to care for and 35 pounds a week rent to find Charmian attacked her problems with a bold entrepreneurial stroke. To the clamoring reporters demanding specifics of the Biggs's remarkably brazen life on the run—it could hardly be called "in-hiding"—she said, "How much?"

Sixty-five thousand pounds was the eventual answer from News Limited of Australia who were happy to hive off the British rights to the *Sunday Mirror*, the largest selling Sunday tabloid in Britain. Charm threw in her photograph album too, priceless pictures of the kind she and Ron had never been able to resist taking of each other: Biggs with the moustache he grew when they were hiding out in Bognor after the jailbreak and Charm demure in her frilly nightdress; Biggs wearing a joke mask in Paris after the plastic surgery; sun-bathing in the backyard at Hibiscus Road with Sadie their labrador; all five Biggses on the beach. It made an engrossing newspaper serial that wove a welcome new episode into the mighty epic.

Even now Biggs tells a circumspect and sanitized account of what he did and where he went after leaving Hibiscus Road. He knows what he owes to his friends. But by the early days of 1970 while his name was still a headline staple in both countries he was aboard the Chandris Lines ship *Ellinis* bound from Melbourne to Britain on the eastward route via the Panama Canal and incapable of waiting longer than the third day out to tell a pretty English divorcée that he was not really, as the passport he now carried said, Michael Haynes, artist.

Breathlessly she recalled the moment for the indefatigable Vine as soon as he had got himself back to London from Rio with the address for her which Biggs had handed out to MacKenzie.

"He got the conversation round to crime for some inexplicable reason," said the young woman, "and began talking about the Great Train Robbery. I started to put two and two together.

"And the day I told him who I thought he was we were standing on deck. Just as I said the word 'Biggs' the ship's siren sounded. He pulled me across the deck toward the sound but he had heard me. He said, 'Yes I am. You're a bright one.' We spent the next eighteen glorious days together. . . ." Bon voyage Terry. Ronnie. Michael.

Biggs left *Ellinis* in Panama, went to Caracas, Venezuela, for a couple of weeks where he got a tourist visa for Brazil and then flew down to Rio. One thing he had done before leaving Australia was to follow Charm's profitable lead into confessional literature. While he had been at sea a Melbourne solicitor, who by yet another affirmation of the powers of coincidence had once been a Scotland Yard detective, offered for sale a manuscript account of his previous adventures authenticated by signature and thumbprint.

That was the series of articles bought in 1970 for 20,000 pounds by *The Sun* who published it only after lengthy and repeated assurances to its readers in London that the money had been paid in such a way that no one but the Biggs children would be able to benefit by it. On the day the first installment appeared in London (*Ronald Biggs Talks* said the solid black handbills everywhere) poor old Tommy Butler M.B.E. died. Far off amid the coffee colored consolations he had found in such abundance at Copacabana Biggs drank to that good omen.

13

"The detection and capture of any criminal, Brazilian or foreign, in Brazilian territory is the task only of the security forces of Brazil."

Foreign Ministry,
Brazilia, 7 February 1974

●

Once the script was back on the tracks in Rio and London was sure the trap would be punctually sprung the preparations within the black glass palace in Fleet Street went ahead with practiced and professional orderliness. Certain things had to be done on the Thursday and inevitably the number of people included in the knowledge that there was a big story in the making had to be increased. But to their perceptible chagrin they were still not given the slightest hint of its nature.

Slipper's insistence on striking early was an unfortunate hindrance to the paper's chances of making the most of its powerful exclusive. Saturday is the worst day of the week for newspaper sales. All national papers are at their smallest, the number of pages being governed by the amount of advertising space sold, and there is the greatest commitment to "must" features in the shape of weekend television programming with accompanying comment and a larger than usual share must go to the sports and racing section.

Monday, on the other hand would have been perfect. Never mind. This was a story for any day of the week.

Even so the tooling up that had begun was aimed at printing an extra 800,000 copies—a total of over 4 million, a figure the *Express* had not aspired to for twelve years—on the Friday night, and even more for every day of the following week when the story Biggs was pouring forth to MacKenzie would be devoured by an excited populace.

Putting on that number of extra copies is not the simple matter of letting the presses run a little longer. They must all be printed within the same time in order to be ready for the trains that take the various editions to their dispersal points and which, since they are contracted for by all the newspapers jointly, wait for no one. Missing the trains means making expensive additions to the fleet of trucks that fill in the gaps left by the railways with the risk still remaining of getting short shrift because of late arrival at the wholesalers.

No one has ever been able to count the number of retail outlets for newspapers in Great Britain. But the wholesalers who supply them will try to press as many copies on them as possible (in the quaint but archaic unit of quires: bundles of 26 until creeping metrication made it 25) of any paper they know to have some special appeal that day. In addition each newspaper has its own itinerant circulation representatives who keep up pressure to get the retailers to order more when they think a particular day's paper will sell well off the counters.

The *Express* made all the necessary arrangements. But with a good deal more difficulty and less conviction than usual since no one concerned had the slightest idea what the special sales attraction might be. Take our word for it, was all anyone could say, passing on the little they themselves had been provokingly told. As if it wasn't hard enough anyway to sell something that's a different product every blessed day.

The production department had its own logistics, too. Printing more papers on a given night would mean using more machines and therefore more men to tend them. The extra machinery must not be immobilized by maintenance. It meant bringing in more paper. Few Fleet Street offices have space to store more than a day's anticipated consumption so the required number of giant reels of newsprint had to be trucked up the narrow alleys and unloaded with wall-shaking thumps. Ink too. An extra half a million copies would use 100 gallons so the tanks must be topped up. And a big run would mean less time to spare for routine troubles like paper breaks. The engineers clambered diligently among the frames and cylinders.

Once the story got onto paper it was as good as delivered on every other newsdesk in the Street. The *Express* office would begin to leak like a rusty bucket. In order to extract the greatest possible advantage from its agonizingly enviable scoop the *Express* had to ensure that even when it had arrived in the office the story passed through the minimum number of hands in circumstances of the maximum security that could be imposed.

McColl and the Deputy Editor McDonald made their dispositions with the composing room and Hitchen his with the newsgathering side all quite masterfully watertight and all of them infuriating and frustrating even more members of the staff. Hitchen had arranged with the supervisor of the Tape Room, the communications center of the paper, for a Telex machine that was normally used only for outgoing communications, to be cleared. And he had given its number to Vine in one of the phone conversations they had been exchanging almost every hour.

In the era of satellite communications Telex is frequently more efficient and reliable than the telephone since the intervention of operators is reduced to a minimum. It is, simply, a teleprinter that can be dialed through to another teleprinter in exactly the same way that two phones become connected.

Slipper had set 11 A.M. on the Friday Rio time—3 P.M. London—as his zero hour and as soon as possible after that Vine was to send Hitchen a Telex message of one word only from their code. "Anvil."

Hitchen slept in the office by the gents again that night using his battered old briefcase as a pillow. It was full of all the clippings on Biggs and the train robbery that he and his secretary had been discreetly and systematically withdrawing from the *Express* library for the past two weeks.

The *Express* part of the enterprise in Rio was also being conducted on a fairly orderly basis. Vine, vividly aware of the urgency of getting their precious pictures back to London, had taken all the exposed film that Lovelace had shot to the airport. Too late for the onerous formalities of air-freighting the package he looked, as desperate newsmen will in far-off parts, for a "pigeon" to carry it home. He picked his man with experienced care and they discussed the matter civilly, one manifest Englishman to another.

"How do I know it's not a load of pot?"

"Ha ha," said Vine, "it would hardly be going to the *Daily Express*. It's some pictures for a travel feature." Not entirely an untruth. But he opened the package and showed the 35 millimeter cassettes.

"All right then, I'll take them. Anything for the good old *Express*," said his chosen pigeon, the commercial attaché from the British Embassy.

The British Embassy in Brazil and its prestigious mother institution back in Whitehall, the Foreign and Colonial Office, were quite unaware that a pair of London coppers had been sent off on a mission so fraught with potential for giving international offense. But then again the boss of the Yard, Commissioner Sir Robert Mark, had not even told *his* boss, Home Secretary Robert Carr, that two of his men were dabbling in such dangerous diplomatic waters.

And Scotland Yard in its infinite caution had not only kept the rest of its own side out of the secret, but all of Brazil as well—including that fine body of men with whom relations would sooner or later have to be established: the Frontier Air and Maritime Police. The *Federales*.

Neither was Slipper going to give the game away prematurely out there. Aware of the prying habits of foreign police forces he and Jones had not produced their passports when checking into the Metropole. Their occupation was entered in them. They phoned the details down to the reception desk from their room. They told the clerk they were from "The Met." Metropolitan Police of course. Presumably they hoped it might be confused with the Meteorological Office.

Slipper and Jones got their first inkling of the depths into which they had ventured when they took their first outing from the hotel on the Thursday morning. No matter how loudly and clearly they addressed the natives in English no one understood a single bleeding word. Faced with smiling but nevertheless complete linguistic incompatibility on all sides they appealed to Vine. Where could they turn for help?

"For heaven's sake," said Vine wearily, "call the British Embassy."

There no longer was a British Embassy in Rio, actually, since Rio was no longer the capital of Brazil. Britain's had been one of the last foreign missions to move to the remote and sterile new capital Brasilia. But it had been unable to hold out longer, not because of any danger of a rupture in diplomatic relations but because the Brazilians began to drop grave official hints that privileges such as duty-free liquor were too valuable to risk so lightly. When the ambassador, his secretaries and staff finally trekked off morosely to the bureaucratic wastes inland their tranquil and civilized old quarters in Rio became a mere Consulate, a kind of branch office in which dealings between countries finally come down to the untidy and inconsequential exchange of people and their problems. Biggs dropped in there a couple of times a week to read the British papers.

So Slipper's distress call brought diplomatic intervention in the form of Her Majesty's Consul, Mr. Henry Alfred Neill and profoundly puzzled he was by the unlikely story he was belatedly told. He got to the Metropole shortly after Vine had arrived there.

Although he was fifty-nine, Neill was not one of your polished old-school diplomats. He was a rumpled and workmanlike retread from the erstwhile Commonwealth Service which in 1965 had merged with the far more elitist Foreign Service to form the present-day Diplomatic Service. Before that he had served time in the Air Ministry and the Ministry of Transport and knew a figure of authority when he saw one. After Slipper had explained the purpose of his unorthodox visit Neill readily answered the questions Vine put to him. Name, age and rank for the record. And did he have serviceable Portuguese? When Vine disappeared into the bathroom for a moment Neill asked Slipper, "That's your boss, is it?" "Is it, bloody hell," Slipper exploded. "That's the bleeding *Daily Express*."

MacKenzie and Lovelace were working on Biggs like a resuscitation team. MacKenzie had been appalled by his new orders but knew that there was no chance of delaying the inevitable. If he was to salvage anything of his original grandiose hopes every valuable word had to be wrung from the victim before he was wafted off out of reach. MacKenzie set his fine jaw and went about it, wondrously relieved to find how eager Biggs was to enter into negotiations.

Biggs had weighed things as carefully as he could and arrived at a harshly realistic conclusion. He was forty-five. If he surrendered then, and recommenced serving his sentence, he was willing to gamble on having to put in no more than ten years of it, thus leaving him enough life left-over to be worthwhile living. Whereas if his present precarious beachcomber's life dragged on for a few more years and he was discovered then he would leave prison only as a very old man. He was aware that several of the train robbers would soon be eligible to apply for parole, having reached the halfway point in their sentences, and his simple faith in being somehow able to share in the bounty of this newly instituted system that he did not really understand showed time and again in the earnest discussions he had with his new friends.

"Who knows what might happen in the next few years?" he kept saying to them. "When I was last inside there wasn't even such a thing as parole. But now you can apply for it when you are halfway through. They might just open all the doors one day. Who knows?" MacKenzie and Lovelace knew.

But what was pushing Biggs most forcefully toward an immediate decision about his future was the fact that he no longer had any valid identity documents, something far more important in Brazilian life than food, shelter or mother love. The thought of becoming a fugitive again was too much. He had been too many people for too long. He was ready to go back to being Ronnie Biggs.

All right. They would get together a book about his fascinating life as a kind of Anglo-Saxon Papillon. He would give himself up to MacKenzie and Lovelace and fly back to Britain. Would that do them for a story? But first he would have to telephone Charm to see if she thought it would be the best thing for him to do. There would, of course, be money in it?

Lovelace took this welcome prospect to Vine, hoping to stay Slipper's pounce. He and MacKenzie were sure they could get Biggs back to London even without a passport now that he was willing to

go. Not a chance, said Slipper. Biggs belongs to me. Slipper treated
Vine and Jones to a dress rehearsal of the moment on the morrow
when he would confront his long-sought quarry. The moustache
comb darted above his flashing teeth as he paced up and down the
room. "Do you think he'll recognize me?" he demanded. "After all
it's been a long time. 'Long time no see,' that's what I'll say. Might
as well keep things friendly."

Back at the Trocadero wallowing in unaccustomed hospitality
Biggs was saying, "We don't have to rush things do we Colin? Take
it easy. You're in Rio, now."

As Michael Haynes, Biggs had become a well-established fringe
member of the small English-speaking community in Rio since he
first infiltrated nearly four years earlier. He was a "fixer" in the most
legitimate sense, an odd-job man who soon showed he could paint,
renovate and repair a good deal more reliably and cheaply than the
capricious and careless local labor. His name got passed around
among the expatriates and so did he, at least at the less intimate of
their parties, one of which had brought him together with the
serendipitous Benckendorff.

For a while things had been good and he had even been able to
keep a small band of Brazilian laborers in work. But the foreign
colony had begun to shrink, intimidated by the terrifying spiral of
Brazilian inflation that in a year drove down the value of the dollar
by 40 percent and turned the pound pallid and there was not
enough work to keep him going. Biggs was so broke that when
Benckendorff rang he had been on the point of moving out of his
apartment because the power had been cut off and he could not pay
the bill. But he had never stolen anything.

He took the *Express*men back to the seedy and dilapidated
building at 330 Avenida Prado Junior, above the Tico Tico
nightclub, where Apartment 1207, two rooms and a bath for 50
pounds a month had been his home for two years. Since, in fact, he
met Xu Xu. Pronounced Shu Shu. Who? said MacKenzie and
Lovelace still bemused by the lissom and complaisant Lucia.

"My girl friend," Biggs explained. " 'Xu Xu' is what Brazilians
call their chicks. Her real name's Raimunda. She's out of town

visiting her mother." He pronounced it correctly *Hi-munda*, justifiably proud of the serviceable Portuguese he had acquired with her help.

In the apartment he started to haul out bundles of letters, postcards and photographs from drawers; tapes, too, that documented the busy correspondence he had been able to keep up with Charm and the kids over the years. MacKenzie and Lovelace were delighted. Pure gold. They dug into it like conquistadores.

"I take pictures myself, you know, Bill," said Biggs. He showed Lovelace an amateurishly posed nude of a thoroughly alluring tawny-skinned girl. "Raimunda," he said. "Best lay I ever had in my life, bar none."

MacKenzie and Lovelace were genuinely appreciative. But two girls could lead to complications. The *Daily Express* was not the kind of paper to welcome too many salacious details, nor Ian McColl the kind of Editor.

The reason that John Monks and Albert McCabe had been plucked from the deck of *Britannia* before getting their gin-and-tonic with the Royals was, of course, to break the news to Charm in Melbourne that her old man had reached the end of his lengthy tether, something she knew he must do one day as surely as a fireman at the top of the brass pole knows he will hit the bottom. The performance would not be complete without her participation. Not only must her comments be recorded first by the *Express* but she must be persuaded, if possible, to offer them exclusively as well as extensively. She might also be induced to make an appearance in London for a brief reunion with Biggs on his way back to Wandsworth or whatever top-security nick he was headed for. What a picture!

In the embarrassment that had followed Biggs's neatly timed departure from Melbourne the Australian authorities got rather shirty with his wife. There was strong talk of deporting her and of charging her as some kind of an accessory to something but in the end they just hit her where at that time it probably hurt most. They levied 40,000 pounds tax on the 65,000 pounds she had collected for her instructive memoirs.

But from the moment the train robbery loot had been spilled out on her living-room carpet Charm had been learning to thrive on her lonely troubles. Events after her arrival in Australia kept her in training. Biggs had invested some of their money in a doomed boarding-house partnership with a woman he had been playing tenant-and-landlady with. Charm made his friend *her* friend as well, and promised to call the next Biggs baby after her if it was a girl. When the boarding-house scheme collapsed and the money ran low Charm went out to pack toilet rolls in a factory for 20 pounds a week. Before and after Biggs's flight her tenacious devotion kept the family together: never did she reproach, criticize or fail to defend her husband for any one of his hapless felonies.

And there was far worse to come. The cruelest shock thrown off by the forces that powered their hazard-prone and tempestuous marriage blazed between the two distant poles of it in 1971. Just as Biggs was settling down nicely with Raimunda in Rio Farley the eldest son was killed by a car in Melbourne.

"Wherever you are," said Charm resolutely, via the panting media—knowing perfectly well by then where Biggs was if not exactly what he was doing—"stay there. Do *not* come back. Now or any other time."

With iron determination the headmaster's daughter set out to improve her prospects as a single parent. She won an adult admission to the University of Melbourne. With an Arts degree she too could become a teacher. She got together enough money to buy a comfortable suburban-Spanish bungalow in a relatively untrodden part of Melbourne called East Doncaster. She reverted to the name of Brent which she had legally taken back in Britain soon after Biggs had gone inside for the robbery and little Farley and Chris went to school untroubled by their dad's unquestionable but unquenchable charisma.

Every detail of this cloistered, intense existence Charm relayed to Biggs in extraordinary letters eight and nine pages long in which the mature undergraduate reverted to the eager little clerk who had abandoned herself to Biggs's raunchy charms on the lumpy mattress of the Bertasso Hotel; passionate, girlishly arch and fatuous True Romance letters. She was besotted with the man she was writing to and to hell with the English Department at Melbourne University.

"My darling own special husband,

I am still increasing my love for you minute by minute and long for you and need you desperately. You and I are part of one whole being and unless we are together life is inwardly meaningless for both of us. . . .

"Gee I wish I'd been a fly on the wall, darling, about an hour ago. I was reading your letter to the boys for the umpteenth time before they went to bed and Farl knows his off backwards. When you ask him if he'd like some more drawings he's sort of bustin' to answer before I even read the question. And at the end, in a real angelic little voice with a seraphic smile to match, he says: 'Night night, dad.' . . .

"Are you ready with the applause? I got honours in British History, Honours in European History and a pass in French and I'm still impatiently waiting for the English results. How about that? Not bad for an oldie, I thought! I ought to get the English 'cos it's my best subject. . . .

"I love you now more than ever before. I miss you, need you and yearn for you with ever increasing fervour.

I am yours, alone for now and for all time."

MacKenzie pocketed the letters appreciatively. Urgency was encouraging a professional ruthlessness Hitchen would applaud. Lovelace "collected"—in the sturdy Fleet Street euphemism used to cover anything ranging from purchase to pilfering—all the pictures in sight. Now, tomorrow. Pictures on the beach with the lovely Lucia? Change in Benckendorff's room? 10:30? You chaps work too hard. But whatever you say Colin. You're the boss.

In London, Friday morning was devoted by everyone involved to the entirely futile effort of pretending that nothing out of the ordinary was happening. A few more people had discovered what was afoot. But not *where*. Hitchen had headed off one of the most skillful feature writers Brian Cashinella and his own deputy Arliss Rhind as soon as they arrived in the office and led them off to the office by the Gents. Not without some understandable smugness he told them what the main story in the paper that night would be and that they would be lending it vital support. He left them in the little office with the door locked, riffling wonderingly through the sheafs of clippings from which they were to write the background stories of the robbery and Biggs's subsequent odyssey as far as Melbourne that would appear in the inside pages.

Rather than have the package of film that Vine had sent by their obliging diplomatic courier collected by the usual motorcycle messenger, Hitchen had sent a reporter Colin Pratt and a photographer Paul Felix to meet the "pigeon" arriving from Rio on his overnight flight. When the two of them got back from the airport Hitchen was locked up with the background writers who were now hammering away with the manic indistractability that only the combination of a close deadline and a story worth meeting it with can engender, and not to be found. McDonald discovered the men with the precious film wandering at large around the Big Room and after snatching the package from them imprisoned him in their own office. No lighthearted gossip was going to find its way around the ravening rest of the staff about a mysterious package from Rio.

In Rio the morning, eighty degrees at 7:30 and rising fast, found Slipper as fretful and impatient as any *Express*man. The thought of Biggs so near, yet so mobile, elusive and frighteningly assimilable in the unruly local ambiance had added to the tortures that his displaced stomach had inflicted on him during the night. Only action could restore his customary state of phlegmatic assertiveness. But he had got the position clear after some detailed discussions with Neill about the technicalities. He was not going to have the pleasure of actually arresting Biggs. He could not arrest anyone for anything *anywhere* outside the jurisdiction of the United Kingdom. However, if Biggs really was willing to give himself up, as the case seemed to be, there was no reason why he should not accompany Slipper and Jones to the airport of his own free will and fly back to London with them. The Consulate could easily provide—as indeed it would have done had Biggs wanted to go with MacKenzie and Lovelace—a oneway travel document to get him out of the country. The Brazilians? They ought to be bleeding glad to see him go.

But what if Biggs did not *want* to go? If he had changed his mind? If he and the *Daily Express* had all this time been trifling with the dignity and power of the force that Slipper and Jones represented, alas so impotently at that instant. Once again they needed help.

Into the unprepossessing Twelfth Delegation police station at Copacabana the pair of Sweeneys strode, sweat-streaked even in their new summer suits, but confident of a fraternal welcome. "I am Chief Superintendent Slipper of Scotland Yard and this is my associate. We would like to speak to the officer in charge."

Nothing.

"Somebody here must speak English."

It seemed not.

They produced their Warrant Cards, undisputed keys to many a door where they came from. The photostats that told the story of Biggs's misspent life. The photostat of the warrant. The letter from the Yard. Nothing.

But as the Copacabana cops stood moving their lips over the credentials, Slipper's loud perseverance got two phrases across that coppers the world over understand. The sonorous and universal words "Scotland Yard." And the last feeble cry of the desperate English globetrotter "British Embassy." Neill came to get him accompanied by Francisco Costa, a Brazilian vice-consul and, after some slightly superficial explanations, two plainclothesmen from the Twelfth Delegation joined the party leaving for the Trocadero. Ninety degrees and rising. God they were hydraulicked.

For a while it looked as though the Scoop of the Century would be heralded by an unseemly bout of fisticuffs in the Big Room. No one in the place could be unaware of Hitchen's compulsive interest in the Tape Room. Since 3 P.M. he had worn a track between it and the Gents, to the annoyance of the operator assigned to monitor the provocatively mute Telex machine. And on one of his trips a playful newsdesk hand waved a piece of copy at him and cried out, "We know what it is. Your secret's out!" Bad joke. Harsh words. Temper.

But it was all over by then. The perfidy complete. The watchers in the hotbox of a car on the Avenida Atlantica had known which room to look for. They had asked for a signal such as a towel on the terrace rail or something done with the shutters. But what they got was infinitely more reassuring; Biggs himself, bold in scarlet trunks and a light tan, flexing his muscles against the primeval thrusting splendor of Sugar Loaf, and the great swathe of enticing honey-colored beach vivid with lollipop-colored umbrellas and rich with a sprinkling of chocolate-colored bodies.

"Just one more, Ronnie." Lovelace's heart was heavy. But he did what he had to. Focusing the side-angle lens of his Nikkon on the carefree idol of the *matin* Lovelace watched the men below cross the road toward the hotel, microscopic avenging images in the background of his picture.

And a few minutes later there it was in Hitchen's trembling hand. It came up not on the carefully reserved Telex but on the keyboard that was the terminal of the direct cable link with the New York bureau. Six words on pink paper. *Prohitchen, London. Anvil happened okay. Tout.*

Tout? Tout? Who the hell was Tout? The New York Bureau Chief Ivor Key, piqued at being left out of the game, had chosen himself a code name. He too had once shared a horse with Vine.

Even now only a few more names could be included in the London in-group. John Ellison the Foreign Editor finally discovered why he had sent Monks and McCabe to Melbourne. He told them what to do next.

They got to East Doncaster with the dawn. And the milkman. It was eleven hours earlier in the day out there. Charm came to the back door in her quilted dressing-gown, red hair trailing, hostile and, when she heard their news, sorrowful and bitter. She spoke to them through a fly-screen door.

"It's like telling me he's dead," she said. "No, it's worse."

Would she go to London?

"How can I? I will never have enough money. And besides he made me swear I would stay here and bring up the children."

Monks intimated that money might not be a problem. Ardently but gently he and McCabe pressed her. They knew they could offer at least 20,000 pounds for her cooperation. To their wonder and discomfiture Charm turned them down flat. No more newspaper deals, she said. No more newspapermen. Piss off.

A picture, please. The photographer could not shoot through the screen door. No thanks, said Charm. Get lost. McCabe and Monks were both seasoned in their calling. Monks had the wisdom of heredity going for him too. His father had been a famous Fleet Street foreign correspondent, who, among others, successfully sued Evelyn Waugh for caricaturing him in *Scoop*.

They started to go. Monks picked up the waiting milk bottles and turned back with them. Thanks, said Charm, opening the door. Click. Thank *you*, Charm.

It was two days before anyone remembered the Glasgow sports writer penniless and mystified in his hotel.

14

"There's an awful lot of copy in Brazil."
Dermot Purgavie,
Daily Mail

•

Some of the best jobs in Fleet Street are in New York City. And some of the people who have them are the best surviving examples around that town of newspapermanship as a wayward and unpredictable way of life.

It was a newspaper*woman*, actually, who felt the first tremor from back home on Friday February 1, 1974. Anthea Disney; small, long dark hair, frequently renovated tan, the kind of look MGM used to fix up for Pocahontas parts. The tom-toms started to beat just as she was about to leave her desk in the *Daily News* Building on East 42 Street where three New York bureaus of British newspapers are housed.

The journalistic conurbation of New York and Washington is the most prestigious of foreign assignments for a British correspondent just as London is the top slot for Americans. Each is the news market place and communications clearinghouse for the other half of the English speaking world; each supports a floating population of the other's newspaper, television and radio correspondents in a kind of extraterritorial media ghetto.

The three dozen or so British staff reporters in the United States march in step to the extent that their days are dominated by the pressure of the five-hour time lag behind London and the complexities of a dual vocabulary. But most of the time they are heading in different directions—or taking, at any rate, different routes to a common end.

Americans are often bewildered by their first sight of British newspapers. To begin with, in an era in which only two American cities have as many as three dailies, there are so many of them. Everyone has heard of *The Times*, of course, and its good greyness is reassuring. And the *Manchester Guardian* comes easily to the lips, even though it has not been called that for years, just *The Guardian*. And there is the *Daily Telegraph* which looks dull and familiar enough to be acceptable to readers of say, the *Boston Globe* or the *St. Louis Post Despatch*. The most unfamiliar quality about these three, the "heavies," is their pathetic thinness. The *Telegraph* averages 26 pages a day—the L.A. *Times*, 80.

But what is this outlandish and brazen scatter of loud-voiced rags that everyone in Britain actually seems to be reading on the buses and in the Tube trains? This explosion of jagged make-up, strident, jumbo-sized headlines, rampant nipples and stories usually no more than a hand's span in length? That's the popular press, cousin, the *Daily Mirror*, *The Sun*, the *Daily Mail* and the *Daily Express*. All fourteen-million-a-day of them.

(The *Telegraph* sells one million and a half but *The Times* and *The Guardian* only reach a scant 351,000 and 353,000 respectively. *The New York Times*, for example, sells, 850,000, the *Toronto Star*, 540,000.)

And this? *Sporting Life*. Oh, yes. And the pretty pink one? *The Financial Times*. Of course. And this one, the *Morning Star*? The Communist Party paper? How interesting.

All these papers are in competition to some degree. But the most intensive battles for circulation are fought out with a single opponent in the same consumer class, the *Mirror* v. *The Sun*. The *Express* v. the *Mail*.

It was the *Mail* that Anthea Disney worked for and which, at about four o'clock in the afternoon she was getting ready to forget for a couple of days. It was already 9 P.M. in London and Friday night, when the smallest papers of the week were being prepared by a largely second string staff, rarely saw a remarkable event.

But her Foreign Desk in London was worried. Spooked. "We don't know what is happening," they told her on the phone. "Let alone where. But we do know that the *Express* is putting on half a million copies tonight. Anything out your way that it could be?"

"Maybe they've found Martin Bormann," she said brightly.

All the "pops," apart from the *Daily Express* are tabloids, a definition genteel American newspaper consumers doggedly equate with "sensationalism." They often use another charming old-fashioned term at the sight of one—"scandal sheet." Although why that should be pejorative even if it were accurate is mystifying. Should scandals be kept out of print?

In Britain as it happens they often are thanks to the *de facto* censorship enforced by the overprotective libel laws and a diabolical piece of legislation called the Official Secret Act. There is none of your luxurious First Amendment, Freedom of Information Act or free-wheeling *Washington Post* Woodstein*ismo* in those parts, more's the pity.

As for sensationalism, happily real life does not leave British newspapermen very much choice despite the thorough official precautions. Sensational events *will* keep coming along as regular readers of such unsensational papers as *The New York Times* and the *Post* can hardly have failed to note.

But it is true that in the British pops news value often means, frankly, amusement value for they consider themselves to be part of the entertainment industry: a daily few minutes of diversion, as much as a mere medium of information. Mass circulation figures are not built on stories about Khmer Rouge politics or the Consumer Price Index.

So to expectations conditioned by American papers, heavily burdened as they are with wire-service copy—old Speed-Graphic style photograph—and three-decked political reportage—city, state and federal—much of the contents of the British pops consists of stories of a distinctly unconventional kind; heavy on exotica, bloodshed, mating habits, showbiz, pets, cars, royalty, popular medicine, homemaking, advice, fashion. Politics is reduced, whenever possible, to personalities.

Although all four pops do a relentless job of political pamphleteering the readers get only as much (meaning, as little) about serious politics, international affairs, science, commerce and the arts as the editors believe them able to digest, neatly folded well within the gaudy, graphic rest. "The Sugar Pill," T. S. Matthews, a former editor of *Time* magazine, astutely labeled the formula in his book of the same title that analyzed the performance of the *Mirror* compared with that of *The Guardian*. It is because so many of the ingredients of both the Pill and its coating are found in such abundance in the Americas that so much British energy and expertise is spent harvesting them there.

Early in the evening several Fleet Street offices had picked up the vibrations of a big-one-in-the-making at the *Express*. But the skillfully tailored wraps stayed on. The first leaks came not from the *Express* office but from the advertising agencies which handle television commercials for the various papers and whose intercession was necessary when the *Express* decided to book time on commercial television that night to boost their epochal scoop. In the end they did not bother to make use of it; simply sat back and watched the momentum of the story win them hundreds of thousands of pounds worth of TV promotion.

Up and down the street newsdesks had rung around correspondents in Britain and abroad to see if they had any idea what the *Express* might be up to. The *Mail*, which had most to lose by an *Express* triumph, was particularly rattled.

Editor David English had gone off to the Continent to ski, putting off the decision whether to have MacKenzie on his gossip column. But since he had left the *Express* to run the *Mail* the rivalry between the papers was a profoundly personal matter to English. His staff knew that he would particularly not appreciate a licking from that direction. They did not know how much worse he would feel when he heard about the by-line.

Disney checked as best she could; read the latest wire-service copy, called the Washington correspondent, the Toronto stringer, and even put in a call to Buenos Aires. Who knows? Maybe somebody else found Martin Bormann?

She did all this in a spirit of dutiful compliance rather than any real hope; there was no reason to suppose that the cause of London's unease was even within the hemisphere covered by the New York bureau. But because she was a compulsive reporter who found it hard to stop work, and because she was glad of an excuse to delay going across to Costello's bar and grill where her colleagues were already getting the weekend under way, Disney went a step further. She telephoned the *Express* bureau to see if she could pick up a hint from them, a delicate process in which the conversation had to be as circuitous and exploratory as the first plea-bargaining round in a district attorney's office, neither side saying anything that could later be held against them; each knowing that what was not said at all might well provide the true clue. There is such a thing as not wanting to scoop a rival too badly to allow them to catch up. Tomorrow always comes.

The only person Disney found in the *Express* office was Ivor Key, the bureau chief. And even if he had been willing to tell her anything there was very little he knew. He was aware now that *something* was going on in Rio but the cryptic message about "Anvil" he had passed on from Vine could have been related to anything anywhere anytime. The sudden departure of Vine from New York *did* come back to Disney's questing mind. When she had arrived at Yvonne Dunleavy's party two day's earlier to find the guest of honor missing she had certainly not believed the excuse. "Vine couldn't care a shit about his sister," she said.

By 5:30, fretful but unable to think of anything more she could do for the moment, she was about to head for Costello's when London came up on the phone again.

"It's Briggs!" said The *Mail* Foreign Desk irascibly. "The *Express* has got him in Argentina."

"Who?" asked Disney.

"Briggs the Great Train Robber."

"Oh, *Biggs*. I bet it's not."

Costello's is one of the few joints in New York to survive a transplant. It moved from Third Avenue around the corner to East

Forty-fourth Street without even losing a cockroach. It certainly never lost one of the hard-core clientele on which it has gratefully depended since two of the native newspapers that provided it with its original patronage the *Daily Mirror* and the *Journal American* shut down ten years ago and the *Daily News* started to hire college graduates. Throughout the week it is used, with relaxed consistency, as a local pub by all the British correspondents within walking distance, but on Friday afternoon right-of-asylum is extended to a few scattered castaways such as the *Telegraph* men from Rockefeller Center and an inordinate number of Australians from the *National Star,* which provides *The Sun* in London with its U.S. service as part of the same multinational operation.

Assimilated, but not in the slightest absorbed, by the city and with their profusion of accents and exotic vocabulary intact, these unruly habitués are much more of a reward to curiosity seekers than the Thurber murals which, alas, did not relocate with Costello's as well as the animal life.

The Friday afternoon conclave is a kind of implicit thanksgiving rite to celebrate the expatriates' joy at being able to ply their craft in a place that puts so few impediments in the way of it; where information is available to a degree often superfluous and enthralling events follow one another in satisfying succession; where the telephones work and the language is not too hard to learn. It is just not like that back home. In Britain—and Australia—telephones are frequently an effective *barrier* to communication because of defective technology and in any case because few official or private citizens are any too obliging about satisfying public curiosity.

What the British correspondents cannot understand is how, given such helpfulness from so many sources and such a wealth of bewitching raw material, the local newspapers manage to be so plodding and funless. But while deploring the waste they are delighted to feast from the laden table themselves, keeping up a steady supply of choice morsels to readers whose appetites are already whetted to a nice edge by the universalities of Kojak, Hawaii Five-O, Wagon Train and Marcus Welby M.D., covering the country—indeed the hemisphere—almost as though they were local reporters. They are not, in the main, perspective seekers.

Many Americans would see a British correspondent among them

personified by the urbane thoroughly transatlanticized and largely retired Alistair Cooke. But a better model for the Costello's crowd would be Cooke's contemporary Don Iddon whose weekly *Daily Mail* column was for years the best guide Britons have ever had to their alternative culture. Iddon set himself securely on the road to fame early by spending his spare time cycling around the provincial town where he worked as a young reporter posting fake readers letters to the editor in praise of his own work. And when he had finally made it to Fleet Street he ensured himself the favorable attention of the *Mail*'s proprietor and principal tennis enthusiast Lord Rothermere by walking around the office with a tennis racket under his arm. Never neglect the obvious, remember.

Since the telephone satellite circuit replaced the submarine telegraph cable as the main communications link between the two countries the correspondents' work habits have become even more erratic than they were by nature. The day often begins prematurely with a call from someone in London who is incapable of understanding that it is not the same time all over the world. And it ends only when nothing short of the return of King Kong could justify a replate on the final City edition.

The Britons order their own movements and are largely left to exercise their own judgment on what they write about for jobs as prized as theirs usually go to nature's self-starters. Their loosely strung together microcosm reflects the loyalties and rivalries of the mother congregation in Fleet Street to a nicety although its small numbers amplify feuds—men drink side by side in Costello's who have not exchanged a friendly word in ten years. And journalistic reflexes, incessantly exercised against the five-hour time lag stay in surprisingly good shape. Even on a Friday none of them would have any difficulty in homing in on a story that they needed or in slapping it together against the fast advancing morn on the other side of the Atlantic as briskly and surely as a pool hall marker racking the balls together in his wooden triangle.

Even as Disney was calling Varig Airlines the two telephones in Costello's started to ring themselves off the walls.

In London the disarray among the *Express*'s competitors was total. The electrifying name of Biggs had finally trickled out of the building just before the first papers came off the presses, far too late for all the others apart from the *Mail* to get even a sniff of it in their first editions. For an insupportable length of time no police reporter could get a word of confirmation from his usual sources for the excellent reason that no one but the original small group at the Yard knew anything about the operation. Finally the press office confirmed. Ronald Biggs had been apprehended in Rio de Janeiro. With the aid of the *Daily Express*.

Rio? That was not in Argentina. Hasty patched together wire-service reports were carrying Argentina. No, said the Yard. Rio was correct. And by the way, forget the bit about the *Daily Express*. That part of the statement was now "withdrawn." Inoperative? asked the coldly furious students of Watergate among the crime reporters. The *Express* had merely been carrying out "parallel inquiries," said the Yard. Oh, sure.

By the time the other papers could start replating—interrupting the critically timed run of the first edition to change their front pages—the champagne was flowing at the *Express*. Apart from the successful preservation of the Scoop of the Century they had plenty to celebrate in its brilliantly improvised handling. The original plan to receive all the copy from MacKenzie by Telex had lasted only as long as the first three takes of the story to arrive. The Telex connection collapsed. Vine came up on the telephone soon afterward. He would dictate MacKenzie's copy as it was written. But to whom? Hitchen was not ready to trust any of the copytakers who would normally take a reporter's call. In the end Cashinella and Rhind—the impressed writers by the gents—telephones shouldered into their ears, took down every word of the thousands that Vine, expertly maintaining the coherence of MacKenzie's piecemeal account, poured over the wire throughout the afternoon. As cramp threatened to immobilize them they abandoned the typewriter and took dictation in shorthand, page after spidery page of it.

Alternating, they transcribed the notes and gave them to Hitchen who decoded the names and places and passed the copy for final editing to McDonald and McColl. In the composing room only three Linotype operators were given the copy to set in type and only two compositors, working at a "stone" well isolated from the rest of the forms being readied for the paper, made up the front page and the exultant overflow into pages two, three and four. In

Manchester the suspense was ended only when the fast train from London delivered the "flongs," moulds of the metal set up in Fleet Street, for them to make their own pages from.

The first man to hit the street out of Costello's was Dermot Purgavie the *Mail*'s bureau chief, the glint of battle in his one good eye. The other one was glass, sacrificed to the quaint British notion that cricket is a desirable preparation for real life. Another hallowed game in British newspaper circles—as in foxhunting—is The Chase. And as the telephones had rattled on hysterically the blood of all the correspondents summoned from the bar already warmed by the afternoon's customary exchange of hospitality and saw-toothed professional badinage, began to rise at the prospect of a memorable pursuit of Biggs. It was not yet clear in London how completely the *Express* had netted the quarry and left only the scent. For that night of shameful defeat a patched-together story would have to do the opposition. But men had to be got to the spot for the counter attack. Livid and vengeful *Mail* executives were loading reporters and cameramen onto planes like a cut-rate charter firm. At one point at least seven pursuers were in motion simultaneously.

Behind Purgavie in Costello's inspiring scenes took place. *The Sun* wanted to send its most frequently consulted correspondent among the News Limited staff, Neal Travis. Or, if he could not be found Steve Dunleavy *The National Star's* news editor and, technically, husband of Yvonne the Vine partygiver. But one was Australian and the other a New Zealander. Each knew he needed visas for Brazil since Britons did not, a Briton had to be found among the overexcited *Sun* delegation. And there was one, Phil Bunton a subeditor, deskbound and unaccustomed to working out of doors, but even less accustomed to such dramatic changes in his plans for the evening. No money, no air travel card, no prospect at all at first glance of getting as far as Penn Station let alone 5,000 miles overnight. John Gallagher the Irish manager and Freddie Percudani the bicycle-riding Italian barman and even Herbie the World's Worst Waiter cleared out the till and started to pile their pocketfuls of wet change on the bar.

In the *Mirror* office a few floors above the *Mail* in the *News* building the bureau chief Ralph Champion was, in accordance with his invariable custom, deeply absorbed in a late-afternoon nap. He had already put in his time at Costello's that day and was preparing to go home. The panic call from London was taken by one of his staff, Sydney Young, who hopefully booked himself a seat to Rio and phoned his wife to pack a bag.

Ian Ball the *Daily Telegraph* bureau chief was also an Australian who would have visa trouble so their mobilization call was switched to Washington where Richard Beeston was the duty correspondent. The two television services—the BBC and the Independent Television News, which had been keeping correspondents in the nation's capital since the first Watergate headlines—also went from there. At Kennedy Airport the paths of these scurrying voyagers crossed like a madwoman's knitting.

Purgavie and the *Mail* photographer Mike Brennan checked with Disney before they boarded the 8 P.M. Varig flight. She told them they were on their way to Rio rather than Buenos Aires as they had thought when they left town. Jesus Christ! No, it's all right. Same plane. But by then copies of the *Express* were in the *Mail* office in London and she could tell them of the devastating extent to which the story already seemed to have been disposed of.

Purgavie and Brennan got on their plane deflated and depressed. There is no more hateful task for a newsman than to mop up after someone else has pulled off a successful exclusive. There was not another *Mail* until Monday—it has no Sunday edition—and by the sound of what Disney had said Biggs would be safely back in Britain by then. Purgavie cloaked himself in a blanket and sulked all the way to Rio.

The next plane was a Pan Am at 10:30. Darryn Hinch the bureau chief of the *Sydney Morning Herald* was the first to check in. He too was a New Zealand citizen and he too needed a visa. But he was not going to let that stop him. The capture of Biggs was as big a story for his paper as it was for any in Britain. It was from Australia still that the most bizarre reports of his fate still emanated: he had been murdered and dismembered by a gang who had contracted to smuggle him to Indonesia; he had been buried in the outback by crocodile hunters who had tracked him down for the loot he still had with him; he had escaped with a beautiful young girl to Red China, Manila, East Africa, Tunisia. What passport do you hold, sir? British!

Hinch was surprised to be joined by Ralph Champion. The *Mirror* bureau chief was a distinguished looking white-haired and ruddy-faced man approaching retirement age who maintained a somewhat stately attitude to his duties, leaving the more exacting assignments to his staff of younger men. But when he awoke and heard from Young what was happening he was more interested in *where*.

"I've *never* been to Rio," he told Hinch.

Champion had held his job for 22 years and as the time to leave it drew near he had become gripped by a determination to go everywhere in the bureau's territory that he had never previously visited, a resolution which occasionally distressed his nominal superiors back in London since once he had assigned himself to a situation and arrived where he had wanted to go he frequently decided to leave again immediately and usually did so, unilaterally declaring the story over. While younger co-practitioners assessed the success or failure of a trip by the amount they had been able to get in their paper or the outlandishness of the adventures to which they had been exposed, Champion's evaluation was invariably based on the price and availability of the least dispensable amenity in his life, Teacher's scotch whiskey. But he was an agreeable traveling companion even if he and Hinch were not reunited until they reached Rio. Champion always traveled first class.

The vainglorious *Express* accounts in London of the events of that Friday in Rio were not exactly an anagram of what really happened as newspaper accounts sometimes manage to be. But no matter how often the component parts were rearranged there were still intriguing gaps left between them. It did not escape the many baleful but erudite eyes scouring the boastful pages that while some of the pictures of Biggs being led from the Trocadero were, as they would have to be, wirephotos the others had clearly been made from original prints which must have been available in the *Express* office on Friday, and therefore must have been taken in Rio the day before that at least.

The story that carried MacKenzie's enormous by-line did little to satisfy anyone's curiosity about how long he and Biggs had spent together, although the official line that the *Express* developed in London as a reply to the deluge of aggressively suspicious inquiries from every point of the media compass was that MacKenzie and Lovelace had got to Biggs only "an hour or so" before Slipper. Nobody believed it.

The following morning alas, Associate Editor Robin Esser, delegated to deal with the unstoppable flow of inquirers from rival newsmen over the weekend, concentrated on putting out unequivocable denials that the *Express* had paid Biggs any money. Which they had not. The pictures? "They all arrived in the office yesterday." Friday that was. Then they left Rio on Thursday? But Esser was still finding out himself what had actually been going on.

The MacKenzie story, which bore the mark of many hands other than his, gave a far from thorough account of what had transpired after Slipper and his entourage made their melodramatic entry into Room 909. But it did provide an explanation of the fortuitous presence of both the *Express* and the Yard that both parties thought they could live with for the moment. Of course for the moment both parties thought they were going to get Biggs back to Britain, a cause for overweening satisfaction to Slipper as long as the impression lasted and of corrosive distress to MacKenzie who had barely collected enough material for the next week's papers, let alone a book. It was also a cause for the gravest concern on the part of Biggs. Biggs was thinking things over.

When Biggs found himself looking up Slipper's flaring nostrils his first reaction was not that he had suddenly lost the game he had been playing with such astonishing success for 3,128 treasurable days; not defeat but shame and disgust. It meant that rather than being able to direct the final gripping sequence himself (staying in close-up to the last) a peerless gesture of renunciation, in which he was seen to be doing what all the coppers in Christendom had failed to bring off—give Britian back her most wanted man—Biggs would now go back home as a defeated, disgraced and helpless prisoner. A failure. A loser. A fool.

No thought of betrayal had yet crossed Biggs's mind. He was completely taken in by Slipper's virtuoso performance as he gave all present a demonstration of The Sweeney's special brand of sergeant-majorish bullying. MacKenzie, who had had his head in the small black refrigerator in the corner of the room looking for a Coke when the door burst open, got the first blast.

"Who are you?" roared Slipper theatrically. When MacKenzie

told him, stuttering through his own part in the farce the blast of invective that followed nearly took Biggs's mind off his own troubles. Slipper had been saving up a few things to say about the *Daily Express* and he bawled them out with loud satisfaction.

"And *you?*" Lucia in her minuscule flesh-colored bikini was tremulous and bewildered. Despite the temperature outside Slipper had put on his jacket and tie for the formalities of the climactic moment and his face was mottled and sweating. She, quite reasonably, burst into tears.

"Go to your rooms!" Slipper ordered them all. And, leaving it to Jones to see that they did so, hustled Biggs into the bathroom.

"Put your trousers on, Ronnie," he said, calmer. But his hands were trembling with tension.

"There's nothing to be afraid of," said Biggs, cheekily.

"I'm not afraid!" snapped Slipper. "Get dressed." He produced the purloined handcuffs.

"Oh, no!" said Biggs. "Not those! Don't put those on me." At least he could walk out of there without becoming a spectacle.

One of the Brazilian coppers had come to the door and, instinctively tuning in to the exchange, opened his jacket to let Biggs see the pistol on his belt.

"Go on then," sneered Biggs in a burst of hopeless bravado. "Shoot me then you son of a bitch. Shoot an unarmed man!"

As soon as they went back into the bedroom Henry Neill, who had been containing himself heroically throughout the excitement, made an apologetic dive for the bathroom.

In the end they took Biggs down in the temperamental elevator with Slipper holding his trousers belt at the back. Lovelace did go to his room but only to get another camera. By the time the others got downstairs he was there to shoot them coming out. He took a couple of pictures with a long lens then dumped that camera under a car and moved forward with the second one. He had no idea if the Brazilians would stop him from taking pictures or try to grab his film. If so they were welcome to the second camera now that he had some insurance safe in the first one. Lovelace knew what he was doing. MacKenzie came out of the Trocadero and joined him. They ran alongside Neill's dark-brown Morris shouting. "It wasn't us, Ronnie. It was those bastards in London."

Vine appeared from the Metropole where he had been straining for a glimpse of activity. It was MacKenzie's first sight of him since they had been in Rio. They had work to do. It was "Anvil" time.

In the car Biggs said to Slipper. "I hope you're not going to be hard on that MacKenzie. He's a nice young fellow."

Slipper and Biggs continued the conversation they had begun in the bathroom. It was on a level considerably below the rarefied diplomatic heights at which the lack of an extradition treaty might be brought up. "You could hang around until I got a deportation order, Ronnie," said Slipper. "Do you fancy six months in a rat-infested cell like they've got here? Or you can have a nice plane ride with me and Peter and tomorrow it'll be the green fields of old England again."

"I won't be seeing much of the scenery," said Biggs, "but I haven't got much of a choice, have I?"

Not much. The seats were booked, The Yard alerted—by the *Express*, naturally. A welcome of unparalleled intensity, not to say nature, was even then being prepared for the return of the celebrity, his captors and his biographers. Fame, admittedly fleeting for poor Biggs, awaited. Glory. An imperishable place in the lurid history of our times and the reporting of it.

Neill had drawn up a document for Biggs to sign declaring that he was leaving the country voluntarily to conclude his interrupted sentence. He could sign it at the police station. The good old Twelfth *Delegacia*, where by now they knew full well who Detective Chief Superintendent Slipper of the Flying Squad was and would no doubt be fascinated to meet his illustrious prisoner. There, Slipper and Jones had left their packed bags and carefully folded raincoats ready for departure. Well, no, actually. Those were the Civil Police down at the Twelfth who kept the peace on behalf of the city. Brazil, like many other countries, had an overlapping system of city, state and federal police forces. Sometimes the beggars spent as much time fighting off each other's encroachments as they did enforcing the law. Situations involving foreigners came under the jurisdiction of the Federal Police which the Consulate had been in the process of consulting. In fact a particularly chronic state of jealousy prevailed between the *federales* and the rather knockabout local coppers who now had Biggs in custody.

Slipper's hunter's spirit which, as he had emerged into the open air with his strong right hand clamped on Biggs's belt, had soared like one of the Copacabana kites with exhilaration and relief, not only at getting his man literally within his grasp but at achieving control of the bizarre and irregular situation for the very first time, suddenly stalled. Fluttered. Plunged. They had gone to the wrong coppers? Oh, dear. Oh dear, oh dear, oh dear. Wise and weathered himself in the impervious ways of bureaucratic jealousy and obstruction Slipper knew that trouble certainly awaited him now. Delay, reiterated explanations, the re-presenting of credentials were the worst possible things that could happen at that delicate moment. All his professional craftiness and cunning told him that the chances of getting the three of them on the plane that night had suddenly been cut to half of what he would have put them at when he had walked into the Trocadero half an hour earlier. As they flung themselves into the torrential stream of crazed traffic that surged toward the shabby rococo redoubt of the Catete Palace prison Slipper's raddled stomach began to bobble and churn like the morning's crop of lightly strung buttocks spread along the Copacabana sands.

No taunting scent or hip-quickening tingle of approaching *carnaval* reached the leaden hearts of Purgavie and Brennan as they stumbled, sour-mouthed and jet-shattered out of Galaeo Airport on the following morning, Saturday. They had spent much of the 10-hour flight in a woebegone analysis of their hopes of distilling something from the left-overs of the situation that might distract from the *Express*'s walkover on Monday morning and concluded that they might as well have stayed in Costello's. They did not even know where they should head for when they got to Rio. But they might have known that when they *did* find out where Slipper and Jones were staying that the first faces they saw would be those of Vine, MacKenzie and Lovelace. "Hello Brian," said Purgavie, striving for a mote of cool in the face of steeply rising humiliation. "How's your sister?"

Purgavie and Vine were old friends and well-matched opponents, both of them expansive bar-room jousters and abrasive, bad winners. They knew how to hurt each other with skill and precision. Brennan and Lovelace were bound by an equally strained rivalry. When Lovelace had won the draw in Calcutta the year before for the single available Indian Air Force seat that had borne him to his prizewinning destination in Bangladesh, Brennan had been one of the photographers to lose and stay behind. Worse, driving home from the Photographer of the Year party after celebrating Lovelace's award Brennan had been "breathalyzed" and subsequently deprived of his driving license.

The *Express*men were simply unbearable. Insufferable. Patronizing. Smug. Complacent. Condescending. All through the night as pride in achievement swelled a wider and wider circle of chests in London, the satellite circuits to Rio had been clogged with "herograms" the effervescent form of congratulatory message in which *Express* executives specialized. Miserable as a pair of squashed *cojones* the *Mail* men offered their own polite but restrained compliments and demanded that Vine buy the drinks.

"I really don't know why you've come all this way, old chap," said Vine to Purgavie with finely calculated pomposity. "The whole thing's sewn up tight. You'll never get a look in."

"Sorry Mike," said Lovelace to his forlorn counterpart. "Biggs will be back in London before you could get a picture to the office."

MacKenzie, whom neither of the *Mail* men knew, was a good deal less offensive. He seemed distracted, and for someone who had pulled off such an admirable feat, preoccupied. But the two others accomplished enough between them. Too much, in fact for sensitive and dedicated seekers after truth to bear without complaint. Purgavie and Brennan went quietly on their way, their flabby hopes for a fortunate accident transmuted by the nonchalant taunts they had swallowed down with their adversaries' beer into steely resolution, vowing revenge and costly retribution. Somehow the Reprisal of the Century was going to have to be arranged.

15

"Who blew it? Did Slipper slip up? Or did the Yard bungle
the whole operation before it even got off the ground?"
Daily Mirror,
February 7, 1974

•

When you are as far in the lurch as Purgavie and Brennan found
themselves the only place to start is at the beginning. Then the
smallest step feels like progress. They booked into the hotel where
they had found Slipper and Jones. It was called the Novo Mundo
and it was in downtown Rio far from the zephyrs of Copacabana.

Mr. Neill the Consul was not much forthcoming even though he
had already received a stern reproof from the *Telegraph* for his
misleading them by denying all knowledge of Biggs. He now
conceded that the events of which Purgavie spoke had in fact
taken place. Purgavie then got Slipper on the phone and received
an awesome burst of officialese full of "acting-on-information-
received" and "proceeded-in-the-direction-of" but not the answer
to the questions that most concerned him: where was Biggs at that
moment? When was he to be flown to London? Had he known it
Slipper was waiting in a state of some consternation to find precisely
those things out for himself. The reason that he and Jones had

moved into the Novo Mundo was to be as close as possible to Catete where, a disconcertingly brief time after their arrival the previous day, Biggs had been blandly but conclusively removed from their care.

But although Slipper refused to see reporters from any newspaper other than the *Express*—Vine, MacKenzie and Lovelace had just been to call when the *Mail* men stumbled upon them—he had not been able to resist the flattering lure of the television camera. John Humphreys the BBC reporter from Washington had been admitted to the room and the result, aired in Britain on the Sunday night, gave Biggs's fellow countrymen the first chance to form their own conclusions about at least one of the principals in the drama that had enthralled the nation. Students of the *milieu* did not fail to note that Slipper in the interview chose his words carefully, like a man aware that what he said might be taken down and used in evidence against him. He hoped, he said, to have Biggs back in Britain very soon. *Hoped*, eh? Yes, Biggs was a character all right. Look, he told Humphreys, how he had managed to come to terms with this culture here which, frankly, left Slipper and his partner baffled. And, with Jones sitting silently beside him and the telephone in the background off the hook, Slipper in his shirt sleeves gave the viewers at home a touching account of the unexpected difficulties to be surmounted in conducting such an intrepid operation in a strange and distant land. The language barrier. The unfamiliar surroundings. The climate. The difficulty in getting taxis. But he thanked the Brazilian authorities for the courtesy with which he had been treated and for their cooperation. Another key word, *cooperation*.

And where was Biggs now? Why in the care of those courteous and helpful Brazilian authorities.

Yes but *where?* Purgavie, putting that off for the moment turned to the next obvious source, the local Reuters bureau. The major wire services—Associated Press and United Press International; the American ones; Agence France Press; the French; Reuters; the British—trade in routine news in and out of the countries in which they have offices and are usually helpful in guiding newly arrived special correspondents around the outlines of an unfamiliar story.

Specialists often used their teleprinter circuits to file copy. Oblig-ingly Reuters passed on the home address that Biggs had given the *federales*. Purgavie and Brennan got to 330 Avenida Prado Junior a few minutes after Derryn Hinch and Ralph Champion.

It had taken Hinch about two hours to convince the immigration officials at the airport to let him in without a visa but Champion had waited for him companionably and they had rented a taxi together, fleeing from Bunton of *The Sun* and Beeston of the *Telegraph* who had also been on the plane. Champion and Hinch were able to collaborate since they were not in competition with one another as each of them would have been with Bunton who represented papers in both Britain and Australia and the moral support was welcome so far from home. Although when Hinch, an energetic spade-bearded young man had called Reuters and begun to speak in clear and careful English for Foreigners, he was greeted by an irreverent riposte in the English of the Antipodes. The Reuters bureau chief Uli Schmetzer was an old acquaintance from those parts. It's a small global village.

Hinch, aware of the hazards of conducting inquiries in an alien tongue, hired as an interpreter a Brazilian youth who turned out to have a distinct taste for the game on which all of the correspondents now embarked. The superintendent of number 330 was wary and unhelpful at first, refusing to answer questions and claiming that he had no key to Apartment 1207. A look inside and some secondhand information about Biggs's living habits would at least have given the desperate scavengers something to write about. But Hinch's Brazil-ian helper worried away at the superintendent, Jose Gomez De Oliviero, as though he had been born to it and eventually induced him to produce a card file in which, to the considerable pleasure and advantage of all, the relevant details of the tenants were recorded as the law, it seemed, required. The "A" List it was called.

The correspondents scribbled gratefully. Michael John Haynes, artist, married, date of entry 17.4.71, previous address 78 Leigham Court Road, London SW10, passport number 3417570. Raimunda de Castro, identity card number 58896, age 26, secretary. Now that *was* something. The *Express* story had mentioned a second girl but not her name. Where was she now?

Superintendent Jose was softening up. Brennan took his picture a few times to flatter him. The reporters made international sign language around their pockets. Jose told them what he could of his unlucky tenant Mike the *finu*, the gentleman, who had given him 30 cruzeiros at Christmas. He told them of the *federales* taking Raimunda off the previous night as soon as she had returned from the visit she had been making to her mother. And of the foreigners that she left with after she had come back from the police. The *Express*, of course. There would not be a bloody thing left upstairs. But Jose produced a key after all. Might as well have a look.

The reason Slipper had excellent cause to be cautious about his chances of ever getting his hands on Biggs again was called Carlos Alberto Garcia and he was the *federales* chief in Rio. He was a small man with fashionably long, piebald streaked hair and usually a couple of days' growth of beard. A pearl handled .38 revolver jutted from a holster low on his hip and he smoked long brown cigars. Swarthy chap. Not the kind of copper you see in Britain at all.

Garcia had been waiting for them in his office in the wing of Catete occupied by the Maritime, Aerial and Frontier Police and he listened with intense, brown-eyed interest while Slipper, Neill, Costa—and Biggs—explained the singular undertaking in which they were by then all united: getting Biggs on the British Caledonian flight to London that night. The consular document was produced. Biggs signed it. Slipper showed Garcia his letter. His Warrant Card. His plane tickets. They were ready, Slipper explained, to leave. Once they got their gear back from the *Twelfth Delegacia*.

Garcia was too courteous to wince. They would understand, he had no doubt, that the matter had been drawn to the attention of the Maritime, Aerial and Frontier Police only somewhat belatedly. They would appreciate that since their compatriot had been residing, illegally it appeared, in Brazil for some years that it would be of interest to have some information from him on his activities during that period. It would be necessary to question his acquaintances. The girl Raimunda, for instance, and this young man Benckendorff. They had already been sent for. He would also speak to the English journalist MacKenzie. No, he regretted that it would not be possible for them to leave today, gentlemen. Perhaps tomorrow. Monday at the latest. In the meantime they could enjoy the pleasures of this beautiful city of which they did not appear to have seen a great deal. He could recommend the Novo Mundo Hotel nearby.

With their main story filed the *Express* team dared not rest on their rather prickly laurels as long as Biggs was still in Brazil. On Saturday the Sunday *Express* would expect to be supplied with its share of the story. Lucia, recovered from the unhappy events of the morning and back in her clothes was energetically distraught at the thought that Biggs was about to disappear from her life forever. MacKenzie and Lovelace took her to Catete and persuaded the *federales* to let her in for a farewell visit. Duly reported. The Sunday *Express* got its account of the touching encounter in a story that included a boldly spurious interview with Neill which MacKenzie wrote as though no *Express*man had been within miles of the scene when Biggs was collared, "He stayed pretty calm when we entered the hotel room" Neill said, according to MacKenzie. "He was most helpful and cooperative and fully admitted who he was."

In London a Mr. Ronald Salinger, a trichologist who lived at the address given on the "A" List, had to explain to reporters from the Sunday *Mirror* that back in the 1950s Biggs had indeed rented the premises during a brief interlude between prison sentences. And the Yard began looking for one Michael John Haynes, the original owner of passport 3417570, the man to whom Biggs had sent the document to be renewed and who had never returned it, stranding him.

With more and more journalists trooping into Rio and the local press gradually waking up to what was happening the *Express*men, unexpectedly compelled by the unfortunate delay to protect their advantage by keeping vital sources like Biggs's girls and Benckendorff out of the way found themselves in danger of overstretching their resources.

Reporters and photographers were beginning to fall from the sky like autumn leaves. The *Mail* had another pair on the way to Rio from London and still another pair in Lisbon the first touchdown point in Europe for flights from Brazil. And when they realized that

Friday night had passed and Biggs was still there Anthea Disney, sitting in New York feeling scorned and resentful, was not forgotten either.

The thought of the approaching waves that they knew must be building up had not been far from the mind of any of the first four rivals as they trooped pessimistically through apartment 1207. A reporter without a lead is always haunted by a formless dread of what someone else somewhere he does not know about might be on to. But there had been a good deal more to see than anyone had expected and they moved about, noting that the bookshelf had a copy of *All You Ever Wanted to Know About Sex* by David Reuben and that the men's clothes in the wardrobe had London and Melbourne labels in them. ("If you want any new clothes let us know your current measurements," Charmian had written in one of the letters Biggs had given MacKenzie.)

There were clothes of Raimunda's too, flimsy and stimulating garments, and the account books Biggs had used in his modest decorating business. Champion and Purgavie concentrated on the superintendent chatting with him through the enterprising interpreter. Brennan and Hinch spent all their curiosity on the apartment itself.

Without knowing it they had walked into Leatherslade reincarnated. When MacKenzie and Lovelace had expected Biggs to leave for London with Slipper and Jones and Biggs the previous night they had intended to be on the same plane. Vine, whose back-up duties would then be over, was to stay behind and look after loose ends like clearing up the apartment. But events had moved too fast and in an unexpected direction. The Dustman of the *Daily Express* had never made it to Avenida Prado.

Brennan pulled open the drawer of a flimsy white wood bureau against one of the bedroom walls. It contained a few tape cassettes and a cheap Japanese player. He looked the tapes over. When you have nothing you want, everything becomes interesting. *Carnaval in Rio. James Last Plays for Lovers.* The third was a battered noncommercial cassette labeled in awkward lettering, "How Much We Love Need and Miss You." Brennan pocketed it like a flash.

Out in the street, before he had a chance to tell Purgavie about his find Hinch said to him. "I saw you, Mike. I know you've got it."

"Well for Christ's sake don't say anything to Champion," said Brennan. Australia was a long way off. But the *Mirror* was an enemy at close quarters.

It was not simply his preoccupation with the demands of the Sunday *Express* that had kept MacKenzie hopping about so distractedly on the Saturday. Like Slipper he had begun to sense the possibility that all might not go according to the Scotland Yard master plan. But unlike Slipper, MacKenzie stood to gain. Once Biggs was back in Britain every hope of profitable collaboration would disappear with him behind the waiting tall iron gates. But every day of delay improved the chances of MacKenzie and Biggs bringing off the original Biggs book project. Brazilian prisons were not as inaccessible as British prisons for outsiders sharing serious business propositions with insiders and MacKenzie had already begun to ingratiate himself with the police. There was just one additional difficulty. Biggs had told him, "*You're* all right Colin. But no more deals with the *Daily Express*. One was enough."

And by Sunday the prospect of Biggs regaining control of his own destiny had brightened dramatically even though by then he was being kept alone in an eight foot by four foot cell in a federal prison near the airport. After the *federales* had finished with him on Friday they had sent him to the detention center known as Praça Quinze where he was put in a cell with three other foreigners awaiting deportation. Naturally they all fell to discussing the pleasures of life in the country they would soon be leaving.

"Have you got a girl friend?" one asked Biggs. Is there a grain of sand on Copacabana? A star in the Southern Cross?

"What a pity she's not pregnant," said the friendly cellmate. "They can't chuck you out if you're the father of a Brazilian kid."

"Funny you should mention that," said Biggs.

Long before he had the slightest idea of what was actually on the tape Hinch was determined to get a piece of it. If it was, as seemed possible, the voices of Charm or the Biggs's kids and it had come from Australia it would make an even better story for him than it would for the *Daily Mail. Mail* trophy though it might be Hinch considered that he had established rights to it simply by knowing of its existence and not mentioning it to the *Mirror* man, a Fleet Street competitor. And anyway Brennan would never have found it had not Hinch's interpreter talked them into the apartment. Never.

The tape was not getting out of Hinch's reach. He left the interpreter to a slightly wondering Champion together with the car and driver and for the rest of the day stuck to Purgavie and Brennan wrangling persistently with them. Purgavie was interested in hearing the tape but he was already beginning to think out an elaborate descriptive piece of a kind he did particularly well. None of them had a cassette player anyway. Nor could one be found in any of the shops still open.

Finally when he could no longer delay a trip to the Reuters office to file a woefully thin story to Australia, Hinch said to Purgavie, "There must be a recorder down there."

"Take the bloody thing then," said Purgavie exasperated, flicking the cassette across to Hinch's yearning fingers. "It's probably a plant. Brian Vine singing *Rolling Down to Rio*."

If the men striving to overturn the odds in favor of the *Express* were having a hard time the frustration had been even greater for Disney. At least *they* were on the spot. She could only hang around New York watching the silent telephone and snapping at her boy friend and the male secretary she had wangled for her office. When she had been posted to New York she had been promised that the biggest and best stories would be put her way and they usually were, Purgavie having the preoccupation of a daily column. But here was the mother of them all being greedily mopped up by the bureau chief himself. Typical.

A lot of women have done well in Fleet Street. But only, until very recently, in specialized jobs such as columnists and editors of women's pages. They were never encouraged to work on the tactically powerful night staffs of the national papers. And when they were reporters considerate news editors tended to "spare" them the big stories which, almost by definition, were gory, ghastly, lubricious or rough-and-tumble. They often found themselves looking after a protagonist's nonparticipating wife or being sent along to barter off sex appeal for entrée. Only a very very few ever got to be foreign correspondents.

But when the time came on the *Mail* for a New York replacement to be made, Anthea's dues were demonstrably as paid up as anyone's. Every other role she had played in her ten ferociously ambitious years of reporting had been built into a star part—she once dyed her skin to live as a Pakistani immigrant—and there was no sign of her stopping. By the time the phone rang she could almost have made it to Rio on the pure power of umbrage. Who needs Pan Am? She did not even mind arriving at the same time as the transatlantic reinforcements reporter David Pryke and photographer Bob Aylott. If the *Mail* could not beat the *Express* at least it could outnumber it.

On the Saturday, executives in London were perpetuating the frenzy of Friday night from their homes. Few of them had any idea of where the first correspondents they had sent to Rio were to be found. The new arrivals had to go from hotel to crowded hotel looking for them. At the Novo Mundo Disney saw at a glance that it was an unlikely place for someone as fastidious as Purgavie to be staying. It was a cracked and peeling dump. But checking the register she found Slipper and Jones among the guests.

She and Pryke went to knock at the door of the room that, once again, the two Sweeneys were sharing. She knew better than to answer when a voice inside wanted to know who it was. Just kept knocking. Eventually Slipper opened the door, an unforgettable figure clad only in his underpants. "Oh my Gawd!" he said in anguish. "I'm not decent, Madame."

Finally Purgavie and Brennan—and Hinch, an amiable friend of them all in New York with whom they did not normally find themselves in conflict—were tracked down in the Leme Palace Hotel. One night in the Novo Mundo had been enough. And Disney walked into a playback of the previous day's tape saga.

Purgavie, having spent the night moping over the draft of his color piece realized that it would take something a little more concrete to lambaste the insufferable Vine and MacKenzie. He had begun to worry that he might have been hasty, even careless, in letting the tape out of his hands. He went looking for Hinch whom he found in an irritable and crestfallen condition. "Well, what was on it?"

"*I* still don't bloody well know." Hinch's problem of the night before had been to find a way to play the tape without letting his old friend and benefactor in communications Uli Schmetzer—or anyone else—know that he had it. In the Reuters bureau he had quickly spotted a recorder on Schmetzer's desk. But he dared not ask to borrow it. So he took an interminable time over preparing his copy even though he needed plenty anyway since the less a reporter has to write the longer and harder it is to write it. Instead of giving his story to a teletype operator he sat at a keyboard himself and painstakingly punched the tape that, fed as a perforated strip into the machine, would transmit his raw-boned and unscrumptious tale over 11,000 grimly expensive miles. It would all have to be replaced (but there would be no thought of cost or recrimination) if the promise of the tape was fulfilled. And an instinct as certain and persistent as a developing ulcer told him that it was going to be. Uli Schmetzer go home!

By the time Schmetzer did call it a night Hinch had been reduced to faking breakdowns with Sydney and rerunning the tape to give him an excuse to stay behind.

Allowing a decent interval for Schmetzer to get out of the building and trying not to attract the overnight operator's attention he strolled nonchalantly back to the bureau chief's office, zeroing in through the glass panel of the door as he approached on the tape recorder, an electronic icon of hope and salvation squatting on the desk. Locked. The bloody door was locked. Hinch pressed his nose against the glass like a store detective on his first day at a two-way mirror.

"What tape?" Disney demanded, hungry as the bracing Brazilian glances that had marked her every comely footstep since she landed. Disney was not a woman likely to settle for equality when sex gave her an advantage. But at that moment the one who had the advantage was Hinch. He had the tape in his pocket and he had no intention of giving it back to Purgavie until a clear understanding had been reached about his stake in it.

Hinch was also under pressure to file again. He was servicing both morning and evening papers in Australia and out there Monday morning was on the way. It was getting late in London, too. Purgavie had no time to waste. In the brisk and badtempered negotiations that followed, Hinch's rights to whatever the tapes might yield were confirmed and the cassette itself was surrendered to the *Mail*. Hinch would not give it to Purgavie but he did let Disney have it. While the others went off to write what they could in the way of preliminary stories, she would find something to play it on. Silly fools couldn't have been *trying* very hard.

Two hours later Disney had tried very hard indeed and totally failed. In the first place Brazil worked even less on Sundays than most parts of the world do. And in the second Copacabana was not exactly Times Square where every second shop window overflowed with the kind of gadget she so desperately needed now at only 35 bucks apiece. Despite the barbaric extravagances of its wafer-thin upper crust, Brazil is a poor country and consumer frivolities like cassette players are sparsely distrubuted.

There was none to be found within miles in any of the shops that were open. No such luxurious tool of trade was known to the local newspaper reporters now swarming, fascinated but utterly confounded by the story, around their foreign counterparts. And the local radio and television stations used only tape recorders with open reels. Useless for cassettes.

But every reporter knows what must be done when every other lead has foundered. Ask a taxi driver. Draw diagrams if necessary. One driver with a few words of English looked at the sketch in Disney's notebook and at the tape like a man accustomed to seeing such things every day. "My brother . . ." he said. "The brother of my sister . . ."

Disney acclimatizing fast jumped into his cab as imperiously as any of the girls from Ipanema. "Take me to your brother-in-law," she said.

The plane that brought the fresh *Mail* forces from London also delivered a photographer from the *Daily Mirror* Eric Piper who promptly began his own search for Ralph Champion. By late Saturday it had become clear in London that the earliest Biggs could be flown out was Monday and the other papers began to sense that things were going wrong.

All day television and radio retold the tale of the capture with gratifyingly frequent references to the *Daily Express* and the *Express*'s sister of the evening, the *Standard* reprinted MacKenzie's story by the yard. And all day Esser, running a full scale information defensive with a girl friend Tui France pressed into service to cope with his telephone, repeated in interview after interview that the *Express* had not paid Biggs, had not paid Charm. Scotland Yard, besieged, put up the shutters. There would be a press conference upon Slipper's return.

Piper found Slipper as he was manfully trying to keep up the distant end of his thinly stretched line of communications with the Yard. At the Novo Mundo outside telephone calls could not be put through to guests' rooms. To keep his harassed superiors in touch with what was going on—or as much of it as he was aware of—Slipper had to descend to the lobby, which was awash with tourist traffic every hour of the day and shout into a completely exposed phone by the reception desk. "Well, Commissioner. . . ."

The taxi driver's relatives turned out to be a charming and hospitable middle-aged couple who were delighted to entertain a young *estrangiera* even one displaying such a slight interest in the courtesies as Disney. Midday in Rio was 3 P.M. in London. Getting late. Whiskey? Coffee? Cakes? Please don't think me rude, Disney implored across the language barrier. Can I just sit here with your handy little gadget and listen to this cassette? Certainly *senhorita*. Coffee? Cigarette? Our cousin Annunziata has been to London. You know Buckingham Palace? Have you been to Brazil before?

Impatiently Disney clicked the tape into the player, a battered rudimentary model. It was over a hundred degrees outside and the windows of the un-airconditioned apartment were wide open to the torrent of Sunday traffic blaring and thundering its way to the sea. The persistent offers of hospitality went on being shouted over its fiendish roar. But Disney was oblivious to anything but the sounds on the tape. And through the din the scarred and corroded heads of the old recorder suddenly brought to her overjoyed ear the tinny encapsulated voice of Charm herself, the tones of Streatham Ballroom smuggled halfway around the world to the land of the samba.

After an hour of cramped and agonizingly difficult listening Disney knew she had a story that would overjoy the *Mail* and rout the opposition. Between the quality of the tape and the player the distractions of the traffic and the constant interruptions of her considerate hosts it had taken her that long to transcribe the first half of the cassette. But at the very least she was now in possession of a gloriously revealing and intimate one-sided conversation in which Charm assured Biggs of her undying love despite the time and distance that separated them. The *Express* would be furious. And there was more to come from the other side of the tape.

She needed help. She telephoned Purgavie back at the Novo Mundo. Warn London. Send Pryke to her in a taxi. She would come back and dictate the first half of the transcript in time, hopefully, for the first edition. Pryke could do the second half of the tape. Hinch, who had stuck mistrustfully close to Purgavie in Disney's absence began to calculate his own relentlessly recurring deadlines. Three in the afternoon in Rio was ten o'clock Monday morning in Sydney, fast approaching edition time for *The Sun* his clamorous evening tabloid which would eat up every syllable of this, and must at all costs be served with it hot, and copiously.

When Pryke got back to the hotel with his part of the tape the *Mail*'s countercoup became even better. Charm, her affections restated at some length, turned to practical matters. The courier who had been carrying tapes between her and her husband had reported that Biggs was depressed and broke. But he must not forget the safe deposit box in Melbourne she reminded him, if he needed money. Wow! Robbery money?

And gossip. How a chum of the family Biggs had managed to diddle the income tax authorities in Australia out of a small fortune. And the future. They could not go on like this forever. Charm had been reading. She had discovered *The Day of the Jackal* and become fascinated by the rather hoary old routine used in it for someone to acquire a passport in the name of someone else of the right age and origins who had considerately and inconspicuously died before applying for one himself.

She would send the book to Biggs. It would inspire him. He could return to Melbourne and hole up in the hills. She would visit him. No one would dream he was back in Australia. *Wonderful* gloated the shareholders assembled in Purgavie's room. Wonderful unbeatable stuff.

When these matchless treasures had been telephoned across from Purgavie's hotel room the *Mail* was indeed delighted. The editors decided to withhold the story from the first editions of the paper to make it all the more difficult for the *Express* or anyone else to contrive a matching story before the night ran out and they urged the team in Brazil to observe the utmost secrecy meanwhile. Purgavie was sure it was exclusive? Superb. The *Express* would go bananas. Tormented Hinch, the scribbled transcript he had been waiting for them to finish with all but in his hand found himself looking into three suddenly guarded faces. Sorry, said Purgavie. We're not going to be able to let you have this just yet. He picked up the sheets of copy. Hinch on the brink of disintegration tried to play it calmly. Reasonably. A gentleman among colleagues. For a few minutes longer.

They had, he reminded Purgavie, a deal. Both of them knew what the catch was. Both could see that if *The Sun* in Sydney got the story into print claiming it as an exclusive before the *Mail* in London was ready to come out with it could be picked up by Fleet Street correspondents in Australia and filed to London. Perhaps even to the *Express*.

Arguing as fervently and unscrupulously as a car salesman Hinch maneuvered toward the sheets of copy that Purgavie had by then given to Disney. She went to the bathroom taking them with her. Pryke and Purgavie circled Hinch uncertainly like a pair of guard dogs prematurely graduated from obedience school. "Look Dermot," said Hinch no longer a gentleman, "you can't stop me. I've heard you dictate all your copy and I've read most of it. I have enough in my head to write a story for Sydney, and that's what I'm going to do. Right now."

"Wait a minute," said Purgavie. "Let's talk to London again." He called Brian Fremantle the Foreign Editor of the *Mail*. Disney, back in the room, forgetfully put the copy down on a table. Purgavie warily snatched it up again as Hinch began to tack toward it and placed it firmly under his hefty bottom as he sat at the telephone. Hello, Brian. The problem is that we have an arrangement with this, er, Australian. Let *me* talk to him, said Hinch. And from a position of some strength he negotiated a grudging truce. Hinch would agree to hold off from his first Sydney edition too. But the *Mail* would hand over the copy. Just as well. He needed it. Its value was in its word for word originality and, despite his bluff, he had committed none of it to memory.

At the Trocadero where MacKenzie, Lovelace and Vine had maintained their headquarters other delicate areas of cooperation were being re-evaluated. The *Express*men had accepted that the growing size of the opposition presence would make it impossible for them to retain control of their collaborators, particularly if Biggs was to be released again, or publicly produced. They were overextended anyway since the number of people they needed to keep to themselves had expanded. MacKenzie had become aware of how strong Raimunda's claim was to be the number one lady in Biggs's life. Good for the book. Worry about the logistics tomorrow.

Industriously MacKenzie wrote Raimunda's part larger in the reams of copy he was filing to help the *Express* increase its already seemingly unchallengeable lead. His exclusive revelations about the alluring Xu Xu—it means sugar beet—the exotic half-Indian daughter of a washerwoman from the wilds was safely in London by early Sunday evening when, to his horror, she suddenly blossomed out of the hotel television set entwined in the arms of the incarcerated Biggs himself and pouring out, for anyone who understood Portuguese to hear, a good deal more than she had so far told the *Express*. One thing in particular. She and her Mike were going to have a baby.

The program called *Fantastico* was put out by the TV station belonging to the Rio newspaper *O Globo* which plainly had no difficulty in enlisting Garcia's assistance after both the *Express* and the Yard had been shown out of Catete. The background of the tender scene was his office. Aghast at the duplicity of it all the *Express*men watched their assets dwindling away.

Biggs, relaxed and elegant in cream trousers and a blue shirt, nuzzled Raimunda's ear and let her do most of the talking. "The Brazilian people hope Mike will stay," she said, speaking unhesitatingly for all 100 million of them. "And I hope he will become a Brazilian. He has been a good man in Brazil and it does not matter what he has done in England."

Irrespective of the damage the entirely unforeseen TV interview did to the *Express*'s privileges of exclusivity it settled one thing about the future strategy. There was definitely not going to be room anymore for the first girl Lovelace had photographed, Lucia the lovely student, in the authorized version of the Adventures of Ronald Biggs. But she must still be kept out of the clutches of the

Express's marauding contenders. Benckendorff, another embarrassment now he had served his purpose, was ordered to escort her out
of town thus removing himself from the danger zone as well. What
was Lucia studying? As it happened, journalism. And learning fast.

The *Mail* team and Hinch, cordial relations among them all
restored, went off to a vine-covered *churrascaria* to celebrate their
table-turning with a few litres of Chilean wine and steaks the size of
a sob-sister's heart. They had become rather belatedly concerned
about their possession of the tape which had, after all been acquired
in ethically dubious circumstances—which Purgavie had justified by
writing in his story the classic line: "The *Daily Mail* yesterday
handed to Scotland Yard. . . ." But they did not want to run foul of
the *federales*.

Purgavie had actually gone looking for Slipper to give him the
cassette but had not been able to find him. Slipper, oblivious to the
startling and ominous appearance of Biggs and Raimunda on
Fantastico and assured that there would be no developments before
the following Monday, was enjoying the hospitality of the British
consul. "I'll give it to him in the morning," said Purgavie to the rest
of the *Mail* team.

On their way out to dinner they had met Ralph Champion in
another group of colleagues. There was no Teacher's to be had in
Rio, but plenty of his second choice, Vat 69.

"We found this smashing little restaurant," Champion told
Disney whose company he had often enjoyed in Costello's. "Marvelous shrimp. Anything happening Anthea?"

Disney was always ready to trade but no one got anything for
nothing. And it had been a long hard day.

"Yes," she snapped. "There's quite a *lot* happening. And you can
bloody well find it out for yourself."

"Pushy little bitch," said Champion to his companions. He had
been acknowledged as the best reporter on the *Daily Express* before
he joined the *Mirror*. Before Disney had been able to reach as high
as a typewriter keyboard.

With cheerful malevolence, Purgavie was waiting for Callback
Time, the dread hour when the Back Bench in London spots a story
in an opposition paper that ought to have been in its own and

reaches an aggrieved hand for the phone. It was delayed that night because of the *Mail*'s first edition prudence. But it came as surely as the morning light.

The *Mirror* called Champion. He called Slipper who by then was back in the hotel. "I have received no such tape," said Slipper. "Never heard of it." Confidently Champion refuted the *Mail*'s story and went back to sleep. A sound and uncompromising official denial. The *Telegraph* called Beeston. *The Sun* Bentley with similar results. But Purgavie did not care about those three. With epicurean timing he arrived at MacKenzie's hotel room door just as the *Express* had got through to their new young star and was inquiring with some heat how they came to have been scooped on their own exclusive. "Would you care to join us for a nightcap, Colin?" asked Purgavie.

"No thank you," said MacKenzie, his upper lip stiffened to the stress point. "I find I still have some work to do."

So far as the *Express* was concerned if the *Daily Mail* said there was a tape there *was* a tape.

16

"The imagination calls up an image of two innocents hunting a notorious criminal in a foreign country—as if our nation was part of the ancient British Empire—without any knowledge of the laws and customs and without any contact with the police."

Jornal do Brasil
February 6, 1974

•

The static Fleet Street converse of a great Chase is A Doorstep. The newsmen are outside some place or building and the person whom they wish to see—and who usually does not want to see them—is inside. A bleary and baffled expatriate press posse, awaiting the outcome of the negotiations that Slipper and Jones and Neill and Costa had begun in order to get their man back, doorstepped Catete on a Monday morning when the temperature was heading for 100 degrees. For once they had only one question—as indeed did The Sweeney—would Biggs leave for London that night?

Actually the reporters and cameramen had infiltrated well past the doorstep itself and into a narrow passageway leading to a reception area from which they were cut off by a locked and barred gate. On the other side of the grille the foremost of them could see Garcia strutting around with his now-familiar air of lawman *machismo*, Slipper and Jones sitting dejectedly on a hard bench looking as though they were the ones to have been collared, and—to their anguish, dismay and resentment—their distinguished young colleague Colin MacKenzie making the best of his fast-improving command of Portuguese.

Nothing is more likely at the best of times to stir growls of discontent and frustration in the throats of a pack of marauding newshounds than seeing that one of them has been able to go where the others may not follow. And MacKenzie was not one to use his advantage discreetly. Even to the kindest eye, that of Lovelace jammed in the steamy jailhouse corridor with the rest of the pack, he was *swaggering*. He did have something to swagger about, apart from having been favored with the freedom of the part that held Biggs. On his instructions Raimunda had walked into Catete a little while earlier for a reunion with her lover untroubled by the restive doorsteppers who, of course, had no idea what she looked like. But MacKenzie still had to get her out of there.

Notable new arrivals included a second young English woman Jan Rocha, who was married to a Brazilian lawyer and lived in São Paolo, and Arthur Steel, a bearded photographer from *The Sun* who had arrived from London only that morning. Like Mike Brennan, Steel too had been among the losers of Calcutta when Lovelace drew his prizewinning trip to Bangladesh.

Rocha, on the other hand, was thrilled just to be there. She was only beginning to break into journalism as a "stringer," a part-time correspondent for the BBC and the *Daily Telegraph*, and she had never before been involved in excitement like this.

Not only were the BBC staff man John Humphreys and the *Telegraph* man Richard Beeston, her contacts, delighted to see her—so was everyone in the corridor with the possible exception of Lovelace. She spoke excellent Portuguese and her cordial readiness to do so on behalf of a united front of her new found confreres did a lot to erode the *Express*'s remaining privileges. She had put her talent to merciful use earlier when she had arrived at the Novo Mundo to find Slipper and Jones unable even to make the staff understand that they wanted a cup of coffee.

Some of the new arrivals were having similar difficulty in getting themselves to the Catete. Time after time throughout the day another sweaty and exasperated voyager would turn up after delivering an approximation of the name to a taxi driver and being taken to some other *palacio* at the farther end of town. It happened to some people several times running. No one ever did find out what the other place was.

Rocha also became the main link with the Brazilian reporters, none of whom spoke adequate English. Over the weekend they, like everyone else, had been too stricken by the retirement of Pele, the world-renowned superstar of soccer (the second-ranking national preoccupation) to bother about the arrest of a *gringo* nonentity. But by Monday the *Fantastico* program and the stories being received from London by the Rio papers left no doubt that a criminal of international stature was safe in their own Catete. The Great Train Robbery was an event well-known, if not in precise detail. It had inspired the Brazilian film *O Assalto Do Trem Pagador.* Something else also seemed clear to the locals. The British, indifferent as ever to the rights of nations that lacked her haughty past, had attempted a flagrant circumvention of Brazilian law. One paper reported over-enthusiastically that the Federal authorities in Brasilia, the capital, had ordered the arrest not of Biggs but of Slipper and Jones.

This was one of many pieces of misinformation traded between the two groups in the jammed corridor when the Brazilians, also finding themselves confined to the wrong side of the bars, decided that the antics of the invaders from the northern hemisphere made almost as good a story as *O Ladrao Do Trem Postal.* But Fleet Street got the best of the trading. One of the Brazilians was tipped off by a *federale* that Biggs's pregnant girl friend was inside. And that there was only one way out and that they were inconsiderately blocking it. Doorsteps have been known to last for days.

In London, neither Scotland Yard nor the vastly displeased Foreign and Colonial Office was saying anything, let alone offering odds on whether or not the Brazilians would hand Biggs over. But Hitchen was planning for the worst. He summoned a reporter named Michael O'Flaherty. Most pops have their own Heavy Mob in the house for the times that someone who has put himself under one paper's care and protection has to be protected from the intrusive intentions of a rival publication. In times gone by, especially in Scotland during the heyday of Ian McColl's editorship there, the *Express*'s—and therefore everyone else's—was as well-trained and belligerent as a line of Rugby forwards. In the milder climate of the South and of more recent times the heavies had become smaller and less formally organized. O'Flaherty was a kind of one-man heavy mob, a good reporter to whom people enjoyed talking but, despite his affable good manners, brimful of brutal Irish *joie-de-vivre*.

"How far can I go?" he asked when Hitchen explained that he would be sent out to help MacKenzie and Lovelace defend the *Express*'s interest in Biggs—should he be released—and Raimunda. "What if I have to thump someone?"

"It's a long way from home," said Hitchen.

"Lovely," said O'Flaherty. "Why don't you send me on more foreign trips?"

There was still a good deal of crossness in the air about the *Mail*'s coup with the tape. The *Express*'s own offering from Charm's correspondence, a wedding anniversary card her husband had just received, looked fairly anemic in that morning's paper beside her reckless outpourings on the cassette, even if it did record yet another of her piquant pledges of undying devotion.

"My darling husband," she had scrawled around the pre-packaged sentiment printed on a commercial greetings card. "Sometimes February 20, 1960 seems like an eternity ago: and yet sometimes it could have been just yesterday. I love you much more now than then in many different ways and yet even then I loved you totally and with every fiber of my being."

But the *Mail* had been unable to match Lovelace's superb series of pictures of Biggs entwined with Lucia. And there was intriguing additional evidence being readied for future issues of the *Express* of how little Charm's single-minded dedication had been requited.

"Rio is a marvelous place," Biggs was saying in the recollections MacKenzie had been hastily piecing together as Slipper and Jones bore down on them. "And if I give myself up it won't be until after *carnaval* next month. Even at my advanced age I can honestly say I have never scored with as many chicks in my life."

Lovelace had originally stayed outside the bars for the same reason that all the other photographers were there. He too needed a

picture of Biggs coming out with Slipper and Jones. If he *was* to
come out, something that was beginning to look increasingly
improbable to Lovelace who could see the faces of the two Yard
men growing longer as Garcia repeatedly conferred with consul
Neill and his assistant and they passed on what he had said.

MacKenzie inside could keep fairly closely in touch with what
was going on. Garcia had had sufficient authority himself to deport
Biggs on the grounds that he had entered Brazil illegally. But since
he had chosen not to do so immediately, and since the affair was
now attracting such attention (and providing Garcia with instant
fame, since every newspaper account mentioned his name pro-
fusely), the Ministry of Justice in Brasilia was now taking a close
interest. They would make the final decision. Things looked bad for
the Yard MacKenzie saw. But jolly good for the literary rights.

However, the two *Express*men had to coordinate their strategy
over Raimunda now that the others knew that she was inside.
MacKenzie joined Lovelace amid the impatient throng on the other
side of the bars and was immediately subjected to a mocking but
intensive interrogation to which, thoroughly flustered, he responded
with the banal cant phrase reporters hate more than any other two
words in the language. It might have been the first time one of them
had ever used it to another. "No comment," said MacKenzie
pompously to the outstretched microphone of Mike Brunson, the
Independent Television News reporter. "No comment."

The outraged and derisive uproar this provoked brought Garcia
to the grille, pearl-handled pistol on hip, hand on pearl handle. No
noise, he said. Silence. Although the language was not their own
everyone understood. They understood too when he glared at the
photographers and added, "And no pictures. Forbidden!"

Eric Piper of the *Mirror* was the first to react like a red-blooded
Fleet Street boy and take a picture of Garcia. The barred door flew
open like a starting gate and to the accompaniment of a spirited
running commentary from their chief a pair of uniformed jailers
plucked Piper from the midst of his fellows and bundled him inside.
In Brazil, the local newsmen explained helpfully, it is against the
law to take the picture of the policeman. Piper did not mind much.
He doubted that they would put him in front of a firing squad right
away. And if Biggs was inside he was now a giant step closer to him
than he had been out there. The chums he left behind were soon

farther away than ever. Garcia banished them to the ornamental gardens next door to the building while the telephoning to and from Brasilia went on.

Some regrouping was taking place in the ranks of the visiting press. Neal Travis, *The Sun*'s man from New York, had flown down after all. If one New Zealander could get in without a visa, said his frantic office, so can you. But unlike Hinch Travis could not. At Galeo Airport the Brazilian police put him on the first plane back to New York, a 10,000 mile round trip. The *Mail*, realizing that their New York bureau had been cleared out of all but the male secretary, sent Purgavie back leaving Disney and David Pryke to report in Rio with Mike Brennan and Bob Aylott to take pictures. Disney, recognizing leverage when she spotted it, struck up a friendship with Jan Rocha. The *Mail* chief reporter, Brian Park, was still waiting in Lisbon, with photographer Bill Cross.

Vine slipped out of Rio like a saboteur who had successfully completed his mission, sparing not one glance for the twisted ruins and the confusion he was leaving behind him. Champion went to Hinch for he realized now that he had been badly outmaneuvered and said, "There's just one thing I'd like to know about that damned tape. Did you get it from the apartment while I was in there?" Hinch tempered the blow. "No, Ralph. It just Came Into Our Possession. You know. Like *The New York Times* and the Pentagon Papers." Everyone in Rio booked a seat on every plane leaving for Europe within the next 48 hours.

As doorsteps go, the one at Catete was not too unendurable. There were constant diversions. There was an invigorating confrontation with MacKenzie and Lovelace over Raimunda once the doorsteppers discovered that she was inside. "She's not going to come out while you are all here," said MacKenzie with proprietorial authority. "I don't know why you don't go away."

"Don't be bloody silly, Colin," said Disney like a patient teacher. "None of us is going to leave until *everyone* comes out no matter how long it is."

Lovelace, the veteran of many an imperishable doorstep, grinned at them from behind his distracted young colleague. He was acknowledging what MacKenzie had not yet grasped. It was the *Express* which was on the defensive now.

The Brazilian television teams with their deadline approaching, the daylight fading, and no action in sight faked a rush back to the main entrance. The British stampeded after them. The Brazilians filmed them and aired this example of quaint foreign journalistic custom on the next news bulletin.

Eventually MacKenzie, his nerve going, decided to try to rush Raimunda out. It was nearly nightfall and inside Catete tempers were giving out. Neill had already stormed out of the building, his face crimson, and driven off without speaking to anyone. While the value of this as an omen was being earnestly debated the *Express*men made their stealthy preparations.

A taxi was telephoned for. Lovelace loitered casually around the doorway. Out charged MacKenzie towing a small sultry brunette by the hand, her braless nipples jiggling in a flimsy halter as she followed him on the trot. Glare of television lights, ripple of strobes, excited cries. MacKenzie tried to shield Raimunda's face with his hands to mar the opposition pictures. Brazilians and British alike pelted her with questions like the flower throwers of *carnaval*. Lovelace, grim-faced but good-natured, shouldered his way through the mob to open the cab door. No cab. Gone. The vigilant opposition had paid it off and sent it away. Lovelace the old campaigner knew when to advance and when to retreat. "Let them take their pictures, Colin," he said. "Otherwise we'll never get out of here."

The next appearance was made by Piper the incarcerated photographer. Jan Rocha had gone to negotiate his release with Garcia. And also to find out if Piper had got a glimpse of Biggs. He had not. Nor had Slipper nor MacKenzie. Garcia had moved him to another jail. Garcia took the opportunity to display his musky charm to Rocha. But certainly the *Senhor Fotografo* could rejoin his friends outside. He had, after all, been adequately punished for his transgression. Oh? How?

We gave him a cup of coffee. That's punishment? The rest of us have been trying to get something to eat and drink all day. "You should taste the coffee they make here," said Garcia. Musky sense of humor, too. "Bring your friend next time you come in," said Garcia. "Anth*ee*a."

At last came Slipper and Jones, white-faced, tight-lipped, haggard. No Biggs. A living wall of impatient newsmen waving mikes, cameras and notebooks barred their path. What's happening

Mr. Slipper? We hear that you will be going back to London without him. There were more questions than answers. Or, rather, the same question reiterated in a dozen permutations. Six P.M. Rio was ten P.M. London. First edition time gone.

The two Sweeneys paused by a battered old black limousine that the *federales* had whistled up for them and that had been immobilized by the sheer weight of the milling press. Slipper spoke slightly. Yes, he said, they were going back on the late flight that night. Twice a week British Caledonian Airways, the private enterprise competitor of British Airways the state airline, flies to London direct from Rio. It left at 11 P.M. Getting the words out of Slipper was like drawing teeth.

They got in the car. Fists drummed on the windows. The Brazilians shouted for a translation. Startled, Slipper lowered the window a crack. Brunson jammed a mike toward it and in his most authoritative television reporter's voice demanded, "Chief Superintendent *are* you taking Biggs back with you?" Soft, low and despondent Slipper spoke one word.

"No."

The car drove off, running over Lovelace's foot.

Immediately Garcia became the focus of attention. He appeared outside to read a statement. Rocha translated for the British. Biggs was to be sent to Brasilia the following day. He would be detained there while the Government awaited a formal request for his extradition based, in the absence of an extradition treaty, on reciprocity. The fine legal point of that was lost on the reporters. But the immediate effect, they realized instantly, was a very good story to be going on with. All at once Biggs seemed to stand a strong chance of never having to serve out the 28 years he owed Britain.

MacKenzie panted out of the Catete too late to hear what Garcia had said. Lovelace, hopping about on one foot, had not been listening carefully. Humphreys of the BBC kindly played his tape back for him, but MacKenzie had difficulty in giving it his undivided attention. His troubles were multiplying. Biggs, he had discovered, had told Garcia that he now repudiated the consent form he had signed for Neill. That was good for the book project. But Biggs had been doing some thinking. He had also told Garcia "I was betrayed." That was bad.

"What you need," MacKenzie had told him, before they parted on the Friday, "is a lawyer."

"What I need," said Biggs, "is a deal with another fucking newspaper."

Geography was getting to be a problem for everyone. Once the night's story had been filed—something that almost everyone found easier to do than MacKenzie because the Trocadero where he and Lovelace had remained had an old fashioned telephone switchboard that caused infuriating delays in getting calls out—a tactical reassessment was called for. MacKenzie and Lovelace decided to abandon Rio and transfer their base of operations to Brasilia taking Raimunda, for the moment their only remaining exclusive asset, with them. The *Express*'s New York bureau chief Ivor Key could be brought down to cover their rear in Rio.

The *Mail* chose to split its adequate forces. Disney and Bob Aylott would go to Brasilia. Pryke and Brennan would board the plane with Slipper. A few words outside Catete were not enough to get the Yard off the hook. And Slipper would hardly be able to keep them at bay all through the long flight home. It was not entirely logical that Aylott, the London-based photographer, should stay in Brazil while Brennan, the one from New York, flew to London. But Brennan had proposed an idea for a classic picture which the Pictures Editor John Lyth had endorsed with enthusiasm. Brennan's idea. Brennan's assignment. The Code of the Street. Arthur Steel who had only arrived in Rio that morning would also fly back with Slipper and Jones. Not everyone in Fleet Street gets day trips to Rio de Janeiro.

While Brennan and Pryke were on their way to the airport Slipper and Jones and Neill and Costa were having dinner at their hotel with Garcia who had arranged the occasion not only to console his crestfallen brothers in duty, but to explain to them in detail what the decision that had come down from Brasilia meant. It meant only one thing to Slipper—as it had to the reporters—but he listened politely if glumly while Garcia spelled it out, the food before him as unappetizing as a condemned man's breakfast, and took plenty of notes. Once again he was going to have to do some laborious explaining back at the Yard.

A Brazilian reporter from *O Globo* who had worked up a trading relationship with Disney peeked into the dining room and came back, tracing the eloquent universal slaughterhouse gesture across his *café-au-lait* gullet.

"Slipper?" asked Disney.

"Garcia," said her useful friend who had shown himself to be in the police chief's confidence to an impressive degree, "too much publicity. Brasilia no like."

David Pryke cut an unexpected figure when he represented the *Daily Mail* abroad, which he had done frequently as a "fireman," a London-based veteran reporter dispatched when and wherever trouble strikes afar. In an earlier professional incarnation he had achieved some eminence as Pryke of Luton, the proprietor of a private news agency in an important provincial center north of London, which he ran so successfully that he was able to sell it while still in his 40s and retire.

But finding leisure quite unsupportable he took a part-time job on the *Daily Express* foreign desk while David English was in charge of it and when English went to the *Mail* as editor Pryke was one of the people he invited to join him there.

English is an admirer of energetic men. He is one himself. And energy shines from Pryke like the beam of a lighthouse flaring across the surface of a darkened sea. On an assignment he is a blur of sound and motion, constantly questioning, scribbling, quarreling, demanding, telephoning. He *runs* everywhere. He files every detail.

But even if he were completely different in temperament, even if he affected the stylish languor of a Purgavie or the cheerful insouciance of a Champion, Pryke would never go unnoticed among his peers. Not because of his regimental moustache, clipped to a pattern Slipper could never find fault with. But because no matter where he was sent, nor how often, part of Pryke remained incontrovertibly Luton where bright sunshine and foreign parts were treated with equal suspicion and prepared for with precautions that had altered little since the days of Empire.

In Honolulu Pryke once appeared in vintage-style khaki shorts and long matching socks with colored tabs sprouting from the garters that held them up. Once he boarded a Mexican airliner in

Acapulco, half the world away from Luton, and with touching faith, called confidently for a pot of tea and a copy of the *Daily Mail*. And Pryke always knew how the natives should be treated.

He and Brennan were not comfortable companions. Once after they had worked together on a job in London Pryke had asked the Picture Editor to assign some other photographer with him whenever the occasion arose again because he found the length of Brennan's fashionably cut hair offensive. Brennan, an easy-going, sharp-witted young man, did not suffer Pryke's attitudes too gladly after that. But as they swayed and jolted against each other behind the suicidal Brazilian taxi-driver speeding them to Galeo they were far too elated and smug to be provoked by each other's company. Lovelace and MacKenzie's preoccupation with their other clients had left the *Mail* with exclusive title—since they did not regard *The Sun* as a foe worthy of Arthur Steel—to the highly desirable extension of the original story that was now developing: Pryke with the first exclusive interview with Slipper, Brennan with his cunningly thought-out picture. Another stinging retaliatory blow for the *Express*.

The British Consulate had seen to it that Slipper and Jones, even though they were flying back to London empty-handed, should return in the first-class splendor that had been arranged for Biggs rather than suffer the additional indignity of reverting to economy class. And the plane which had begun its route in Buenos Aires was being held for them while they finished their dinner. But the Sweeneys had arrived, checked in and boarded with VIP treatment, Pryke on their heels at a breathless gallop, before Brennan focused down on exactly what the Brazilian clerk at the British Caledonian desk was explaining to him. His American Express card did not represent anywhere near enough credit to cover the $813 ticket he needed to join the others. And he had very little money.

A Fleet Street man denied a seat on an airplane is a fearsome sight. The world over bumptious airline managers, blameless female booking clerks, steely-eyed air force generals and beribboned captains of aircraft carriers alike have known defeat before their theatrical outrage or their insidious, relentless, shameless wheedling. Somehow obstacles crumble. Elderly refugees are evicted from seats, hallowed rules ignored, a boarding pass thrust in choking exasperation into the hand of the panting, importunate pest who has turned up devoid of reservation, authorization, money or perhaps even passport. Fleet Street men usually get where they want to go. And someone is usually glad to see them leave.

Brennan was well into a classic performance of the well-established role when he realized that by uninhibited Brazilian standards it was being received as nothing more than the standard rhetoric of a frustrated traveler adjusting to disappointment. He had just decided that it would be best to clout the clerk with his camera bag and storm the departure gate when the Caledonian lady flight purser came out looking for the passenger adrift from her manifest. Horrified at the threat to Anglo-Brazilian relations that she found developing, she bolted to get Pryke while Brennan, desperate, continued the choleric stand-off. Finally, in an appalling welter of racial epithets, restated threats and banknotes of varying currencies, which Pryke pulled out of a series of wallets, the ticket was scrawled in the clerk's enraged and shaking hand.

"You are all bad persons. Bad English persons," the shattered Brazilian stammered in a defiant attempt to have the last word.

"Bloody wog," retorted Pryke, having it.

The confrontation was more than Caledonian could possibly bear. After all, *they* would be coming back to Rio. The flight had to be delayed even longer while the distracted purser negotiated a reconciliation.

"Shake hands and be friends," she demanded with the ancient wisdom of a nation of nannies. Disarmed by this manifestation of traditional British fair play the ticket clerk extended his hand in courteous forgiveness. Brennan gave it a weak but willing squeeze. He would have kissed the Brazilian's bottom had he needed to to get the ticket.

In the very front of the Boeing's forward cabin Slipper sat in seat 1F by the right-hand side window and Jones in 1E, the seat originally reserved for Biggs. Adrenalin still surging through their veins like the fuel that began to stream into the engines that were impatiently fired up the moment the door had slammed after them, Brennan and Pryke tumbled into the row behind. The rest of the passengers, surly from the long and inscrutable delay, glared at the strays resentfully. So did their friend Arthur Steel. If Brennan had not been able to make the plane *he* would have been the only photographer on board.

With 13 hours to go before they got to London Brennan could afford to bide his time. In fact he had to, because the symbolic little tableau that he planned to immortalize needed time to arrange itself. And besides, he had no intention of alerting Steel to what he had in mind. But just as Lovelace had understood in his cautious preliminary flirtation with Biggs, the photographer must solicit his subject's confidence long before he takes a camera out of his bag. Brennan introduced himself as soon as the seat belt signs went off and the first drinks came along. "Hello there, Chief Superintendent. Did you enjoy yourself in Rio, then?" The warm and cheery tone was all right. But he could have picked a better opening.

Slipper was exhausted. He was baffled. And he was chastened to the very core. He was a proud man, unaccustomed to defeat or humiliation. And he had just spent the most miserable and frustrating few days of all his time in the Force. He now felt free to acknowledge that fact.

"Well," he said, pinioning Brennan with the piercing, ice-blue glare that had helped many a scoundrel to sharpen the recollections of his misconduct, and speaking distinctly like a seasoned professional witness, "I have traveled a very long way, having left home at very short notice. It has been rather uncomfortable these last few days, having to share a room with my colleague here in this awful bloody heat. I have had quite a lot of difficulty in finding my way around in a strange place where I did not speak a word of the language. I am returning to London, in spite of everything without my prisoner, Ronald Biggs. And I have had a nasty dose of the shits. So I hope that answers your question, sir. No, sir, I did *not* enjoy myself in Rio de Janeiro."

In Brasilia the British Embassy had been bestirred from its original lofty indifference to a squalid consular matter. The ultimate significance of the pronouncement that Garcia had delivered would have to be carefully weighed on the finely balanced scales of diplomacy. And in the meantime, since this development went far beyond the matter of Biggs himself, the details had better be transmitted to the Foreign Office. A burden dumped in someone else's lap is a burden shared.

As Slipper downed his first nightcap far out across the South

Atlantic the diplomatic teleprinters chattered late into the time difference. What did the Brazilians mean by "reciprocity"? Were they proposing that an extradition treaty be negotiated on the basis of this single case? One of the reasons Britain had not been particularly interested in the subject in recent years was the nature of Brazil's Federal Government—military, authoritarian, politically repressive.

Or did the Brazilians have in mind a one-shot exchange? If so, with whom? There was not, so far as anyone knew, a single Brazilian in a British prison. Nor were there any Brazilians living in Britain who were known to be wanted by the authorities in their own country.

But of course if a reciprocal agreement *was* reached Brazil might then prefer charges against someone and request their extradition. Someone whose alleged crime might be a good deal less tangible than Biggs's. Those damn policemen had really stirred things up.

Slipper tried to explain something of this to Pryke in mumbled weary snatches through the night, or as much as he had been able to grasp himself of Garcia's interpretation as it had been translated to him. "It's all a matter of repro . . . repos . . . repiros . . . What's that bloody word, Peter?"

In his dedication to the task of debriefing Slipper, Pryke was pitiless. Not only to Slipper but to everyone else trying to doze in their expensive seats. For the first half of the night he administered a rigorous and repetitious grilling through the space between the tilted-back seats in front of him, his moustache pressed against the victim's tortured ear, his ballpoint skittering across his notebook like the needle of a seismograph that had been hit with a hammer. For the second half he typed up the meager results of his interrogation with manic concentration hammering at the keyboard of his portable as it clattered around on the plastic seatback table with fingers as straight and stiff as a spastic pianist. Pryke typing is a sight, as well as a sound, not easily forgotten. And, even if Slipper would only talk about things that had happened after he had collared Biggs, he had an exhilarating story to write. But as Caledonian bore them all toward the approaching sunrise Pryke too nodded off. Brennan awoke.

Peter Jones got up from Seat 1E to go to the toilet, leaving Slipper undisturbed. Brennan slipped from the seat behind to one across the aisle from Slipper. Gently he eased up the plastic window shade, flooding the fore end of the cabin with clear, shadowless illumination from the lightening sky. On his Nikon he had a 28mm wide-angle lens that to the unprofessional eye looked just like any other. If Slipper awoke and looked across at him as he framed the shot he would realize only that he was having his picture taken. But at that range of a few feet the greedy lens embraced a panorama from the tip of Slipper's toes snug under Caledonian's tartan blanket to the seats in the row behind where Pryke now slumped beside his still-warm typewriter. Click. Click. Click. Click. Just four frames, the exposures bracketed for safety. Brennan pulled down the shade and was back in his seat before Jones returned. Or before Steel awoke.

Attacking his lavish breakfast with inimitable English zeal, Slipper was a changed man: appraising his surroundings and treatment with the *savoir-faire* of the seasoned voyager he had now become. The first-class temptations of mid-morning champagne delighted him and by the time the seat belt signs went on for their landing at Lisbon he was as pleased at the prospect of getting back to London by afternoon as, for their own excellent reasons, were Pryke and Brennan. The night's rest had put him at peace with himself. He had done his best: his duty as he had seen it.

Pryke and Brennan were a good deal less happy however when the plane took off an hour later for the last leg of the flight. For they had been joined by the *Daily Mail* contingent that had been cooling its restless heels in Lisbon for three days waiting for the action to reach them: Brian Park the paper's chief reporter and yet a third photographer, Bill Cross. Park, a lean, heavily spectacled whippet of a newshound operated on a competitive drive as supercharged as Pryke's, but far more suavely controlled. He was incapable of letting another reporter get away with a story even if he did work for the same paper. Pryke had no idea Park had been kept on in Lisbon. As he saw him enter the first-class cabin his typing knuckles whitened. He would rather have sighted the *Daily Express*.

Slipper by contrast accepted the additional attention graciously.

At Lisbon he had seen the British papers, documentary evidence for the first time of his new celebrity status. And he was only slightly hurt by the emphasis he had detected in most of the stories. Park hovered over him as he gnawed his way through Caledonian's roast duckling lunch. And to do it he had to lean across Pryke in the seat behind Slipper. "Look, Park," hissed Pryke resentfully up at him. "Don't try to upstage me. This is *my* story. It's all sewn up."

But Park was putting in his own stitches. What did Slipper think of what he had read?

"Very interesting," Slipper allowed. "There is a lot being said, isn't there?

"But this is not the time or the place for me to talk about it," he said cautiously, if a mite reluctantly. "I do not wish to add anything to the strange stories that seem to have been going around." There would be a few more going around Scotland Yard soon enough.

Cross, too, was determined to make some impact on the operation. Would Slipper mind being photographed while he was dealing with his airborne bird and bottle? Not at all.

As Cross clicked away Brennan, cameras swathed around his neck, weaved and bobbed craftily, to make sure he was included in the background of each frame his colleague exposed. Picture editors hate shots with other photographers in them. Brennan did not want any competition to his own safely buttoned-up exclusive.

At Gatwick Airport 30 miles outside London, where Caledonian inconsiderately makes its base, Commander John Lock, the chief of the Flying Squad, was waiting to greet Slipper who readied himself for the encounter with a final defiant flick of his moustache comb. Lock had not had champagne and duckling for *his* lunch. He had no cheery farewell for his companions from the press. The two top Sweeneys drove off heading straight for the Yard, while Park and Pryke were still rattling out their separate stories from adjacent phones in the baggage claim area.

Two kinds of photographs make unforgettable news pictures. The one where the photographer has encapsulated the quintessential split-second of a movement; eye and shutter finger perfectly co-ordinated by reflexes as sure as the camera mechanism itself. Lovelace's shots of the oblivious caresses between Biggs and Lucia were perfect examples. The other is taken when a picture that is an eloquent story in itself forms in the photographer's mind long before the elements of the final image come together in his patient viewfinder. Among those the picture that carried Brennan's by-line and dominated the *Mail's* story the following day (on which the names of Pryke and Park were solomonically linked) would be hard to beat. The seat that should have held Biggs, empty. And beside it the reclining form of the worn-out empty-handed pursuer. *The Sun* carried an almost identical picture. Steel had taken it when Jones went to the john while Brennan himself was asleep.

17

"We don't admire hard work so much. But we do admire a successful trick."

Dr. A. H. Fuerstenthal,
Brazilian psychiatrist

•

In Brasilia, Lovelace and MacKenzie were devoting themselves to seeing that Raimunda got everything she wanted. And she wanted plenty. She did not understand everything that was happening but she had come to realize how vital her own part was and that of the baby that she had now been assured she was going to have in seven months' time.

Raimunda was not a stranger to childbirth. She had her first in a carefree, warm-blooded fashion at the age of fourteen and another a couple of years after that, leaving them with her mother when she went to live in Rio. She had also miscarried several times. The prospects of her producing a child safely were really quite thin, her doctor said. But the lawyers that MacKenzie had begun to consult confirmed the cell-block counsel that Biggs himself had been given. By a well-meant piece of 19th-century legislation still on the books, a man with Brazilian-born dependents could not, in principle, be deported. The *Express*men saw that, when Raimunda was not shopping with the fistfuls of *cruzeiros* they consoled her with, she rested a lot with her feet up.

Disney was the first opposition reporter to follow them there. She travels faster who travels alone in search of advantage, although Bob Aylott the photographer was with her. Disney still wanted what no one but MacKenzie had yet got: an interview with Biggs. With Slipper and Jones gone the *Express*men were the only people in the country, apart from the police, who had even *seen* Biggs. British diplomats had no idea where he was. In Rio, Neill had been told by Garcia that he had already been taken to Brasilia. In Brasilia the Embassy had been assured he was still in Rio.

Brasilia, the Federal capital, is one of the world's more noticeable cities. It was designed as an administrative monument to the future by Oscar Niemeyer. On an enormous high plain far inland he traced out the shape of an airplane and in the fuselage raised the public buildings, ministries, foreign embassies and a cathedral. In the wings on either side he built a university, schools, hospitals and enormous monolithic *edificios* each with its shopping center and recreation area in which to house the bureaucratic denizens. At a distance it has a certain pretentious grandeur, but at close hand it is shabby, unfinished, sterile, a space-age slum of grubby concrete in-the-making. When on Tuesday, about the same time the British Caledonian flight got to Gatwick, Disney arrived in an unending warm drizzle, she felt as though she had landed in the middle of a giant, very wet, Erector set.

The following morning she called on Nelson Marabutu Dom Miguel, the portly and elegant functionary who acted as spokesman for the Federal police from the sixth floor of his particular *edificio* in the South Banking Sector. Disney pulled her chair up to his desk, unveiling thighs rounded and browned to the most demanding standards of Copacabana. When in Brazil. . . . Marabutu was an exile from Rio himself and his job something of an unengrossing sinecure up until now. But this *gringo ladro do trem* was livening things up. Of course, if it were to be possible, Disney could have her interview. Of *course* it could be exclusive. They would see when Biggs arrived. Then he was not, in fact, in Brasilia? Not yet. When? Disney would be the first to know. Marabutu wrote her name down in a Gucci notebook. Anth*ee*a.

But it was Thursday before Biggs caught up with Disney and then he was preceded by the army of doorsteppers from Rio who had kept up the siege of Catete until, his resistance waning, Garcia tipped them off to the plane they should try to meet. There were some new faces. Frank Taylor, the *Daily Telegraph* staff reporter from Buenos Aires who had been on leave when the story broke, had returned, freeing Richard Beeston to go back to Washington. Neill Travers, a visa fresh in his New Zealand passport, had returned from New York. A numerically overwhelming local press corps formed as Brazilian newspapers and television became increasingly intrigued by the cliff-hanger which was evolving. O'Flaherty too arrived and opened up communications with the other *Express*men, but for the moment he infiltrated the opposition. Lovelace knew that even such a public occasion as Biggs's airport arrival could be turned to profit by a judicious deployment of resources and the *Express* was fighting for every inch of ground it could gain.

Biggs got off the plane, towering above his escorts except for one man, a *federale* called Brito who was known in the circles in which he moved as The Animal. Brito had not been moved by pleas as Slipper had. Biggs's wrists were manacled together in front of him, the hardware hidden by a folded jacket. He grinned cheekily up at the mass of reporters and cameramen lining the terrace of the terminal building above him.

"Do you want to go back to Britain?" they bellowed through the whine of taxiing jets.

"No!"

"Then why did you sign that document?"

"I was put under great pressure."

From behind the line of newsmens' backs MacKenzie, who had made an unobtrusive and well-timed arrival, released Raimunda from his side like a pigeon fancier launching a champion bird. Homing in on Biggs she shouldered through the mob to the rail where O'Flaherty waited, throwing out her arms, raising her nipples taut against her thin red blouse. "Michael!" she shrieked. "Michael, *te amo.*" From his strategically chosen corner Lovelace's Nikon chattered.

"Is she really pregnant, Colin?" the others asked MacKenzie

when, with Raimunda safely restored to her hotel room, they were able to catch up with him. "Sick every morning," he replied with satisfaction.

For Maributu the fun had been brief. Instead of flirtatious little chats with Disney he was now swamped day and night by reporters demanding to see Biggs who had been locked up in a small detention block with another potential deportee for a neighbor, Fernand Legros, an alleged art swindler who was wanted in France. But Disney kept dropping in and on Friday Marabutu at last offered her an assignation. Come to headquarters at two o'clock this afternoon. I shall be waiting in my car at the back of the building. We will go to Biggs. You can have ten minutes with him alone.

Jubilantly Disney danced back to her hotel to call London. But when the phone rang it was not her connection but Marabutu, apologetic and embarrassed. The chief of the Federal police himself the fearsome General Antonio Bandiera had intervened. With so many importunate reporters after the same thing he was afraid there would be a riot if anyone, especially a foreigner, were to be given an exclusive interview. Marabutu could let them all in or continue to keep them all out. It was up to him. But no one must see Biggs alone. Marabutu was mortified. What should I do Antheea? I will give the choice to you. All in or no one? That was no choice at all to Disney. No one. Cat in the manger.

Marabutu was not the only one feeling the official heat. In London the Home Office, most impervious and mysterious of British ministries, blandly let it be known that Sir Robert Mark, the Police Commissioner, had taken it upon himself not to tell Home Secretary Robert Carr the Cabinet Minister in charge of his department about Slipper's secret mission to Rio. They could therefore not be blamed.

The Foreign Office let a good deal more pain show. "We were not told in advance. We were not even asked to apply for Biggs's extradition," said their spokesman stiffly. "Sometimes these things can be done on the police network. But you could hardly expect the Brazilian Government to turn a blind eye to this."

It was a gag rather than a blindfold that the Brazilians were putting on. In dutiful response to Disney's instruction Marabutu called a general press conference. No one would be permitted to interview Biggs, he announced, nor would he be permitted to make any statements. Biggs would remain in the custody of the Federal authorities until his fate had been decided. We hope you have enjoyed your stay in Brasilia, ladies and gentlemen.

The decision was something of a relief now that everyone had indeed had a chance to assess the threadbare delights of the capital. The two television teams, BBC-TV and ITN received their orders to pull out with relief. Television stories need film and all they had so far, apart from the John Humphreys's interview with Slipper, was Biggs's brief appearance at the airport and a few thousand feet of traveloguish exteriors. Ralph Champion decided it was time for him to go. He had seen Rio de Janeiro and thoroughly enjoyed the experience. There is an old maxim of foreign correspondence about never being the first to quit the story. But the man who first uttered it had never been faced with the prospect of a weekend in Brasilia.

Even the *Express* team decided to go back to Rio. MacKenzie wanted to find a lawyer who could really provide Biggs with some clout. O'Flaherty wanted to see a doctor. Coming back from dinner on his first night in town, his muscles barely flexed by the brief flurry of strong-arming necessary to minimize Raimunda's contact with the others at the airport after she had waved to Biggs, he had tumbled down a hole in one of the many unlit and incompleted streets and given his leg a nasty bruising.

The *Express*men were still in Rio on that Monday when the *federales* reversed themselves and produced Biggs. Disney and Frank Taylor of the *Telegraph* were the only foreigners beside the dozen or so Brazilian reporters whose insistence had brought it about and Biggs was so irritated at being hauled out of his cell for their delectation that he sulked and would answer only in grunts and monosyllables.

He had settled down comfortably inside, sharing the expensive meals that Legros was having sent in from Brasilia's lone French restaurant. Just like old times in the hospital wing at Aylesbury.

It was late at night when the two stories reached London. But they made the final editions of the *Telegraph* and the *Mail* and, sparse though they were, it *was* the first Biggs interview since he had become Brazilian property. Hell was raised in the offices of the papers that had missed out, especially the *Express*. And raised a good deal higher the next day when it became known that Charm, after having turned the *Express* down, had accepted a considerably less generous offer from the Sydney *Daily Mirror* and was heading for Rio to be reunited with her Ronnie. Michael? What did she call him now? ITN sent Mike Brunson back from Washington saying it was all their fault. The *Mirror* sent Ralph Champion back from New York saying it was all his. MacKenzie and Lovelace brought Raimunda up from Rio again. Perhaps a deal could be made for the amalgamation of the two valuable properties, she and Charm.

The entire reconstituted press corps staked out Brasilia Airport all day Wednesday waiting for Charm to arrive on a commercial flight from Rio. But Peter Brennan, the enterprising news editor of the Sydney *Mirror* who was with her, had chartered a light plane that disembarked them at another terminal on the field. In full view of the waiting plane-watchers had they turned around he, a photographer and Charm—unmistakable with her barmaid bouffant of flaming hair—tip-toed to a taxi and drove into town. It was a foolhardy challenge.

In the two other great centers of fascination with this globe-circling saga, Great Britain and Australia, appetites had been beginning to flag. Two weeks of almost daily Biggs stories had satisfied the curiosity of most newspaper readers. But the advent of Charm raised some new and gripping questions. What would she say to a man with whom she was still by all accounts as infatuated as she had been in those days before she went to Australia when she would try to assuage her restlessness by visiting his wax effigy in Madame Tussaud's? What would she say to Raimunda if they met, wife challenging mistress on uncertain foreign ground? The story cannoned back onto the front pages from which it had lately strayed.

Freshly inspired, the old-stagers launched repeated skirmishes against the newcomers, searching for a way to sabotage the trade-off that MacKenzie and the Australians were dickering about. Or to get in on it. But the police and the Ministry of Justice were sympathetic to Charm's rights as a wife and Raimunda's as a Brazilian. Both got in regularly—although separately—to see Biggs. But no one else did, although the foreign journalists daily spread through ministry offices like the agents of a *coup d'état*.

Having failed at the relatively low level of Marabutu, sultry Disney teamed up with gamine Rocha for a full frontal attack on his overlords, the Ministry of Justice, with a two-pronged onslaught of short skirts and long glances reinforced by Rocha's persuasive powers of Portuguese. By Friday, when the two determined women finally found the right door to knock on, the men from the Ministry did not stand a chance. Back at Marabutu's office a disconsolate and mutinous assembly of reporters heard of the change of heart in mid-pronouncement. There would definitely be no interview with Biggs or his *Senhora*. Repeat, there *would* be an interview with them for those who were interested at three o'clock that afternoon. *"Gracas a Deus,"* said General Bandiera, who had dropped in to complain about the infestation. "Give the *gringos* what they want so long as they promise to go home."

A howl of outrage swept Marabutu's office. *Not* at 3 P.M. on a Friday! Not for Fleet Street anyway where it could only catch the final edition on Saturday morning. And if the interview took place later in the day it would be available to the Sunday papers, which the editors of the dailies—who had waited so long for it at such enormous expense—would regard as the personal failure of their correspondents on the spot to order events properly. No, said Disney firmly, the interview should take place at about 8 P.M. on Saturday, too late for the Sundays but in plenty of time for Monday morning's papers.

Anth*ee*a, said Marabutu, what can I do? The appointment is already arranged for the *Senhora*. Change it, said Disney, merciless in victory. But once he had been spared bureaucratic responsibility for the decision, Marabutu rediscovered his sense of fun. *"You* change it," he told Rocha, getting his secretary to call Charm at her hotel. "But if we tell her she is going to see *you* she will not come. She has assured me."

On the phone, Rocha became an Interpol interpreter with a nicely thickened Portuguese accent clogging her brisk English. It had been necessary to change the arrangements, *Senhora* Charmian. Would the *Senhora* be so kind as to visit the detention block at 8 P.M. the following evening instead. No, nothing was wrong. It was just a matter of the bureaucracy. *Muito obrigado.*

As well as the moonless dark the shades of half a hundred B movies descended on the parking lot outside Biggs's temporary residence on Saturday night. A dozen cars and taxis were lined up there each with its strained and anxious complement of doorsteppers well aware that this was the last chance they were likely to get of wrestling the story to the ground.

Following Marabutu's instructions the correspondents and photographers had assembled in the parking lot at 8 P.M., arriving, in the interests of discretion, separately and with excruciating difficulty since, even more than in Rio, it was difficult to make taxi drivers understand where they were being asked to go. Let alone what they were being asked to do in grotesque situations like this stake-out. The very aura of the detention center made the Brazilians uncomfortable and their mumbles of protest could be stifled only by the subdued rustle of *cruzeiro* notes bearing alarming numbers of zeros.

The full title of the detention center was the *Superintenencia Policia Federal*, and it was, in effect, a police station with a suite of three cells on its second floor. It was one of the few two-story buildings in Brasilia the doorsteppers had encountered, a squat chopped-down shed of a place painted a silly pale blue color and dwarfed by the prematurely dilapidated monoliths of which the city was assembled that reared against the overcast sky like the institutions of a decaying civilization waiting unprotestingly for the creepers to engulf them.

Brasilia nods off early, having limited alternatives. The journalists watched impatiently as across the fancifully delineated city limits *edificio* after towering *edificio* darkened like a white-hot ingot of steel plunged into water and the vast windowed slabs became merely cold and darker patches of the tormenting and suspenseful night. No one had ever managed to get above the ground floor of the detention center, although most of them had tried often enough in the past few days. As its lights, too, flickered off except for one above the back door and one on the top floor back, which they knew was the section that held the cells, it seemed to the tortured watchers of the night that all their trials and frustrations were gathered to burst against its dense and impervious walls.

They knew from Marabutu that Biggs was dining daily with Legros. They knew from a diplomat who had visited him that despite the clinical modernity of the small cellblock it was not air-conditioned nor even well-ventilated and that the prisoners spent most of their time stripped down to underpants.

But a reporter has to see for himself. And despite their thousands of miles of frenzied voyaging and the thousands of words they had written, all that any of them—apart from Disney and Taylor in their brief incursion with the Brazilians—had yet seen of Biggs was that brief glimpse at the airport with its unsatisfying exchange of shouts. This had the makings of the golden moment of the story. Doubly so with Charm, of whom, of course, they had seen little more.

It was 10 P.M. and still no sign of her. Where was the carrot-headed cow? In a taxi that could not find the *Setor Policial Sul* where the *Superintenencia* was situated, that's where, driving around the rutted, pitch-black streets of Brasilia; she and her Australian heavies, completely incapable of describing where they wanted to go, as irritable and exasperated as the waiting doorsteppers. In the end they managed to get back to their hotel to find another cab. He knew where to go because every other driver from the rank was there already, he told his passengers, had they only been able to understand him.

No one was allowed to smoke for fear that *federales*, not aware of what was afoot, would see them, or Charm herself when she drove up. MacKenzie and Lovelace were jammed sheepishly among the others, Raimunda having been left with O'Flaherty. They had not been able so far to set up anything with the Australians because Charm still blamed them for Biggs's capture. Stripped of privileges and advantages they had to share this climactic event—if it could be brought off—with everyone else.

MacKenzie's one consolation was that he had been assured by Raimunda that Biggs in his cell had begun energetically writing an account of his life on the run. It seemed that the fragile contacts he had been able to keep up through the walls of the *Superintenencia* had overcome Biggs's displeasure with the *Express*. They might make their fortune yet.

But there were delicate problems associated with keeping the part of the bargain Biggs was most concerned about—that they should continue to look after Raimunda.

"It's those damn nipples," MacKenzie confided to Disney in the parking lot. "She keeps sticking them under my nose all the time. But if she thinks I'm going to make a pass at her and risk losing everything I've been able to gain so far, she's crazy."

Not crazy, just restless. Raimunda was fast getting over the thrill of life in expensive hotel suites with men who were merely considerate and companionable. She was becoming harder to keep confined, slipping out whenever she got a chance to prattle mischievously to other journalists in a scrabble of Portuguese and mock-English. David Tindall, a BBC-TV reporter who arrived to film a wrap-up documentary, found her wandering in the hotel grounds one day and, after interviewing her as best he could, took her back to O'Flaherty.

"I believe this is yours," said Tindall with the particular relish of an ex-*Daily Mail* man.

"Thank God," said O'Flaherty. "I thought she'd got right away."

Charm drove up in her second taxi and with a flash of bright orange hair in the lone light above the entrance facing the parking lot, billowed into the *Superintenencia*. Bodies slithered out of the stake-out cars hissing with excitement, cameras and tape recorders clattering gently. But even then minute piled on agonizing minute and still there was no sign of Maributu. Disney and MacKenzie were sent as a delegation to search him out. Antagonism submerged in the desperation of common misgiving, they sidled around to the front of the building and found their coconspirator just leaving. "Anth*ee*a," he said, arms thrust out to them with a flash of Cartier cuff links. "Where have you *been*?"

From the pool of promising light the others were beckoned out of the dark. Up the stairs of the stark-walled little building they poured in a soft-shoe stampede to the closed door outside of which Peter Brennan, the Sydney *Daily Mirror* escort, and his photographer-companion awaited them with stunned despair. In Latin countries everyone learns to shrug a lot.

But when Marabutu flashed his cuff links once more and with an elegant jailer's flourish opened the door and they burst in on the quiet *tête-à-tête* Biggs and Charm had just begun, Charm did not shrug. She screamed abuse at the invaders, her ferocity turning aside the first wave to enter the room. It was the same room in which Biggs had made his earlier appearance, a small auditorium used, perhaps, for line-ups, the center of it filled with chairs and at its front a small raised podium on which the unhappy couple sat like actors in a drawing-room farce discovered by the curtain. As the stream of doorsteppers still pressing their way up the stairs rammed the hesitating frontrunners further forward, Charm's vociferous and now noticeably Australianized profanity gave way to tears.

"This isn't what I came 10,000 miles for," she sobbed. "Can't you leave us alone?"

The intruders paused, embarrassed, disarrayed. In their consuming and single-minded zeal to share the event the journalists had forgotten what the event itself was. It was not just a chance for them to talk to Biggs and Charm. It was a reunion between a deeply engaging man and a devoted and dauntless woman whose hearts had remained united through the stupefying difficulties which had kept them apart for so long. Charm was right. She was entitled to be left alone. But there was a story to be got, nonetheless. Confusion.

Biggs put his arm around Charm. "Give us a little while together and then we'll talk to you." A man with a strong sense of the inescapable.

And also a man with a mischievous sense of retribution. This was a matchless chance for Biggs to take out his frustrations on the *Express* and be seen by the world at large to be enjoying it. When the room filled up again and a bizarre mutation of a routine press conference got under way, Biggs launched himself zestfully into registering some public indignation and at the same time demolishing the last fragments of the *Express*'s exclusivity.

"It's good to see you, Bill," he said to Lovelace cheerily. "Why did you do it to me?"

Lovelace squirmed miserably in a ring of self-righteous and accusing stares from his colleagues.

Charmian too wanted to get her own questions in before the reporters could ask theirs.

"Why is Raimunda getting paid?" she demanded of MacKenzie as he in his turn shrank from her glare. "And why aren't I getting anything?"

In fact, although Raimunda was being well kept and was getting generous handouts from MacKenzie every time she needed anything, she was not being formally paid for her services to journalism. At least not by the *Express*. She was learning the slippery ropes, though. She told an Australian woman reporter that her price for a magazine interview was $2,500. Reluctantly the editors in Sydney consented. "*Australian* dollars," said Raimunda sweetly. One Australian dollar equals $1.25 U.S. Well, she was earning for two.

The other reporters were delighted for a while to follow where Biggs so obviously wanted to lead them. Okay, Ronnie, who shopped you? How was it done?

"The only person who knew," said Biggs, cheered by the discomfiture of the *Express*men, "was the chief of that shitty newspaper."

To Lovelace and MacKenzie he said, "You're two nice guys. But you work for a grubby organ. And organ's the right word."

He pressed on, attacking the *Express* unerringly at its weakest point. "What did I expect to happen? I would have left my story with the *Daily Express* for, obviously, financial reasons. And then I thought it would have been a simple process of going back to England to prison."

MacKenzie listened gloomily as Biggs went into more detail of his initial hope of profiting from the new British parole system.

"I wanted to give myself up," he said. "I considered it quite carefully and that is why I contacted Mr. MacKenzie. But it turned sour. Now Brazil has taken over. If I don't get extradited I will fight expulsion."

These were the sturdy bones of the interview which eradicated the last vestige of *Express* control of Biggs. The final dividend had been the story MacKenzie had been able to publish the day before, brought to him by Raimunda—Charm had offered to divorce Biggs so that he and Raimunda could get married to reinforce his chances of staying in Brazil.

But while Biggs was putting his version of his relationship with the *Express* on record for the appreciative audience, the reporters discovered that they were also witnessing an enthralling interplay of emotions between a pair of quite extraordinary people. Biggs and Charm, meeting for only the second time in five years, were all but unmindful, after those first resentful minutes, of the glaring lights, the stabbing strobe flashes, and the turning tape-recorders. When they spoke to the avid reporters they were also speaking to each other across the tortured years, the desperate miles, the aching silence.

"I'm not taking the easy way out by talking of divorce and marrying a Brazilian woman," said Biggs. "The fact is that Raimunda lived with me for more than a year. I have a great affection for her, but no one would ever replace Charmian in my life. Or my children. They and my wife will always be part of my life."

Charm succumbed to her tears from time to time. But when there were questions about the Train Robbery she bounced off the ropes like a true wifely titleholder and came to Biggs's defense.

"He loved his children so much he wanted them to have the things he never had," she said, tearful and indulgent. "Lots of people given the same opportunity would have done the same thing. I considered him worth waiting for. I *love* him."

What would Charm do? Move to Brazil?

"I shall go back to Australia, finish my university course and go on as before. If I divorce him and he married Raimunda and had a child there would be no particular point, would there."

"Let's get this straight," said Biggs, looking at her, not the cameras. "Charmian will never be out of my life. I will love her always. I have a great affection for *Raimunda*. It would not be a marriage of convenience. I have a pretty big heart," he said, thinking perhaps of Lucia, too. "I have a capacity to love lots of people."

An hour and a half later the bemused reporters had an embarrassment of material but their subjects, perfectly relaxed, were reluctant to see them go. The final questions were mere belated courtesies. But Charm put her bruised heart into the answers.

Did she care for the new image of Biggs the playboy of the southern hemisphere? "I'm rather pleased with it," she said. "He's regaining his lost youth." And she gave the reporters a heart-softening glimpse of the girl who would never forget that night after the staff dance in the Bertasso Hotel.

"I'm going to inquire about conjugal visits," said Charm, boldly. "I'm long overdue."

For two weeks the reporters and photogaphers had been battling incessantly not only among themselves and against the police and the bureaucrats, but against the nerve-testing vagaries of the Brazilian telecommunications system. The facilities the wire services offered were efficient. But a story became virtually public property the moment they were used. Pictures even more so. Every visit Lovelace made to the U.P.I. office in Brasilia, the only place from which photographs could be wired abroad, was followed by a procession of his rivals offering ever-escalating bribes to the delighted operator to delay transmission of the *Express*'s exclusive shots of Raimunda.

Everyone came to mistrust the public Telex because they were not allowed to punch out their own messages or watch them actually being sent. Telephone connections to New York, London or Sydney were perfect once achieved. But the operators invariable *um momento* could mean three hours. Prepaid calls got through much faster than collect calls. So in addition to having been reduced by suspense, frustration, tension and the aftereffects of Chilean wine and Vat 69 to worn and ill-tempered shadows of the vigorous and powerfully motivated figures they had been at the beginning of the story everyone was also, at the end of the inanely hectic fortnight, broke. Hinch's hotel bill, mainly for phone calls to Sydney, was $10,000. Plus 10 percent service charge, *senhor*.

But the difficulties the newspapermen had in getting their material out disappeared completely in the black shadows that overhung the prospects the television reporters had of ever getting film back to London while it was hot.

Covering the press conference in the detention block had been Jan Rocha's maiden solo assignment for BBC-TV; the first time she had directed the small movie that makes a television news report. Until then she had done only radio by herself and she had to compete against the seasoned expertise of Michael Brunson, the ITN reporter. Both of them however were equally at the mercy of the unforgiving technology of electronic journalism. Rocha had a Brazilian cameraman and soundman who, speaking no English, had not the slightest idea of which parts of what was being said were important and, consequently, no idea of whether to shoot close-ups of Biggs or Charm, pan the reporters crossing the room or cut to a questioner.

Brunson had had to pick up a crew from one of the British regional companies, Southern Television, which coincidentally had been filling in time in Rio waiting to film British yachtsman Chay Blyth who was heading northward after rounding the Horn in an intrepid race around the world in the opposite direction to the one traditionally preferred. Since they had expected to work only in daylight the crew had no lighting equipment.

Brunson had borrowed a heavy quartz iodide light from TV-Globo—telling them he was going to interview Colin MacKenzie to allay their curiosity about his intentions—and, holding it in his subjects' faces with one hand and his microphone with the other, had done what he could to dominate the interview in the *Superintenencia,* making sure, as a television man must, that the best questions were recorded in his own voice as well as getting the best reactions of Charm and Biggs on film.

The only way Brunson could get his pictures on the air in Britain the following night, Sunday, was to transmit them by satellite beam from the TV-Globo facilities in Rio. He packed the film and headed for the airport to catch the first flight out of Brasilia at 5 A.M. Before he left, MacKenzie came to see him.

"Any chance of getting those harsh remarks about us and the *Express* off the film before it goes to London, Mike?"

"No chance at all, Colin."

The TV-Globo station was completely deserted when Brunson, haggard and weary, arrived there at eight o'clock on Sunday morning. But, whipping couriers off in several directions, laden with *cruzeiro* notes, a few technicians were intercepted on their way to the beach and, assembled, they offered their considered advice. Impossible.

Instead of the usual news-filming practice of recording sound directly on the film the Southern team had been following the technique documentary makers prefer in which it is taped on a recorder that is synchronized with the running film by an ingenious electronic pulse produced in the camera. If the film were to be sent by satellite the sound would have to be synchronized with the images by a similar pulse in the mechanism through which the film runs while being transmitted. At TV-Globo there was no such exotic piece of equipment. And another thing, *senhor,* the motor of the English tape-recorder operates at 60 cycles per second and in Rio the power supply is 50 cycles.

The pathetic state to which Brunson was reduced by this crushing pronouncement moved the warm-hearted technicians to awesome feats of improvisation. Six hideously expensive minutes of satellite time had been booked for 3:30 in the afternoon by ITN and BBC-TV jointly. And the BBC would not suffer from equipment incompatibility no matter what the quality of their film. Brunson began to brace himself for the additional indignity of being wiped out by an absolute beginner, even though Rocha was yet to show up.

All day a young Israeli-Brazilian who had decided to take Brunson's plight as a challenge to national prestige juggled equipment to transfer the sound from the tape to a separate reel of film which might then be synchronized with the ITN print. He finally achieved it after endless attempts, projecting the sequences of the press conference on the laboratory wall while loosening and tightening tension on the turning tape reel by hand as he watched the film until he could roughly synchronize what was being said on one with who was saying it on the other. Just as Brunson was feeling overjoyed not only at the technical triumph but at the absence of his rival Rocha she burst into the studio having waited to have her film processed in Brasilia. Both of them made the satellite cast with minutes to spare. Strangely enough Rocha's Brazilian cameraman had frequently found his lens filled by a clapperboard chalked with ITN data. "Whose bloody film is this anyway?" grumbled the BBC news editor in London.

Mindful of the displeasure of General Bandiera, for they had promised they would leave town once they got their interview, the press evacuated Brasilia, straggling gratefully homeward although MacKenzie and Lovelace lingered in Rio long enough to contrive a strained meeting between Charm and Raimunda. Calm descended on the embattled ministries. And it remained unbroken until hostilities had to be resumed when Biggs's 90 days of detention came to an end at the beginning of May.

During that time the bureaucrats of both Britain and Brazil were not idle. The Foreign and Colonial Office applied through the British Embassy for an extradition order, pointedly avoiding any reference to the principle of reciprocity. The Brazilian Foreign Ministry did not respond. The Home Office held an inquiry into the eccentric methods adopted in Scotland Yard's attempt to retrieve Biggs and blandly announced that no one deserved to be blamed for its failure.

The lawyer who finally took over Bigg's case got busy, too. He was Dr. Sepulveda Pertence, the country's foremost authority on the rights of aliens and a man widely admired for his expensive skills with precedent and petition. Under his guidance Biggs laid the groundwork for a future claim to be allowed to remain in Brazil, confirming paternity of Raimunda's unborn child by volunteering in the Family Court at Brasilia to pay $150 a month. It was a purely nominal sum since Biggs had so little money he would have been living on beans and dry bread in jail had it not been for the generosity of M. Legros and the small amount that MacKenzie left with Raimunda to pay off the jailers on her visits.

MacKenzie himself however was by far the most industrious of all. He landed back in London needing three things in a hurry: an agent, a publisher and leave of absence from the *Daily Express*, should Biggs beat the extradition rap, to do what he had dreamed of from the first moment that Biggs's name on Constantine Benckendorff's innocent lips had, in his ready imagination, levered aside the bonds of Battersea—Write "Biggs: The World's Most Wanted Man." The first two he found without difficulty. For the third he had to apply to his editor.

None of the *Express*men in London who had stage-managed the ensnaring of Biggs had been convinced by the tornado of controversy it generated—especially after Slipper's forlorn return—that they should have acted differently in any way. Andrew Edwards was confident that his legal counsel had been sound. And in the repeated postmortems held in the *Express* office and, more often, in the Golf Club and the Harrow, he insisted that it would be the same if a similar instance arose in the future.

Hitchen and Vine had no reason to regret their parts. They might have dealt with Biggs differently had it been within their power, but they had succeeded in saving for their paper the most covetable exclusive in Fleet Street's collective memory and hundreds of thousands of papers had been sold on the strength of it.

McColl, whatever his misgivings might have been, had the supreme consolation of having obeyed the dictates of a demanding Calvinist conscience. It must have given him a twinge or two about MacKenzie though because he readily granted his request for paid leave on the understanding that MacKenzie would continue to cover developments in the story, offered him in addition an uncharacteristically generous bonus and agreed to a large fee for Benckendorff.

But triumph though it had been, the agitation the Biggs saga had stirred up, the recriminations and the slights—to say nothing of the cost—had added considerably to the vexations of office with which McColl was burdened. Jocelyn Stevens had brought down the axe on the Scottish *Daily Express* (the heartland of the Scotia Nostra ravaged in one cruel stroke) and only enormous sums borrowed on the most exigent of terms were keeping the whole group in being. And already the *Evening Standard* had had to abandon publication on Saturdays as an imperative economy. McColl had troubles enough. If MacKenzie had been expecting praise for his exploits he was talking to the wrong man. "Do you know what I think about Ronnie Biggs?" McColl asked him as they parted. "I wish I'd never heard of the furstie gink."

But the newspaper readers of three continents were about to hear much more about him when a genial reunion of the principal participants took place back at the *Superintenencia* on May 6. Biggs was still in his upstairs cell. His chroniclers were doorstepping outside, once more, MacKenzie, O'Flaherty and Lovelace with Raimunda still in tow. But in the other corner this time was a fresh and well-girt *Daily Mail* team led by Brian Park. Raimunda, now heavily pregnant, wanted everyone to hear about the *promessa* she had made, an ornate vow sanctified by the burning of many candles, that if Biggs was freed the day would be marked henceforth by his putting on a white suit and carrying their baby dressed as an angel to hear nine masses in nine different churches. The photographers made their own *promessa* that if Biggs did that they would gladly make a third trip to Brazil to see it.

The Minister of Justice Dr. Armando Falcao announced that Biggs would be deported for having entered Brazil illegally. Sensation. He added that immediately Biggs would be released on conditional freedom for 30 days to allow him to find a country that was willing to accept him. More sensation. He could not possibly find one. What then? Then, said canny Dr. Pertence, we file for habeas corpus in the federal court of appeals. Meanwhile we apply for the suspension of the deportation order. In a scrum of federales Biggs was flown back to Rio for the release formalities and, by the time he got to the apartment MacKenzie had rented at 602 Rua

Gastao Baiana in Copacabana, he had taken over from Pele as Brazil's top celebrity. Let that be a lesson to *os ingles*.

There was a little fight left in everyone. But not much. Park marshaled the *Mail* forces and dutifully broke into the apartment in which Benckendorff—and his mother—had also been installed. Lovelace and O'Flaherty mounted a counteroffensive and threw them out again. But it was hardly worth the trouble. Biggs refused flatly to give Lovelace or MacKenzie any cooperation that would benefit the *Express*. But he had become enraptured by the idea that his exploits were to be immortalized and he wanted to work on the book every day. MacKenzie found the sections Biggs had written himself very impressive.

A few hours after the abortive raid the *Express*men came down to the grubby little bar around the corner from Gastro Baiana which had become the neighborhood press center, Dos Irmaos—Two Brothers. The freshly repelled *Mail*men were there and, in addition, Frank Taylor, Rocha, David Tindall and his BBC team planning a documentary on Biggs at large; a new face from the *Daily Mirror*, David Wright. Drink was bought. A little later the gathering was discovered there in a flood tide of uproarious reminiscence by one of the Brazilian journalists who had been doing his best to keep up with the tumultuous story since it began and who had just filed to his own paper a colorful but admirably accurate account of the spirited battle between the *estrangieros* he had witnessed with some awe on the stairs of Number 602.

"But," said the poor man, appealing in bottomless bafflement and confusion to Lovelace who was now taking refreshment with men whom only an hour earlier he had been shouldering through a doorway with the impersonal verve of a Japanese subway stuffer, "you *hate* them. *They* hate *you*. I have *seen*."

"No, no," said Lovelace. "You chaps don't understand." He had been in Brazil long enough to be able to use the Portuguese for what he wanted to get across. "We're very good friends, really. *Irmaos*. Brothers."

Upstairs, Biggs another shamelessly sentimental man was listening over and over again to a Nina Simone record he had asked Raimunda to collect from their old apartment. "It's a new dawn," Simone sang. "It's a new day."

For the first time in 11 years he was by official decree a free man. He still is.

18

Stop Press

●

MacKENZIE resigned from the *Daily Express* about a year after he was first sent out to make contact with Biggs. He had finished his book, splitting the proceeds with his collaborator (who always complained he was not getting enough) and decided he could make a living as an author.

BENCKENDORFF set up an import-export business on his payout. When Slipper heard about it he asked, "What is he dealing in? Absconding criminals?"

SLIPPER is still directing the activities of The Sweeney Todd, with particular attention to high-crime areas of London. He still believes that there was no better way to organize the capture of Biggs than to do as he did. He does not blame the *Express* for obstructing his task nor does he think matters might have been better handled by British diplomats. He *does* think that if he had gone to the federal police in Rio in the first place everything might have been different.

McCOLL relinquished the Editorship of the *Express* in the middle of 1974 and ascended to the board of Beaverbrook Newspapers. He also became Chairman of the board of the Scottish *Daily Express* which, alas, is now published from Manchester.

SIR MAX AITKEN and his co-pilot JOCELYN STEVENS seem to have pulled the *Express* out of its financial nose-dive, an achievement welcomed far beyond the black glass. Fleet Street would not be the same without it.

HITCHEN AND VINE are still in charge of its news operations.

LOVELACE is still the best photographer on the paper.

DISNEY is now the Features Editor of the *Daily Mail* and tipped as Fleet Street's first woman Editor.

RALPH CHAMPION retired from the *Daily Mirror* in 1975 having realized a lifelong ambition to travel beyond the Arctic Circle.

GARCIA was transferred to a police station at Niteroi on the other side of Guanabara Bay. It is the home of Rio's British colony.

MARABUTU was made an instructor at the federal police academy.

RAIMUNDA had her baby—a boy, Michael. She took him off to London where she sold her own story to the *News of the World* for $12,000, disclosing that when Charm returned to Rio briefly to bring the older Biggs boys to see their father she managed, at least once, to claim those long-suspended conjugal rights. Raimunda also took Michael to France where Fernand Legros who had himself been extradited (and acquitted) became his godfather. When her Fleet Street hosts asked her what she would like to do for amusement while she was in London she told the interpreter, "I would like to see a blue movie."

CHARMIAN kept her promise. Back in Australia she filed for divorce.

BIGGS, it was eventually decided by the Court of Appeal, *could* be deported. But only to a country that did not have an extradition treaty with Britain. The effect of the decision has been to allow him to remain in Brazil but under a restriction order that prevents him from working.

Because he attracted so much attention from jubilant Brazilians, including the ultimate accolade of being presented nude in a magazine centerfold, the government issued an edict against publicizing the activities of notorious criminals. In addition to the money he got from MacKenzie, Biggs charges whatever he can get for interviews from the procession of reporters from all over the world who come to see him. He and Raimunda left the pulsating delights of Copacabana for a life of blissful beachcombing in a fishing village 50 miles down the coast. Until the restriction order is lifted and Biggs can go to work as a carpenter they will stay there rebuilding a fisherman's house, growing fruit and vegetables and bringing up Michael.

Most of the Great Train Robbers are still in prison. Wretched little Boal died of a brain tumor which might have been the cause of his erratic behaviour. But Edwards and White were granted parole in 1974. If Biggs had been serving out his time he too might be coming out of prison now rather than living on with the thought of the 28 years to come should he ever set foot outside Brazil. But why should he do that? He is safer now than he ever was on the run.

He gave Lovelace a message to take back to London. "Say thanks for me," Biggs told him cheekily, "to Slip-Up of the Yard."